Prophesy the Promises of God

A Collection of Prayers to Align with God's Word

and Release His Power in Your Life

Angelia Mitchell Brown

PROPHECY THE PROMISES OF GOD

Prophesy the Promises of God: A Collection of Prayers to Align with God's Word and Release His Power in Your Life
© 2025 Angelia Brown
All rights reserved.

No portion of this book may be reproduced, stored in a retrieval system, or transmitted in any form or by any means—electronic, mechanical, photocopy, recording, or otherwise—without prior written permission of the author, except for brief quotations used in critical articles or reviews.

First Edition: 2025
ISBN: 979-8-218-72731-4
Published by AMB Publishing
www.angeliaBrown.com

Scripture Notice:

Scripture quotations are taken from various translations of the Bible. **Unless otherwise noted, all Scripture references are from the King James Version (KJV).** Other translations used in this book include:

The Holy Bible, New International Version® (NIV)

New Living Translation (NLT)

English Standard Version (ESV)

New King James Version (NKJV)

The Passion Translation® (TPT)

New American Standard Bible (NASB)

The Message (MSG)

Full copyright acknowledgments for each Bible translation appear in the back of this book under *Scripture Acknowledgments*.

Dedication

To my loving husband, Billy—your unwavering support, love, and prayers mean more to me than words can express. Thank you for standing beside me, believing in me, and covering me in prayer as I walk out God's assignment. You are my partner in faith, purpose, and destiny, and I honor the man of God that you are.

To my beautiful daughters, Alicia and Anesha—I thank God for the incredible women you are and for the purpose He has placed within you. May this book be a testament to the power of faith, prayer, and perseverance, and may you always walk boldly in all that God has for you. May favor, peace and blessings rest upon you.

To my grandson, Branden—I pray that you continue to grow into the man that God has called you to be and know the power of God's Word, the strength of prayer, and the unshakable love of your heavenly Father. May you always walk in divine favor, wisdom, and protection.

To Live Out Your Faith Nation—this movement is more than a ministry; it is a divine calling, a family of faith-filled believers who refuse to settle for anything less than God's best. Thank you for praying with me, standing in faith, and believing for miracles, breakthroughs, and supernatural provision. Your hunger for God inspires me daily, and I dedicate this book to each of you who dare to live out your faith boldly.

To my family, mentors, spiritual leaders, and friends—your wisdom, prayers, and encouragement have shaped me in ways you may never fully know. I honor and thank each of you for pouring into my life, speaking truth, and holding me accountable to the call of God. Your impact is immeasurable, and I pray this book blesses you as you have blessed me.

Most of all, to my Heavenly Father—You are the reason for it all. Thank You for Your unfailing love, Your divine guidance, and the privilege of being a vessel for Your Kingdom. Every word in this book is for Your glory, and I pray that as people read and pray, their lives will be transformed by Your power.

This book is my love offering to my Father God. May it strengthen faith, stir hearts, and ignite prayers that move mountains. With love, faith, and gratitude, Angelia

Table of Contents

Dedication v

Acknowledgments xv

Introduction 1

How to Use This Book as a Prayer Tool 5

Chapter 1 - Prayers for Spiritual Growth & Walking with God 7

   Living a Christ-Centered Life 11

   Abiding in Jesus and an Invitation to the Holy Spirit 13

   Delighting in the Word of God 15

   Writing the Word of God on the Tablet of My Heart 17

   Discernment and Spirit-led Living 19

   Hearing God's Voice 20

   The Gift of Prophecy, Hearing, and Seeing in the Spirit 21

   Holy Spirit Our Teacher 23

   Yielded to the Holy Spirit: Living a Life Led by God 24

   Invite the Holy Spirit into Every Area of My Life 26

   Yielding to the Lord and Welcoming the Holy Spirit 30

   The Fruitfulness of Abiding in Jesus 32

   Walk in Sanctification and Surrender Before the Lord 35

   Walking in Forgiveness 37

   Renewed Fellowship with the Lord 39

Chapter 2: Prayers of Repentance, Surrender and Obedience 41

   A Sincere Prayer of Repentance 45

   Submission and Surrender to God's Will and Calling 47

Abiding in Jesus to Produce Good Fruit	49
Walking in the Fruit of the Spirit and the Gifts of the Spirit	51
Repent and Submit Fully to God	52
Walking in the Spirit	54
Anointed Ears to Hear & Obedient to Divine Instruction	56
Faithful Obedience to God's Calling	58
Faith to Say Yes Again Prayer	60
Listen for the Holy Spirit's Voice	61
Hearing and Following God's Voice	63
Divine Release of the Anointing on Your Life	66
The Lord is My Shepherd	68
Hungering and Thirsting After Righteousness	70
Prayer to Forgive and Release Bitterness	72
Chapter 3: Prayers for Protection and Spiritual Warfare	**73**
Putting On the Whole Armor of God	77
Psalm 91 Declaration	79
Protection and Pleading the Blood of Jesus	81
Binding and Loosing on Earth as it is in Heaven	83
Believers' Scriptural Authority to War Against Principalities	84
Breakthroughs in Stubborn Situations and Strongholds	86
Faith Confessions for Warfare Against Stubborn Situations and Strongholds	87
Declaring the Mind of Christ and Breaking the Enemy's Influence	89
A Prayer for Angelic Intervention and Victory	91
Declaring Psalm 91 & Putting On the Whole Armor of God	93
Resisting the Devil & Drawing Close to God	95

Chapter 4: Prayers for Financial Breakthrough and Kingdom Wealth — 97

Financial Increase Faith Confession — 101

Declarations of Success, Prosperity, Abundance, & God's Goodness — 103

Faith Confession of Abundance — 105

Releasing Money Miracles and Supernatural Breakthrough — 106

Debt Cancelation Accelerator Affirmation — 108

Financial Breakthrough and Money Miracles — 109

Prayer to Pronounce Blessings and Favor Over Finances — 111

Prayer for Growth, Expansion, Increase, and Abundance — 113

Biblical Generosity and Spirit-Led Giving — 115

Building Kingdom Wealth, Entrepreneurship, and Legacy Income — 117

Declaring Blessings Over the Economy and God's People — 119

Financial Resources for Churches, Ministers, & Missionaries — 121

Global and National Economy — 123

Divine Connections, Destiny Helpers, and Supernatural Favor — 126

Chapter 5 – Prayers for Healing and Deliverance — 129

Healing Miracles and Manifestations — 133

Prayer to Command Healing and Rebuke Specific Sicknesses — 135

Daily Prayer for Deliverance and Freedom from Bondage — 138

Divine Cures and Breakthroughs — 140

Freedom from Addiction and Destructive Habits — 142

Prayer for Healing for the Brokenhearted — 144

Prayer for Healing in Mental Health — 147

Holy Spirit and Supernatural Healing — 150

Personal Deliverance and Walking in Freedom	152
Strength to Overcome Sickness and Walk in Divine Health	154
Prayer to Set Captives Free	156

Chapter 6 – Prayers for Family, Marriage and Relationships — 159

Daily Prayer Over My Family	163
Strengthening Marriages, Family Unity, and Restoration	165
Healing and Restoration in Families and Relationships	167
Prayer for Family (People) based on Ephesians	169
Prayer for Children to Walking in Purpose	170
Psalm 91 Declaration Over Our Children and Youth	172
Prayer of Purpose and Wholeness in Singleness	174
Healthy God-ordained Friendships	176

Chapter 7 – Prayers for Purpose, Destiny and Calling — 179

Living a Life of Kingdom Purpose	183
Prayer for Building a Legacy of Faith	185
Prayer for a Purpose-Driven Life	187
Declare the Will of God Being Done on Earth as It Is in Heaven	189
Operating in the Gifts of the Spirit and Releasing His Power	191
Faith Confessions for Operating in the Gifts of the Spirit	192
Perseverance and Boldness to Act on Your Vision	193
Walking in Prophetic Insight	194

Chapter 8 – Prayers for Favor, Blessings and Miracles — 197

Declaration of Blessing Over Our Lives	200
Commanding Favor and Declaring Grace	202
Walking in the Favor of God	204
Divine Connections & Open Doors	206

Divine Connections, Destiny Helpers, and Supernatural Favor	208
Victorious Living in God	210
Prayer to Pronounce Blessings Over the New Week	211
Faith Confessions for New Week	212
Declaring Favor, Breakthrough, and Abundance	215
Blessings and God's Promises Over Our Bloodline & Seed	218
Prayer for Manifestation of Miracles, Signs, and Wonders	221

Chapter 9 - Prayer for Revival & Fresh Outpouring — 223

Baptized in the Holy Spirit and Fire	227
Dead to Sin, Alive to God	229
Hunger and Thirst for God's Word, Prayer, Worship, and Praise	230
More Like Jesus	232
Prayer for Revival	233
Prayer for Revival 2	235
Preparing Hearts for a Fresh Outpouring	237
Graced to Win through the Leadership of the Holy Spirit	239
Revival Fire in Our Lives, Churches, and Communities	241

Chapter 10 – Prayers for Specific Areas and Situations — 243

Anoint Yourself	246
Salvation of the Lost	248
The 7 Mountains of Influence	250
The Educational System – Teachers, Administrators, and Students	252
Prayer for Godly Leadership in Government and Authority	255
Leadership in the Body of Christ	257
Joy and Peace Over the Body of Christ	259
Prayer for the Lost, Hurting, and People in Need	260

Faith that Moves Mountains	262
Prayer for Peace in Our Land	263
Prayer for Restoration	265

CHAPTER 11 – Declarations and Confessions — 267

Declarations and Confessions Introduction	269
Declaration and Faith Confession of Blessings Over the Day	270
Declaration of Victory Over Your Life	271
Declaring God's Rule Over the Day	273
The Power of Speaking Good Things	276
Faith Confessions: The Power of My Words	276
Faith Confessions for Resisting Fear, Anxiety, and Worry	278
50 Declarations and Decrees for Your Prayer Call	280
50 Faith Confessions for Live Out Your Faith Nation with Scriptures	284
Faith Confessions for Live Out Your Faith Nation	288
Declaring Blessings Over a New Year	292
Prayer Declaring Who I Am in Christ	293
Faith Confessions Declaring Who I Am in Christ	293
Declaring the Lord is Good (Psalm 118)	295
The Lord's Prayer Faith Confession	296
Prophetic Prayer to Declare Blessings Over the Day	297
Due Season Declaration	299
Release the Prophetic Anointing and the Gift of Prophecy	300
Declaring the Spirit of Power and Might	302
Prayer for Endurance, Tenacity, and Unwavering Faith	303
A Prayer to Unleash Divine Progress and Provision	306

Declaration: Who We Are in Christ	308
Declaration of Divine Acceleration and Restoration	309
Scripture Acknowledgments	*311*
About The Author	*313*

Acknowledgments

With a heart full of gratitude, I want to take a moment to acknowledge those who have played a part in bringing this prayer book to life.

First and foremost, I give all glory and honor to my Heavenly Father—the One who called, anointed, and equipped me for this assignment. Lord, You are my source, my strength, and my wisdom. Every prayer in this book is a reflection of Your goodness, and I pray that it touches lives, shifts atmospheres, and stirs faith in the hearts of Your people.

To my Live Out Your Faith Nation family—you are warriors in the Kingdom, standing boldly in faith and refusing to back down. Your passion for prayer, your hunger for God's presence, and your unwavering belief in His promises inspire me daily. This book is for you and for every believer who dares to trust God for the impossible.

To my mentors, pastors, and spiritual leaders—your wisdom, prayers, and impartation have strengthened me along this journey. Thank you for speaking into my life, challenging me to grow, and reminding me to always keep my eyes on Jesus. Your obedience to God's call has made an eternal impact on my life.

To my dear friends—Shalon Simpson, Jocelin McElderry, Debra Henson, Cynthia Johnson, Brenda Suggs and so many others—thank you for your encouragement, your prayers, and your steadfast support. True friendship is a gift, and I do not take it lightly. You have lifted me up in prayer, walked with me through seasons of testing, and celebrated every victory with me. I am grateful beyond words.

To the editors, designers, and publishing team—thank you for your dedication, expertise, and attention to detail in bringing this book to life. Your hard work behind the scenes is seen and deeply appreciated.

And finally, to you—the reader—thank you for taking this journey of prayer with me. My prayer is that as you speak these words, heaven responds. That as you declare the promises of God, you see His power manifest in your life. May this book stir your faith, deepen your intimacy with the Father, and remind you that prayer changes everything.

Introduction

The Power of Faith-Filled Prayer

Prayer is not just words. it is a divine conversation, a supernatural exchange between heaven and earth. It is the key that unlocks breakthroughs, shifts atmospheres, and brings God's promises into manifestation. This book is not just a collection of prayers; it is a tool for transformation, a guide to help you stand in faith and boldly declare God's Word over your life.

This prayer book was birthed from our daily prayer calls, which began in January 2023. Every morning, we gathered in faith, lifting our voices as one, declaring the promises of God, and watching Him move mightily. We have seen miracles, breakthroughs, and divine shifts happen as we stood in one accord, believing God for the impossible. The prayers in this book are a direct result of that time; prayers filled with faith, spoken in authority, and rooted in the Word of God.

A Divine Visitation and the Birth of Live Out Your Faith Nation

During the COVID-19 pandemic, I experienced one of the most defining moments of my life. I became very ill with COVID-19, struggling to breathe, weak in my body, and facing uncertainty. It was one of the most intense battles I had ever encountered. As I lay there, fighting for my health, I had a divine visitation that changed everything. God spoke clearly to me, "Do what I tell you to do, nothing more and nothing less. Say what I tell you to say, nothing more and nothing less."

It was a moment of undeniable clarity. A real encounter with the Most High; a call to obedience that I could not ignore. I knew then that it was time to stop hesitating and fully step into what God had placed on my heart. That moment of divine instruction led to the birth of the Live Out Your Faith Nation Daily Prayer Call. It began with our Annual Fasting and Prayer in January 2023, and what started as a simple act of obedience quickly became a global movement. People from various countries around the world joined in, standing together in faith, interceding for one another, and witnessing the power of God in our midst.

As I submitted in obedience, I watched the vision God had given me take shape. This was more than just a prayer call, it was a divine assignment, a Kingdom movement, a gathering of faith-filled believers determined to walk in the fullness of God's promises. Through prayer, I saw lives transformed, testimonies of healing, financial breakthroughs, and supernatural interventions unfold before our eyes.

The Power of Prayer and Faith Confessions

Prayer and faith confessions have completely changed my life. I have walked through seasons where everything around me seemed to be falling apart, where it felt like I was standing in the middle of a storm with no way out. I know what it is to be in financial lack, to struggle just to make ends meet, to feel the weight of disappointment pressing in. I know what it is to face health challenges, to stand in faith for healing when doctors give you a report that shakes you to your core. I know what it is to cry out to God for restoration in relationships, to believe for open doors when everything seems closed, to trust Him when everything in the natural says it's over. And yet, through it all, I have seen the faithfulness of God prevail.

When I lost everything, my home, my car, and found myself moving from living with friends to an extended stay hotel with my daughter, I had a choice. I could either let circumstances define me, or I could hold on to what I knew was true: **God is faithful**, and **His Word never fails**. So, I began to speak faith-filled confessions every single day. I declared God's provision over my life. I reminded myself of what His Word said:

"And my God will supply every need of yours according to his riches in glory in Christ Jesus." Philippians 4:19 (ESV)

"But remember the Lord your God, for it is he who gives you the ability to produce wealth, and so confirms his covenant, which he swore to your ancestors, as it is today." Deuteronomy 8:18 (NIV)

I studied the Word of God and spoke God's promises until my faith became stronger than my fears. And step by step, He began to turn things around. I saw unexpected provision come. I saw doors open that no man could shut. I saw the power of my words shaping my reality.

Believing for the Impossible

Prayer is not just about asking, it's about believing and listening for God's voice. The Bible tells us:

> Mark 11:24 – "I tell you, you can pray for anything, and if you believe that you've received it, it will be yours." Mark 11:24 (NLT)

There were times when I had to believe God for supernatural healing, not just for myself, but for others. I have prayed for family, friends, and strangers who needed a miracle, and I have watched the power of prayer bring healing where doctors said there was no hope.

I remember praying for safety in travel, for divine protection, and for God to order every step. From moments of uncertainty to seasons of acceleration and promotion, I have learned that when I stand in faith and speak God's Word, things shift.

When I believed God for promotion, I declared:
"Father, I thank You that promotion doesn't come from people; it comes from You. So, I release my faith and expectation for promotion. Promotion comes to me now today in Jesus' name. Promotion comes to me now today in Jesus' name. God is speaking my name to people who will propel my life into abundance and goodness. Father, release contracts, new deals, overflow, clients, sponsors, grants, divine help, and angelic assistance. Let Kingdom connections be made that impact generations."

> "For promotion comes neither from the east nor from the west nor from the south. But God is the Judge: He puts down one and exalts another." Psalm 74:6-7 (NKJV)

I watched as He opened doors no man could shut and placed me in positions of influence that I knew only He could orchestrate.

How to Use This Book as a Prayer Tool

Each chapter in this book focuses on a specific area of prayer, whether it be spiritual growth, healing, financial breakthrough, divine protection, peace, or kingdom advancement. You can use these prayers in different ways:

Daily Devotion: Start or end your day in focused prayer by making room for God to speak, lead, and fill your heart with His peace, wisdom, and presence.

Targeted Intercession: If you are believing God for a specific breakthrough, find the corresponding prayer and declare it over your situation.

Corporate Prayer: Use these prayers in group settings, agreeing with others and standing on one accord.

Family Prayer: Stand with your family in agreement; praying together as a family, covering your lives and aligning with God's Word, declaring breakthrough, and building a legacy of faith.

Faith Declarations: Speak these prayers aloud, building your faith and reinforcing God's promises in your life.

Your Faith is the Key

This book is not meant to be read passively. It is meant to be prayed and declared with faith, power, and expectation! Speak these prayers as if you are commanding mountains to move because that is exactly what Jesus told us to do:

"Listen to the truth I speak to you: If someone says to this mountain with great faith and having no doubt, 'Mountain, be lifted up and thrown into the midst of the sea,' and believes that what he says will happen, it will be done." Mark 11:23 (TPT)

So, as you journey through this book, exercise your faith. Declare these prayers with conviction. Stand firm on the promises of God and expect results. My prayer for you is that as you use this book, your faith will increase, your prayers will become bolder, and you will see the supernatural hand of God move mightily in your life.

Let's pray, believe, and receive together. **Let's watch God work!** Blessings, peace and prosperity to You!

Chapter 1 - Prayers for Spiritual Growth & Walking with God

Spiritual Growth & Walking with God

Before we do anything, before we prophesy, declare, or go to war in prayer, we must first prioritize our relationship with God. This is where true power flows from: intimacy, obedience, and spiritual growth. This chapter is not about religious activity; it's about growing in deep fellowship with the Father, Son Jesus Christ, and Holy Spirit.

Spiritual growth is not optional. It's not just for preachers or intercessors; it's for every believer who desires to walk in victory and fulfill their Kingdom assignment. If I'm going to win in life, I have to be anchored in truth, rooted in the Word, and led by the Holy Spirit. Everything else flows from that foundation.

God is calling His sons and daughters into spiritual maturity. No more surface-level faith and mediocre living. No more emotional rollercoasters and lukewarm living. It's time to grow up in the Spirit, to walk with God daily, and to yield every area of our lives to His Lordship.

This chapter is your invitation to come closer to the Father, Son and Holy Ghost. To abide in Jesus Christ. To be pruned. To be filled again. To be refreshed and renewed. To glean from His presence. Whether you're just getting started or you've walked with the Lord for many years, there's always room to grow and connect with God at a deeper level. There is always more. More fire. More clarity. More revelation. More wisdom. More fruit. More grace.

Jesus said in John 15:5 (NLT) – *"Yes, I am the vine; you are the branches. Those who remain in me, and I in them, will produce much fruit. For apart from me you can do nothing."* That's the heart of spiritual growth: remaining vitally united to in Him. He is the true vine.

In this section, we're going to:

- Invite the Holy Spirit to take over every area of our lives
- Ask God to help us walk in discernment, wisdom, and sanctification
- Pray to hear His voice clearly and obey His leading
- Confess our hunger to delight in the Word and be rooted in truth
- Declare a fresh fire to walk with God in full surrender and boldness

You'll find prayers focused on walking in forgiveness, abiding in Jesus, yielding to the Holy Spirit, and living a Christ-centered life. These aren't just beautiful prayers, they are life-shaping tools, in your prayer arsenal. Speak the prayers and faith confessions with faith and boldness, allow the Holy Spirit to do a deep work in you.

You were never meant to walk this faith journey on your own. Spiritual growth doesn't happen by striving, it happens by surrendering. As you walk through this chapter, I challenge you to open your heart wide. Allow the Lord to search you, purify you, and align you with His will, plan and way. The fruit of this growth will touch every area of your life, your family, your decisions, your peace, your authority, and your impact.

Let's grow. Let's be intentional about walking with God like never before. Let's pray from a place of relationship, not performance.

Living a Christ-Centered Life

Heavenly Father, I come boldly before Your throne of grace, with my heart surrendered and eyes fixed on Jesus, the Author and Finisher of my faith. You are my foundation, Savior, and King, and I declare that I desire to live a life fully centered in You.

Lord, Your Word says in Matthew 6:33 that if I seek first Your kingdom and righteousness, everything I need will be added to me. Today, I realign my priorities and place You at the very center of my life. I make room for you and give you first place and the highest priority in my life. You are Most High and I make you Most High over every area of my life.

Father, forgive me for the times I allowed distractions, busyness, and worldly desires to pull me away from Your presence. I repent and turn my heart back to You. Teach me to walk daily in surrender and obedience, not leaning on my own understanding but trusting fully in You.

Lord, Your Word declares in Galatians 2:20 that I have been crucified with Christ, and it is no longer I who lives, but Christ who lives in me. Help me to die to my flesh, pride, and self-centered ways so that Your life may flow through me.

Holy Spirit, guide my thoughts, decisions, and actions. Let everything, I do bring glory and honor to the Father. Strengthen me to live a life of integrity, humility, and compassion. Teach me to abide in You, as it says in John 15:5, for apart from You, I can do nothing.

Father, ignite within me an unquenchable hunger for Your Word, a passion for worship, and an unyielding desire for Your presence. May I never grow complacent in my relationship with You but seek You with all my heart, soul, and mind.

Lord, empower me to reflect Christ's love to those around me. May my life be a testimony of Your grace and power. Open doors for me to share the Gospel boldly and lead others to the saving knowledge of Jesus Christ.

I declare Philippians 1:21 over my life: *"For to me to live is Christ, and to die is gain."* Let this be my life's anthem, mission, and purpose.

Father, fill me with courage, boldness, and unwavering faith. Strengthen me to stand firm on Your Word in a world filled with compromise. Let my life shine brightly as a beacon of light, pointing others to Your love and truth.

I thank You, Lord, for drawing me closer to You, for molding me into Your image, and for giving me the privilege to walk in fellowship with You daily.

I believe, I receive this prayer, and I release my most holy faith to bring it to pass. In the mighty and matchless name of Jesus Christ, I pray. Amen and amen!

Abiding in Jesus and an Invitation to the Holy Spirit

Heavenly Father, in the name of Jesus Christ, I come boldly before Your throne of grace, giving You glory, honor, and praise for who You are. Lord, I acknowledge that You are the true vine, and apart from You, I can do nothing. I thank You for the privilege of abiding in You and for the life, strength, and fruitfulness that come from staying connected to You (John 15:5).

Holy Spirit, I welcome You into this moment, into this prayer time, and into every space I step into. Saturate this atmosphere with Your holy presence. Rest mightily upon me, lead me and guide me into all truth. I give You full control. Speak to me, renew me, and fill me afresh with Your power and Your love. Let Your presence transform and empower me as I learn to abide fully in Jesus (John 16:13).

Jesus, I thank You for being my refuge and my strength, my ever-present help in time of need. I declare that I am a branch, and as I remain in You, I will bear much fruit. I surrender every part of my life to You, knowing that apart from You, I can do nothing. Lord, let Your Word take root in my heart and produce a harvest of righteousness, transforming me and aligning me with Your perfect will (John 15:4-5).

Heavenly Father, I choose to abide in Your love and to walk fully in all You've called me to be. Let Your peace guard my heart and mind and let Your joy overflow in my life as I stay rooted in You. Let the fruit of the Spirit; love, joy, peace, patience, kindness, goodness, faithfulness, gentleness, and self-control, be evident in all I say and do (Galatians 5:22-23).

I bind and cast down every distraction, every hindrance, and every lie of the enemy that would try to disconnect me from Your presence and my relationship with You. I declare that nothing can separate me from Your love, for I am more than a conqueror through Christ who loves me (Romans 8:37-39).

Strengthen me, Lord, to remain steadfast in You and Your Word, even in the midst of trials and challenges.

I delight in Your Word, and I ask that it dwells richly in my heart, transforming, guiding, shaping, and renewing me daily. Let me be like a tree planted by streams of water, yielding fruit in every season, and prospering in all that I do because I am rooted in You (Psalm 1:3; Colossians 3:16).

Holy Spirit, continue to lead me, speak to me, and empower me to abide in Jesus Christ. Let Your presence fill me with boldness and courage to live a Christ-centered life. I thank You for aligning my heart with the will of the Father and for using me to bring glory to Your name. May my life be a living testimony of the power of abiding in Jesus Christ.

I seal this prayer in faith, declaring that I will abide in Jesus Christ, and His life-giving power flows through me, setting me free. I believe, I receive this prayer and I release most holy faith to bring it to pass. In the mighty and matchless name of Jesus Christ, amen! It is so!

Delighting in the Word of God

Heavenly Father, I come before You today with a heart full of honor and gratitude for the priceless gift of Your Word. Your Word is life, light, and truth, and I thank You for giving me access to this divine treasure.

Lord, stir within me an unquenchable hunger and thirst for Your Word. Just as it is written in Psalm 1:2, I desire to delight in Your law and meditate on it day and night. Let me find joy, wisdom, and direction every time I open the pages of the Holy Scriptures.

Father, teach me to approach Your Word with reverence and great expectation. Remove every distraction, every hindrance, and every mindset that keeps me from prioritizing time in Your presence. Let Your Word dwell in my heart richly, shaping my thoughts, attitudes, and decisions.

Holy Spirit, illuminate the Scriptures as I study. Bring divine clarity and understanding so that I can comprehend the truth. Open my spiritual eyes to see the treasures hidden within Your Word. As You commanded in Joshua 1:8, I will meditate on Your Word day and night, so I may live in obedience and walk in success according to Your promises.

Lord, I declare that Your Word is a lamp to my feet and a light to my path (Psalm 119:105). In moments of uncertainty, guide me with Your truth, Your Word is Your truth. In moments of weakness, strengthen me with Your promises and remind me of Your word. In moments of doubt, remind me of Your faithfulness. Hallelujah.

Father, I ask that Your Word transforms me from the inside out. Just as it says in Hebrews 4:12, Your Word is alive and active, sharper than any two-edged sword. Let it pierce through every fear, every insecurity, and every stronghold in my life.

Let my life be a reflection of Your Word. Help me not only to be a hearer but a doer of the Word, applying it in every area of my life. As it says in 2 Timothy 3:16-17, may Your Word equip me for every good work and prepare me to fulfill my God-given purpose.

I pray for boldness to speak Your Word, faith to believe Your Word, and perseverance to live by Your Word. Let my heart overflow with Scripture, and may my conversations be seasoned with grace and truth of Your promises.

Lord, let the seeds of Your Word be deeply rooted in my heart. Protect them from being stolen by the enemy, choked by the cares of life, or withered by neglect. Let them grow, flourish, and bear much fruit in my life for Your Kingdom.

I declare that Your Word will not return to me void but will accomplish everything You sent it to do. I submit myself fully to the authority of Your Word, and I rejoice in the promises it contains. I believe I receive this prayer, and I release my most holy faith to bring it to pass.

In the mighty and matchless name of Jesus I pray, amen and amen!

Writing the Word of God on the Tablet of My Heart

Heavenly Father, in the mighty and matchless name of Jesus Christ, I come before You today with my heart open and ready to receive all that you have for me. Lord, I don't want to just be a hearer of Your Word, I want it to be written on the very tablet of my heart. I want Your truth to be embedded so deeply within me that it governs my thoughts, directs my steps, and transforms every area of my life.

Father, help me to engrave Your Word into the depths of my being. Let it be more than something I read, let it become the very foundation of how I live (Proverbs 3:3).

Lord, I hide Your Word in the core of who I am (Psalm 119:11). Let it shape my decisions, mold my character, and align my life with Your perfect will. When trials come, let Your Word rise up as a shield around me. When confusion tries to creep in, let Your Word illuminate my path and bring clarity and peace. When the enemy whispers lies, let Your Word in me silence every voice that is not from You.

Father, I declare that Your Word is a lamp to my feet and a light to my path (Psalm 119:105). In dark seasons, Your Word is my guide. In uncertain times, it gives me clarity. It is my compass, my roadmap, and the undeniable truth that keeps me grounded. No matter what storms may arise, I will stand firm because Your Word is my firm foundation.

I thank You for the transforming power of Your Word. Lord, as I meditate on Your Word, let it renew my mind, shift my perspective, and break every stronghold in my mind, will and emotions (Romans 12:2). Let it wash over me, cleansing every thought, every attitude, and every belief that doesn't align with Your truth.

I reject every distraction, hindrance, and excuse that would try to keep me from knowing, meditating on, and applying Your Word. I receive a fresh hunger and deep passion for Your truth. Let it be as Jeremiah 15:16 (NIV) declares: "When Your words came, I ate them; they were my joy and my heart's delight." Lord, let Your Word be my delight. Let it dwell richly in me, transforming me from the inside out.

I believe that as I meditate on and declare Your Word, I am being transformed, renewed, strengthened, and empowered to walk in divine wisdom, authority, and victory.

I believe I receive this prayer, and I release my most holy faith to bring it to pass. In Jesus' mighty name I pray, amen!

Discernment and Spirit-led Living

Heavenly Father, in the name of Jesus, I thank You for the gift of the Holy Spirit, who leads me into all truth. Lord, today, I ask for you to sharpen my spiritual senses so that I may recognize Your voice clearly, distinguish between truth and deception, and walk in the fullness of Your wisdom. May my senses be sharpened to comprehend Your direction and leadership.

Holy Spirit, guide my thoughts, decisions, and actions. Let me not be moved by emotions, pressure, or fear, but by the leading of Your Holy Spirit. Give me the ability to discern opportunities from distractions, true friends from fake ones, and wise decisions from foolish ones. Help me to walk in the spirit and not according to the impulses of my flesh.

Father, let me be discerning in my relationships, finances, business, and ministry. Help me to see beyond the surface and recognize what is truly of You. Give me wisdom in stewarding my money, time, resources, and assignments so that I do not fall into the traps of the enemy.

I reject confusion, deception, and manipulation. I declare that my heart is sensitive to Your guidance, my ears are tuned in to Your voice and aligned with the heavenly frequency, and my steps are ordered by You. I will not be led astray, but I will walk in supernatural discernment, wisdom, and understanding.

Thank You, Lord, for the leadership of the Holy Spirit in my life. I yield to You completely and trust that You are directing me in the way I should go. I believe I receive this prayer, and I release my most holy faith to bring it to pass. In Jesus' name I pray, amen!

Hearing God's Voice

Heavenly Father, I come before your throne of grace through and by the blood of Jesus. I enter your presence with a humble and submitted heart. It is written in Your Word according to John 10:27-28 that Your sheep know Your Voice. I am one of Your sheep. I ask You to teach me to know Your Voice and to hear You distinctly and clearly. I ask You Lord to teach me to discern every spirit to know if they are of You. As it is written in 1 John 4:1-2, that I should not believe every spirit but test the spirits to determine whether the spirits are of God. I ask You Father to draw me closer to You so I will not heed the voice of a stranger.

In the name of Jesus, I decree and declare, that my ears are anointed to hear the voice of God clearly. I hear the voice of the Good Shepherd. I purpose to listen to my heavenly Father's voice, and the voice of a stranger I will not follow. I roll my works upon You Lord, commit and trust them wholly to You. You will cause my thoughts to become agreeable to Your will, and so shall my plans be established and succeed. Thank You for Your love and commitment to me, in the name of Jesus I pray. Amen.

I believe that I receive all that I have prayed and release most holy faith to bring it to pass.

The Gift of Prophecy, Hearing, and Seeing in the Spirit

Heavenly Father, in the mighty and matchless name of Jesus Christ, I enter Your throne of grace this morning, thanking You for Your divine presence and Your endless love. You are the Alpha and the Omega, the God who sees all and knows all, and today, I surrender myself to You, asking for an outpouring of Your prophetic anointing upon my life. Lord, I come as Your vessel, hungry to hear Your voice and see with clarity in the Spirit.

Father, Your Word declares in Joel 2:28 (KJV): *"And it shall come to pass afterward, that I will pour out my spirit upon all flesh; and your sons and your daughters shall prophesy, your old men shall dream dreams, your young men shall see visions."* Today, I decree and declare that this promise is alive in me! Pour out Your Spirit afresh, Lord! Open the heavens and let the oil of prophecy flow freely over my life.

Lord, I ask that You anoint my eyes with the seer's anointing, that I may see clearly into the realm of the Spirit. Illuminate my spiritual eyes, Lord! Let the scales fall off and let me see the things You want to reveal, visions, revelations, and divine mysteries hidden in You (Ephesians 1:18).

Father, anoint my ears to hear with precision and clarity. Your Word says in John 10:27 (ESV): *"My sheep hear my voice, and I know them, and they follow me."* Lord, I declare that I hear Your voice above all others. Silence every noise, distraction, and counterfeit word that tries to deceive or mislead me. Sharpen my discernment, so that I may know what is from You and walk in obedience to Your direction.

Holy Spirit, release Your fire upon me now! As it is written in Isaiah 50:4 (KJV): *"The Lord God hath given me the tongue of the learned, that I should know how to speak a word in season to him that is weary."* I ask for prophetic boldness to speak what I see and hear, declaring Your will on earth as it is in heaven. Let my tongue be filled with divine utterance, releasing words that bring life, encouragement, and edification to those who hear.

Lord, just as You anointed the prophets of old, I ask for that same mantle to rest upon me. Let me walk in alignment with Your Word and with heaven's agenda. I surrender my thoughts, my heart, and my spirit to You. Let everything in me align with Your will, and may I never shrink back from the prophetic call You have placed on my life.

Father, I stand on the promise of Amos 3:7 (NIV): *"Surely the Sovereign Lord does nothing without revealing His plan to His servants the prophets."* I ask You to reveal Your plans, Your mysteries, and Your strategies for this season of my life. Make me sensitive to Your Spirit so I can partner with You in advancing Your kingdom.

Finally, Lord, I bind every spirit of confusion, deception, and fear that would try to hinder the flow of Your prophetic anointing in my life. I release the power of the Holy Ghost to activate the seer's anointing, sharpen my spiritual ears, and empower me to prophesy with boldness and authority.

I declare that I am anointed to see, to hear, and to speak what thus says the Lord! I receive this impartation by faith, and I seal this prayer in the blood of Jesus Christ. I believe I receive this prayer, and I release my faith to see it manifested in my life. In the mighty and powerful name of Jesus, I pray, Amen and Amen!

Holy Spirit Our Teacher

Heavenly Father, in the name of Jesus, I come before You with a heart full of gratitude for the precious gift of the Holy Spirit. You did not leave me as an orphan, but You sent the Spirit of Truth to teach me, lead me, and guide me in all things. Holy Spirit, I welcome You! Have Your way in my life. Open my spiritual eyes to see, my ears to hear, and my heart to receive divine wisdom and revelation.

Teach me what I do not know but I need to know. Remind me of what I have forgotten. Illuminate the deep mysteries of Your Word. Lead me in the paths of wisdom and righteousness. I will not lean on my own understanding, but I trust fully in Your guidance. Remove every veil, every distraction, and every hindrance that would keep me from hearing Your voice clearly.

I declare that I am a student of the Holy Spirit! I am not led by the flesh or by the wisdom of this world, but by the Spirit of God who reveals all truth and equips me for every good work. Strengthen me to discern between truth and deception, to operate in spiritual wisdom, and to move in divine understanding. Lord, let Your Spirit rest upon me, the Spirit of wisdom, counsel, knowledge, might, and the fear of the Lord. I hunger for more of You.

Father, I thank You for fresh revelation, supernatural insight, and divine strategies that come from Your Spirit. I receive Your teaching with joy, and I choose to walk in obedience to Your instruction. Thank You for leading me into all truth. I declare that I will not be deceived, distracted, or discouraged, but I will walk in the fullness of the Spirit! I believe I receive this prayer and release my most holy faith to bring it to pass. In the name of Jesus I pray, amen!

Yielded to the Holy Spirit: Living a Life Led by God

Heavenly Father, in the mighty name of Jesus, I approach Your throne of grace with a humble and surrendered heart. Father, I acknowledge that apart from You, I can do nothing, but with You, all things are possible. Today, I position myself to hear Your voice and follow the leading of Your precious Holy Spirit.

Holy Spirit, I invite You to take Your rightful place in my life. Lead me and direct me. Direct my steps, my decisions, my thoughts, and every aspect of my life. I surrender completely, not relying on my own strength or understanding, but fully leaning on your wisdom, understanding, and divine insight. Your Word declares in Romans 8:14, *"For as many as are led by the Spirit of God, these are sons of God."* I affirm today that I am Your child, and I choose to walk boldly and confidently under Your leadership.

Father, give me ears to hear Your voice with greater clarity than ever before. Tune my heart to Your frequency; silence every distraction and remove every hindrance. Let my spirit be sensitive to Your promptings and my heart quick to respond in obedience to your word. Your Word promises in John 10:27, *"My sheep hear My voice, and I know them, and they follow Me."* Lord, I declare that I am Your sheep, I know Your voice, I hear Your instructions, and I follow You.

Today, I yield every area of my life; my dreams, goals, plans, relationships, business, ministry, finances, and future to You. Holy Spirit, take control and establish Your perfect will in my life. I commit to live a surrendered, Spirit-led life, bearing abundant fruit that honors You and advances Your Kingdom.

Lord, remove any resistance, pride, or self-sufficiency from my heart. My sufficiency is in you. Fill me with humility, courage, and unwavering trust to follow wherever You lead. Your path is the path of peace, victory, abundance, and purpose, and today, I choose Your way above my own.

I thank You, Father, for Your faithfulness, Your guidance, and Your love which fails not. I embrace the beautiful life that flows from yielding fully to Your Holy Spirit. Oh Lord, let Your presence saturate my life, guide my every decision, and empower me to walk victoriously every day.

I believe I receive this prayer, and I release most holy faith to bring it to pass. In the matchless name of Jesus Christ, I pray, amen and amen!

Invite the Holy Spirit into Every Area of My Life

Father, in the name of Jesus, I come before You today, filled with gratitude for Your precious gift, the Holy Spirit. I welcome You, Holy Spirit, into my life with open arms and a surrendered heart. I don't just invite You in to visit, today, I invite You to dwell fully in me. I ask you to move in every area of my life, my heart, my mind, my family, my finances, my health, my career, and ministry. Fill every corner and every space of my life with Your sweet presence.

I love You and want to know you more. You are my Friend, my Comforter, my Guide, and the one who empowers me to walk in victory. You are the One who teaches me, leads me, and shows me the will and plan of God. I yield myself to you so that I am fully aligned with You, in my thoughts, decisions, and actions.

Lord God, I remember Your Word in John 14:26 (NASB), *"But the Helper, the Holy Spirit, whom the Father will send in My name, He will teach you all things and bring to your remembrance all that I have said to you."* Holy Spirit, I invite You to teach me. Remind me of God's promises. Open the eyes of my understanding so I can walk in alignment with God's purpose for my life. I trust that You are the one who helps me make sense of everything in my life.

I desire to walk in deeper communion with You. I open my heart to You fully and completely. Your presence is my greatest joy. I don't want to miss a moment with You, and I ask that You move freely in me today. I surrender all control to You. Take over my thoughts, my emotions, my will, and my actions. Use me to glorify God and to fulfill His purposes on the earth.

Romans 8:14 (NIV) says, *"For those who are led by the Spirit of God are the children of God."* I declare that I am led by You, Holy Spirit. I trust that Your guidance is always perfect, and I walk in the direction that you are leading me. I thank You for the wisdom and understanding You give me each day.

I know that You bring peace, joy, and life where there is none. In Galatians 5:22-23, I am reminded that the fruit of the Spirit is love, joy, peace, forbearance, kindness, goodness, faithfulness, gentleness, and self-control. I welcome the fullness of Your fruit into my life today. Let Your love overflow through me, Your peace fill every space, and Your joy be my strength.

I give You full permission to work in every area of my life. I ask that You cleanse me, heal me, and renew me. Bring Your light into every dark place and restore everything that needs to be made whole. You have full access and I trust You with every part of me.

In Ephesians 3:16-17, Paul prayed that we would be strengthened by the Spirit in our inner being so that Christ might dwell in our hearts through faith. I declare today that my inner man is being strengthened, that Jesus Christ is alive in me, and that I am more equipped to do all that God has called me to do because of the power of the Holy Spirit.

Holy Spirit, I care deeply for You, and I desire Your tangible presence in my life. Reveal yourself to me. I trust that as I invite You into my life today, You will move with power, bring transformation, and lead me into greater intimacy with the Father. I surrender to You now. I'm open to Your guidance and correction. I receive your anointing on my life this day. Have Your way in my life. In Jesus' name, I pray. Amen.

Faith Confessions to Declare:
- Holy Spirit, I invite You into my heart. I ask that You fill me with Your love, peace, and joy. Let Your presence transform my inner being so that I reflect the heart of God in every thought, emotion, and action.
- Holy Spirit, I invite You into my mind. I ask You to bring clarity, understanding, and wisdom. Illuminate my thoughts with divine insight and help me align my thinking with the

truth of God's Word. Fill my mind with peace, removing all anxiety, confusion, and negativity.
- Holy Spirit, I invite You into my relationships. I ask You to fill my interactions with love, patience, and kindness. Let Your goodness flow through me in all my relationships. Help me to communicate with grace and wisdom, reflecting Your gentleness and humility in every conversation.
- Holy Spirit, I invite You into my finances. I declare that You bring wisdom, provision, and favor. Teach me how to steward the resources You've entrusted to me with integrity and faithfulness. I invite Your creativity to flow in my decisions and strategies, bringing abundance and blessing according to God's will.
- Holy Spirit, I invite You into my health. I ask You to bring healing, strength, and restoration to my body. I invite Your renewing power to flow in and through every cell, every organ, and every system in my body. I declare that by Your stripes, I am healed, and I receive Your divine healing today.
- Holy Spirit, I invite You into my career and ministry. I ask You to bring clarity, excellence, and favor in all my tasks. Help me to serve with diligence, creativity, and integrity. I invite Your wisdom and guidance into every project, every meeting, and every decision I make.
- Holy Spirit, I invite You into my home. I ask You to fill every room with peace, harmony, and love. Let Your presence be the foundation of my household. I pray for Your protection over my family, and I invite You to guide us in unity, respect, and mutual support.
- Holy Spirit, I invite You into my purpose and destiny. I surrender my dreams and aspirations to You, asking for Your guidance in walking out God's will for my life. Empower me

to live out my purpose boldly and with confidence, knowing that You are the One who strengthens me.
- Holy Spirit, I invite You into my spirit. I open myself fully to Your presence. I want to feel Your comfort, hear Your voice, and experience communion with you. I trust that You will lead me into deeper intimacy with the Father, filling me with the fullness of His love and His will for my life

Yielding to the Lord and Welcoming the Holy Spirit

Father, in the mighty and matchless name of Jesus Christ, I enter Your throne of grace with a heart full of thanksgiving and reverence. I come before You acknowledging that You are my sovereign King, my Redeemer, and the Giver of every good and perfect gift. You are holy, righteous, and altogether worthy of my praise.

Lord, today I yield everything to You, my heart, my plans, and my desires. I submit myself under the authority of Your will, declaring that Your glory will be revealed in my life and in the earth. Let Your mercies, which are new every morning, flow into every situation I face, saturating me with Your peace, favor, and power.

Holy Spirit, I welcome You! Come and invade my life with Your presence. I invite You to take complete control. Fall fresh upon me with Your holy fire, burning away everything that is not like You. I ask for Your power to rest heavily upon my life, releasing signs, wonders, and miracles. Move through me. Renew, revive, and empower me to walk in the fullness of Your glory.

You are the Spirit of truth, the Spirit of power, and the Spirit of life. Saturate my heart and mind with Your anointing. Fill every dry place, heal every broken place, and breathe fresh life into every weary part of my soul. Let the fire of Pentecost fall fresh upon me now, stirring up boldness, authority, and victory within me.

Father, I decree that as Your Spirit moves in my life, chains are breaking, walls are falling down, strongholds are breaking, and freedom is being released upon me. I stand in the victory that was already won for me by Jesus Christ on the cross of Calvary. Your Word declares in 2 Corinthians 3:17 (TPT) that *"Wherever the Lord is, there is freedom."* So today, I proclaim liberty over my life, home, and every situation connected to me, right now, in the name of Jesus!

Lord, let Your favor flow, let Your peace reign, and let Your glory fill my life. Holy Spirit, I surrender all to You, move as You will, speak as You desire, and transform every part of me in this moment. Lord, I believe Your holy fire is falling right now. Your power is flowing through every part of my life, and Your presence is saturating the very atmosphere around me. Nothing stays the same in your presence.

I give You all the honor, all the glory, and all the praise. I believe I receive this prayer, and I release my faith to see it come to pass. In the powerful and matchless name of Jesus, I pray. Amen and amen!

The Fruitfulness of Abiding in Jesus

Father, in the mighty name of Jesus, I come before You with a heart fully surrendered. I honor You as the true Vine, and I declare that apart from You, I can do nothing. Because I abide in You and Your Word abides in me, my life bears much fruit, fruit that remains, fruit that glorifies You, and fruit that impacts every area of my life.

Lord, I submit myself completely to You today. I lay down my plans, desires, and will. I choose to stay connected to You, the source of my life. You said in John 15:5 (NIV), "I am the vine; you are the branches. If you remain in me and I in you, you will bear much fruit; apart from me you can do nothing." So, I make the decision to remain in You, not just in word, but in action, in thought, and in every part of my being.

Because I abide in You:

Spiritually, I am growing in faith, wisdom, and discernment. My relationship with You is deepening every day. I am being transformed into the image of Jesus Christ.

Emotionally, I walk in the peace of God that settles my heart, mind and soul. The joy of the Lord strengthens me and keep me stable in my emotions. No matter the storm, I'm anchored, focused, and unshaken in Him.

Physically, I declare good health, healing, strength, and vitality. My body is the temple of the Holy Spirit, and I walk in divine health.

In my relationships, I cultivate connections rooted in love, trust, and godly purpose. My family, friendships, and partnerships are blessed and thriving.

In my purpose and calling, I have clarity, direction, and boldness to fulfill the assignments You've placed on my life. I am effective, fruitful, and walking in divine alignment.

Financially, I experience provision, overflow, and wisdom in stewardship. I walk in abundance, debt freedom, and opportunities that reflect Your favor and goodness on my life.

In my career and business, I operate in excellence, creativity, and favor. Doors are opening, opportunities are coming my way, and I am advancing with purpose and impact.

As a leader and influencer, I am a light in dark places, a voice of hope, and a vessel of wisdom. I inspire, empower, and uplift others to know You more.

In my legacy, I am sowing seeds of faith into the next generation. My children, my family, and all connected to me will experience the ripple effects of my obedience to You.

For Kingdom impact, I am a laborer in Your harvest. Souls are saved, lives are transformed, and Your Kingdom is advanced through my words, witness and work.

In personal development, I grow daily in character, discipline, and resilience. I'm becoming the best version of who You've called me to be.

Mentally, I have the mind of Christ. I reject anxiety, fear, and confusion. I walk in peace, mental clarity, and soundness of mind.

Father, prune me. Remove anything that hinders my growth. Cut away what no longer serves Your purpose in my life. I don't fear the pruning because I know it's making room for more fruit, more impact, and more of Your glory revealed in me.

I declare that I am planted by rivers of living water. I bear fruit in every season whether in times of abundance or challenge because my roots go deep in You. My leaves do not wither, and whatever I do prospers because Your hand is on my life.

I seal this prayer in faith and bold expectation. I believe I receive this prayer and release most holy faith to bring it to pass. In Jesus' name, I pray, amen!

Walk in Sanctification and Surrender Before the Lord

Father, I come before You today with a heart surrendered and full of gratitude. I acknowledge that You are my everything, my savior, my redeemer, and my strength. I am fully aware that I cannot walk this journey of life without Your grace, guidance, and power.

Lord, I choose to surrender all to You today. I surrender my will, plans, desires, everything that is within me. I lay it all down at Your feet, knowing that Your will for my life is perfect and full of purpose. I trust You with every area of my life, Father. I invite You to purify my heart and cleanse me from anything that is not of You.

1 Thessalonians 4:3-5 (ESV) says, *"For this is the will of God, your sanctification: that you abstain from sexual immorality; that each one of you know how to control his own body in holiness and honor, not in the passion of lust like the Gentiles who do not know God"*. Lord, I desire to live a life that reflects Your holiness and Your righteousness. I ask that You sanctify me, set me apart for Your purpose. Remove anything in me that does not align with Your will. I don't just want to be transformed on the outside, but I ask for a deep, inner transformation, one that only You can do. Let Your Word wash over me and renew my mind, that I may be more like You every day.

I surrender my emotions, my thoughts, and my actions to You. Help me to be led by Your Spirit in all things. In moments of temptation, remind me that I am a new creation in Christ, empowered to walk in Your ways. Let Your holiness be the foundation of every decision I make.

Romans 12:1-2 tells us to present our bodies as a living sacrifice, holy and pleasing to You, and not to be conformed to this world, but to be transformed by the renewing of our minds. Lord, I present myself to You today. Take my life and make it holy before You. I refuse to be conformed to the ways of this world. I choose to be transformed by Your Word, by Your Spirit, and by Your love.

I declare that I am sanctified by the blood of Jesus, and I walk in the power of His resurrection. I thank You, Holy Spirit, for the work You are doing in me. Fill me with Your presence and continue to guide me to walk in purity, peace, and grace. I submit to Your will, and I trust that You will equip me to live a life worthy of Your calling.

Father, I ask for strength to surrender completely, no reservations, and no holding back. Have Your way in my life, Lord. I give You full control, and I trust that as I walk in sanctification, You will be glorified in all things. In Jesus' name, I pray. Amen.

Walking in Forgiveness

Heavenly Father, I come before You today with a humble heart, fully aware of my need for Your grace and mercy. Lord, You are the God who forgives, who casts my sins as far as the east is from the west, and who remembers them no more (Psalm 103:12).

Father, I confess that there have been times I have held onto offenses, nursed wounds, and allowed bitterness to take root in my heart. Today, I repent. I lay every hurt, every grudge, and every offense at the foot of the Cross. Cleanse my heart, Lord, and make me whole.

Your Word tells me in Ephesians 4:31-32 to put away all bitterness, rage, and anger, and instead be kind and compassionate, forgiving just as You forgave me in Christ. Help me to live this out daily. Teach me to forgive even when it's hard, even when it feels unjust, and even when it costs me my pride.

I release those who have wronged me. I let go of resentment, anger, and any desire for revenge. Just as You forgave me, I choose to forgive others (Matthew 6:14-15). I refuse to let unforgiveness block my prayers, hinder my growth, or steal my peace.

Lord, make me a vessel of Your love and mercy. Let forgiveness flow freely from my heart and be evident in how I live and speak. Heal every wound in me caused by unforgiveness; emotional wounds, spiritual wounds, and relational wounds.

Father, give me the courage to seek forgiveness from those I have hurt. Give me the humility to admit where I have missed it, make things right, and walk in restoration. Holy Spirit, empower me to keep forgiving, not just once, but as many times as needed (Colossians 3:13). When the pain tries to rise again, remind me of Your grace and the debt You paid on my behalf.

Lord, I also lift up those moments when I struggle to forgive myself. Help me to receive Your forgiveness fully and walk in the freedom You have already provided. I break agreement with guilt, shame, and condemnation, they no longer have a place in my life.

Today, I declare that I will walk in forgiveness, live in love, and move forward in freedom. Bitterness has no place in my heart. Resentment has no power over me. My prayers will not be hindered (Mark 11:25), because my heart is clean and my spirit is yielded.

Thank You, Father, for the gift of forgiveness and for the example You gave me through Jesus Christ. I declare that I am free and they are free too. I am whole and I am walking in alignment with Your will.

I believe I receive this prayer, and I release my most holy faith to bring it to pass. In the mighty and matchless name of Jesus, I pray. Amen and amen.

Renewed Fellowship with the Lord

Heavenly Father, I come before You today standing in the gap for every believer who has drifted from Your presence. Your Word says in Jeremiah 24:7 that You will give them hearts that recognize You as Lord, and they will return to You wholeheartedly. Today, I stand on that promise and lift them up in prayer, believing for their full restoration.

Father, I ask that You break every chain of guilt, shame, and condemnation that has kept them away from you. Let them know that Your arms are open wide, ready to embrace them just like the father welcomed the prodigal son in Luke 15:20.

Lord, heal every spiritual wound, disappointment, and offense that caused them to drift. Your Word in Hosea 14:4 says, You will heal their faithlessness and pour out boundless love. Pour out that love now over every son and daughter who has wandered away from you.

Holy Spirit, draw them back with Your loving kindness and tender mercy. Woo their hearts again. Strip away every distraction and silence every lie the enemy has whispered. Remind them they are forgiven, they are redeemed, and they are fully restored by the blood of Jesus.

Father, restore the joy of their salvation (Psalm 51:12). Rekindle their passion for prayer, worship, and time in the Word. I speak fresh fire over their spirit. Let every ounce of spiritual weariness be replaced with new hunger and holy zeal for Your presence.

I declare that every stronghold, every lie, and every thought that has tried to exalt itself above the truth of God is coming down right now in the name of Jesus (2 Corinthians 10:4-5).

Lord, lead them back into fellowship with a life-giving, Spirit-led community. Surround them with godly mentors, faith-filled relationships, and divine connections that will lift them, sharpen them, and speak life into them.

Your Word says in 2 Timothy 2:25-26 that You are able to bring them to their senses and free them from every trap of the enemy. So, I declare today that every snare is broken, every lie and deception of the enemy is exposed, and every hold of the enemy is broken off their lives. They are coming out, now. They are free right now in Jesus' name.

I thank You in advance that these sons and daughters are coming home. They are not lost, they are found. They are not bound, they are free. Their hearts are turning back to You. Their hands are lifted again in worship. Their lives are coming into alignment with Your perfect will.

I speak full restoration over them now. They are walking in step with the Holy Spirit, filled with joy, and growing stronger in love for You every single day. I celebrate the testimonies ahead of time.

I believe I receive this prayer, and I release my most holy faith to bring it to pass. In the mighty name of Jesus, Amen and Amen

Chapter 2: Prayers of Repentance, Surrender and Obedience

Repentance, Surrender, and Obedience

If we're going to walk in Kingdom authority, we must first walk in surrender. Yes, we can't have the power of God without fully surrendering and submitting to him. There is no spiritual power without obedience. There is no favor without submission. We cannot carry the weight of our assignment and walk in the fullness of God's promises while holding on to sin, pride, rebellion, or self-will.

This chapter is about humbling ourselves before the Lord, not in shame, but in humility, acknowledging that without Him, we are nothing. It's about repenting for anything in our lives that has grieved the Holy Spirit, hindered our prayers, or held us back from stepping fully into who God has called us to be.

The truth is, repentance is not just a one-time act. Repentance is a lifestyle, a way of life. A heart that stays soft, tender and submitted before the Lord. A posture that says, "God, if there's anything in me that doesn't look like You, take it out." True repentance is not just about remorse; it's about turning back to God's way of living. It's about saying, "Yes, Lord" all over again.

Surrendering to God is so powerful. It's the soil where miracles are seeded and grow. When I surrender, I'm telling God, "You can have it all, my pain, my timing, my dreams, my plans, my gifts and my talents." It's in that place of total surrender that Holy Spirit flows freely through me.

Obedience is where breakthrough is birthed and lives. Obedience opens doors that striving never will. Obedience is not about living legalistic rules and laws. Obedience aligns us with Heaven's agenda and positions us for favor, acceleration, and divine access. Obedience brings freedom. Even Jesus, our perfect example, obeyed unto death and because of that obedience, we now walk in eternal life.

In this chapter, we will:

- Offer sincere prayers of repentance and ask God to cleanse and restore us
- Lay down our will, our plans, and our fears in exchange for His divine purpose
- Pray for a heart that's quick to obey, even when we don't understand
- Ask the Lord to help us walk in the fruit of the Spirit, not just in gifting
- Declare our "Yes" to God again and mean it

According to 1 John 1:9 (NLT) – *"But if we confess our sins to him, he is faithful and just to forgive us our sins and to cleanse us from all wickedness."* We are not praying for forgiveness hoping to earn something, we're praying with confidence, knowing that He is faithful to cleanse us and restore us.

You will find prayers here to submit to God's will, walk in the Spirit, overcome rebellion, hear and obey His voice, and live a life of full surrender. These are not weak prayers. They are prayers for warriors. They are prayers for you. Because every time you bow your heart to God, you rise in greater power and authority.

Let this chapter be a turning point for you. Let it be where generational cycles break, clarity and revelation comes, and fresh fire falls. If you've been holding back, wavering, or second-guessing your calling, this is the place where you say, "Yes, Lord, Yes", again.

Obedience is the place where the oil flows. So, let's humble ourselves, lean in closer, and move forward with power through complete surrender.

A Sincere Prayer of Repentance

Heavenly Father, I come before You today with a heart that is humbled and laid bare before Your throne. Lord, I want to feel the weight of Your glory and presence. I recognize how far I have fallen short of Your perfect will for my life. I acknowledge my sins, my mistakes, and the ways I have allowed my own desires and distractions to cloud my obedience to You.

Father, I repent. With all sincerity, I turn away from the things that grieve Your heart and dishonor Your name. I lay down pride, compromise, and selfish choices that have kept me from walking fully in Your will. Forgive me, Lord, for the times I have put my trust in other things instead of in You. Forgive me for the words spoken out of anger, the thoughts I have entertained that weren't pure, and the actions that have fallen short of Your way.

Your Word says in 1 John 1:9, *"If we confess our sins, He is faithful and just to forgive us our sins and to cleanse us from all unrighteousness."* So, Lord, I confess (say what you are repenting of) _____, _____, and _____. I hold nothing back. Wash me clean, Lord. Purify my heart and renew my spirit. Let the blood of Jesus cover every stain, every failure, and every regret.

Lord, I long to be closer to You. I don't want anything standing between us. I ask You to search me, O God, and know my heart; test me and know my anxious thoughts. See if there is any offensive way in me and lead me in the way everlasting (Psalm 139:23-24).

Father, I need Your mercy today. I need Your grace to carry me forward. Let Your Holy Spirit fill every empty and broken place within me, bringing healing and restoration. I surrender all my guilt, my shame, and my burdens at Your feet. Let Your love overwhelm me and remind me that You have called me Your own.

I declare that I am forgiven, not because of what I have done, but because of the sacrifice of Jesus on the cross. I declare that I am made new by Your mercy and covered by Your grace. Lord, give me the strength to walk in obedience, to turn away from sin, and to live a life that reflects Your glory.

I thank You for Your unfailing love, for welcoming me back with open arms, and for never giving up on me. Lord, I receive forgiveness, cleansing, and restoration. I believe I am a new creation, walking in the freedom that only You can give. I believe I receive forgiveness and cleansing, and I release my faith to see it come to pass. In Jesus' holy and matchless name, I pray. Amen.

Submission and Surrender to God's Will and Calling

Heavenly Father, I come before You with my heart wide open, fully aware that You are the Creator of my life and the Author of my destiny. Lord, I lay everything down at Your feet, my plans, my desires, my fears, and my uncertainties, because I trust that Your will for my life is good, perfect, and filled with purpose.

Father, I surrender to You completely. I let go of control and lean on Your infinite wisdom. I confess that I don't always understand the path You've set before me, but I choose to trust You with all my heart, not leaning on my own understanding (Proverbs 3:5-6). Align my heart with Yours, Lord, and teach me to desire what You desire.

Lord, I submit to Your calling on my life. I know You have created me for a purpose, to glorify You and to walk in the works You prepared for me before I was even born (Ephesians 2:10). I surrender my gifts, my talents, and my abilities to You. Use them, Lord, for Your Kingdom and for Your glory. I lay aside my doubts, my excuses, and anything that would hinder me from fully stepping into what You've called me to do.

Help me to hear Your voice clearly, Lord. Let every step I take be guided by Your Spirit. Remove the noise and distractions that try to pull me away from Your will. If there is anything in me that resists Your plans, I ask You to uproot it. Shape me, mold me, and refine me until I am a vessel ready for Your use.

Father, I trust You with my life. I surrender my will for Yours, knowing that You see what I cannot see, and You know what I cannot know. You have good plans for me, plans to prosper me and not to harm me, plans to give me a hope and a future (Jeremiah 29:11).

Today, I declare that I am Yours. My life is not my own; I was bought with a price, and I will honor You in everything I do. Lord, give me the courage to obey you even when the path seems difficult. Give me the faith to follow You wherever You lead. Let my "yes" to You be sure and unwavering.

Thank You for calling me, for choosing me, and for equipping me to fulfill Your purpose. I believe I am stepping into the fullness of what You've designed for my life. I believe I receive this prayer, and I release most holy faith to see it come to pass. In the mighty name of Jesus, I pray. Amen.

Abiding in Jesus to Produce Good Fruit

Heavenly Father, I come before You in the name of my Lord and Savior Jesus Christ. I humbly submit myself to You, knowing that You are the true vine and I am a branch. Your Word reminds me that without You, I can do nothing. So today, I make the decision to remain in You, to abide in Your presence, and to draw strength, wisdom, might, and life from You alone.

Lord Jesus, I surrender my heart to Your leading. Holy Spirit, I invite You to take full control of my mind, my desires, and my actions. Let me not be led by the flesh, but by Your Spirit, which brings life and peace. I desire to bear fruit that pleases You, fruit that reflects love, joy, peace, patience, kindness, goodness, faithfulness, gentleness, and self-control. Teach me to put off the old nature and clothe myself with compassion, humility, and forgiveness, just as You have extended to me.

Let every part of me be awakened to Your presence. Soften every hardened place in my heart, renew every weary part of my spirit, and call me deeper into a life fully surrendered to Your will. As I remain connected to You, let my life overflow with Your love that binds everything together in perfect harmony.

Father, uproot anything in me that does not glorify You. Remove every distraction, every weight, and anything that tries to pull me away from Your presence. I long to abide in You, to dwell with You, and to remain rooted in Your truth, so that everything I produce reflects Your character and shines Your light into this world.

Holy Spirit, fill every area of my life with your glory and anointing. I yield to Your power and Your gentle guidance. Your ways are higher, Your wisdom is sure, and Your plans for me are perfect. Transform me from the inside out. Day by day, make me more like Jesus so I can walk in the abundant life You've promised.

Thank You, Lord, for choosing me to bear good fruit. I believe I receive this prayer and release my most holy faith to bring it to pass. I declare that I will abide in You, I will be fruitful, and I will walk in step with Your Spirit. In the mighty name of Jesus I pray, amen.

Walking in the Fruit of the Spirit and the Gifts of the Spirit

Heavenly Father, I come before You today with an open heart, inviting Your Holy Spirit into every part of my life. Holy Spirit, You are welcome here. Move freely in my heart, my home, and every space I enter. Fill the atmosphere with Your presence and Your glory.

Lord, I desire to walk in the fruit of the Spirit, just as Your Word teaches in Galatians 5:22-23. Let love, joy, peace, patience, kindness, goodness, faithfulness, gentleness, and self-control overflow in my life. Teach me to reflect these qualities in every interaction. Let Your Spirit guide me in all I do, so that my life testifies of who You are.

I recognize that You have gifted me uniquely and wonderfully. As Your Word says in 1 Corinthians 12:4-7, there are different gifts, but the same Spirit. Stir up the gifts You placed within me. Empower me to use them boldly, not out of fear or striving, but in faith and obedience. I trust that You have fully equipped me for every good work You've called me to do.

Father, I surrender my life completely to You. I open myself to everything You've placed inside of me. Help me to steward my gifts well and build others up, just as Ephesians 4:11-13 encourages. Use my life to strengthen, encourage, and unify the body of Christ. May love guide my actions and Your Spirit lead me.

Holy Spirit, transform my heart, renew my mind, and empower me to live as a true representative of Your Kingdom. I release every plan, every fear, and every doubt, and I place my full trust in Your perfect will. Use my life for Your Kingdom and for Your glory. Let my life be an expression of who You are.

In the mighty name of Jesus, I pray. Amen. I believe I receive this prayer, and I release my most holy faith to bring it to pass.

Repent and Submit Fully to God

Heavenly Father, I come before You today with a humble and sincere heart. I enter Your presence with reverence and awe. You are holy, righteous, and faithful in all Your ways. Thank You for Your mercy. Thank You for Your grace that is new every morning. Thank You for the privilege to stand before You, cleansed by the blood of Jesus.

Father, I repent sincerely, and completely for every sin I have committed against You. Forgive me for the times I have allowed pride, disobedience, and self-will to rule in my heart. Forgive me for harboring bitterness, resentment, and unforgiveness toward others. Your Word declares in 1 John 1:9 that if I confess my sins, You are faithful and just to forgive me and cleanse me from all unrighteousness. So today, Lord, I confess openly and honestly. Wash me. Cleanse me. Purify me. Create in me a clean heart and renew a steadfast spirit within me (Psalm 51:10–12). Always remind me to come back to You.

Lord, today I submit my heart and emotions to You. I honor Your Word and choose to walk in forgiveness. I release every person who has hurt or offended me. Just as You have forgiven me, I choose to forgive them (Matthew 6:14–15). I lay down the weight of unforgiveness and offense, and I ask You to heal every wound in my heart caused by those hurts, pains, and disappointments. I know that You are my Healer, and I trust Your healing power to remove the stench that unforgiveness has left in my life and replace it with the fragrance of love, peace, and joy. I am free, and they are free too.

Heavenly Father, today I surrender fully to You. I lay down my plans, my desires, and my own agenda. I say, "Not my will, but Yours be done" (Luke 22:42). Teach me to walk in total submission and alignment with Your will. Guide my steps. Direct my paths. Lead my decisions. Let my life reflect Your glory and fulfill Your divine purpose.

I recommit myself to You today, my mind, my heart, my body, and my spirit. Your Word instructs me in Romans 12:1 to present my body as a living sacrifice, holy and acceptable to You. So, I renew my commitment to live in obedience, holiness, and faithfulness. This is my true act of worship to You.

Holy Spirit, draw me closer. Remove every distraction, every idol, and every hindrance standing in the way of deeper intimacy with You. Help me to hunger and thirst for Your presence. Teach me to seek You daily in prayer and to meditate on Your Word with a tender and open heart.

Father, let this mark a true turning point in my walk with You. Let this be a season of spiritual growth, personal revival, and deep renewal. Ignite a fresh passion in me for Your presence. Let my life reflect Your love, Your grace, and Your power.

I believe I receive this prayer, and I release my most holy faith to bring it to pass. In Jesus' mighty name, I pray. Amen and amen.

Walking in the Spirit

Heavenly Father, I come before You with reverence and gratitude for the precious gift of Your Holy Spirit. Thank You, Lord, that through Jesus, You have called me into a life of victory, freedom, and purpose. I recognize that in order to walk fully in the Spirit, I must surrender my will and allow You to guide me every step of the way.

Today, I confess that I desire more of You and less of me. I acknowledge the areas in my life where I have been led by the flesh, where I have allowed my own desires, weaknesses, and distractions to take over. I repent for those times, and I ask You to cleanse me, renew me, and set my feet on the path of living fully my walk with Christ.

Holy Spirit, I invite You into my heart right now. Take full control of my thoughts, desires, and actions. I know that apart from You, I can do nothing. But with You, I can walk in strength, in love, and in power. I declare today that I will not conform to the ways of this world, but I will be transformed by the renewing of my mind. Lead me, Holy Spirit, to think on things that are pure, lovely, noble, and pleasing to the Father.

Awaken in me a deep hunger for the Word of God. Let me be one who meditates on Your truth day and night. Let Your Word be a lamp to my feet and a light to my path. Stir within me a desire to stay in constant communion with You, to seek Your voice, to obey Your leadership without delay. Teach me to silence the noise around me so I can hear Your still, small voice leading me in the way I should go.

Father, I declare that I walk by faith and not by sight. I trust in the Spirit of Truth to guide me, to reveal the mysteries of Your Word, and to empower me to walk in holiness. Fill me with boldness to resist the works of the flesh and to live out the fruit of the Spirit, love, joy, peace, patience, kindness, goodness, faithfulness, gentleness, and self-control.

Lord, I lift up every part of me that feels insecure, weak or weary. Holy Spirit, rise up in me with strength. I cast off every weight and sin that is setting me back, and I put on the full armor of God. I declare that I am not alone, I have Your Spirit living within me, giving me everything I need to live a godly life.

Let this not just be a moment of prayer, but a turning point in my life. Let this be a moment of rededication and transformation. From this day forward, I commit to walk in the Spirit daily, to seek Your will above all else, and to live a life that honors You in all that I do.

I believe and receive this prayer in faith, and I release the Holy Spirit's power and glory over my life to bring it to pass. Thank You, Lord, for Your presence, power, glory and guidance. I am strong in the Lord, and I am led by the Spirit in all things. Amen. In Jesus' mighty and powerful name, I pray.

Anointed Ears to Hear & Obedient to Divine Instruction

Heavenly Father, I thank You for the blood of Jesus that gives me access to Your presence and for the Holy Spirit who leads me into all truth. Today, I ask that You anoint my ears to hear. Let every spiritual blockage be removed and let my ears be tuned to the frequency of Heaven.

Your Word says in John 10:27 (KJV), *"My sheep hear my voice, and I know them, and they follow me."* Lord, I am Your sheep. I declare that I know Your voice and another I will not follow. Sharpen my spiritual hearing. Let me hear You clearly above the noise, above the doubt, and above every distraction.

The voice of the stranger I will not follow. I bind the voice of the stranger. I silence the lies of the enemy. I cast down confusion, doublemindedness, and deception. Let there be clarity in my spirit. Let Your voice rise louder than every other voice including my own.

Holy Spirit, I invite You to saturate my life with your presence. Breathe on me with fresh wind. Release divine instruction and supernatural insight. Open the eyes of my understanding according to Ephesians 1:17–18, that I may know the hope of Your calling, the riches of Your inheritance, and the greatness of Your power toward those who believe.

Father, increase my capacity to comprehend spiritual things. Give me revelation knowledge, divine wisdom, and discernment beyond my natural ability. Let Your Word come alive in me, not just as information, but transformation. I don't want to just hear You, I want to obey You. I want to walk in sync with Your Spirit and move when You say move.

According to Isaiah 50:4–5 (NLT), *"The Sovereign Lord has given me his words of wisdom, so that I know how to comfort the weary. Morning by morning he wakens me and opens my understanding to his will. The Sovereign Lord has spoken to me, and I have listened. I have not rebelled or turned away."* Lord, I declare that this is my testimony. You open my ears. You speak. I listen and obey.

Draw me closer to you, Father. I don't want to live distant from Your voice. Let my hunger for Your presence increase. As I draw near to You, You promised You would draw near to me. I press in and incline my ear to hear you. I posture my heart and surrender my will.

Let Your Spirit lead me into all truth. Give me supernatural understanding of what You're doing in this season of my life. Empower me to obey quickly and without hesitation.

I believe I receive this prayer. I release my most holy faith to bring it to pass. In the name of Jesus, I declare my ears are anointed to hear, my heart is surrendered, and my steps are ordered by the Lord. Amen and amen!

Faithful Obedience to God's Calling

Heavenly Father, I come before You today with a humble heart, fully surrendered to Your will. You are the Author and Finisher of my faith, and I honor You as the Sovereign King who directs my every step.

According to Isaiah 1:19, You promised blessings when I am willing and obedient. Today, I declare that I am willing to follow Your voice and committed to obey Your commands, no matter the cost. Lord, I stand on John 14:15, because I love You, I will keep Your commandments. Let my obedience be a reflection of my love and devotion to You. Give me a heart that responds quickly when You speak and feet that move swiftly when You lead.

Father, I will not merely be a hearer of Your Word, but a doer, just as James 1:22 instructs. Remove from me every hesitation, fear, and procrastination. Strengthen me to act boldly and confidently on every word You've spoken to me. I align myself with Deuteronomy 28:1, declaring that I will carefully follow Your commands. As I obey, I trust You to lift me, favor me, and position me in places of influence for Your glory.

Let my obedience be swift and consistent, as written in Psalm 119:60. Teach me to respond without delay, without excuse, and without compromise. I rebuke and resist every spirit of fear, doubt, and disobedience. I cast down every thought that rises against Your instructions and declare that my heart is aligned with Your will.

Holy Spirit, guide me every day. Speak to me with clarity and help me recognize Your voice clearly. Give me the courage to follow through on every assignment, even when the path is unclear or the task feels beyond me.

I believe that obedience opens the door to blessings, favor, and Kingdom advancement. I refuse to settle for partial obedience or delayed obedience. I will walk boldly, knowing that every obedient step I take leads to breakthrough. Father, use me as a vessel for Your glory. Let my obedience inspire others to walk by faith and trust You fully. May my life be a testimony of what happens when Your servant says, "Yes, Lord!" I surrender my plans, dreams, and desires to You, trusting that Your ways are higher and Your plans are perfect.

I believe I receive this prayer, and I release my most holy faith to bring it to pass. In the mighty and matchless name of Jesus Christ, I pray. Amen and amen!

Faith to Say Yes Again Prayer

Father, in the name of Jesus, I come before You with a surrendered heart. Thank You for never giving up on me. Thank You for being faithful, even in the moments when I have wrestled, hesitated, or sat still longer than I should have.

Today, I ask You to restore the fire, the focus, and the willingness to say yes again. Not just with my lips, but with my life. I don't want to move in my own strength or say yes out of obligation. I want my yes to come from a place of love, trust, and alignment with Your will.

You know the battles I have faced. The moments of weariness and feeling like giving up. The times of feeling disappointed. The unexpected delays. But today, I shake off the residue of the last season. I lay down fear. I lay down pride. I lay down the need to have it all figured out. I say yes again, not to people, not to pressure, but to You.

I say yes to the calling. I say yes to the next assignment. I say yes to the stretching. I say yes to being used by You in a fresh way. Father, breathe on my yes. Strengthen my yes. Anchor my yes in purpose and in faith.

I declare that I will not draw back. I will not shrink. I will not sit on what You placed inside of me. I step into this next season with bold obedience. I trust that if You're calling me, then You've already made the way.

Let my yes unlock doors. Let my yes bring breakthrough and freedom to others. Let my yes release joy back into my journey. Lord God, let everything I do from this point forward bring glory to Your name. I believe I receive this prayer, and I release most holy faith to bring it to pass. In Jesus' name I seal the prayer, amen.

Listen for the Holy Spirit's Voice

Heavenly Father, in the mighty name of Jesus, I come before You with a heart full of gratitude and reverence. I thank you for the privilege of walking in the Spirit and living a life that reflects Your glory. Lord, I desire to develop a lifestyle of obedience that honors You in all I do. I declare that I am fully surrendered to Your will, walking in alignment with Your Word, and allowing Your Holy Spirit to guide me every step of the way. Father, teach me to follow Your commands with joy and trust, knowing that obedience leads to Your blessings and favor. (John 14:15; Psalm 128:1)

Lord, I lift up my relationships and ask for Your grace to walk in love and unity with others. Your Word says that love binds us together in perfect harmony, and I desire to live in that love daily. Help me to be a peacemaker, to strive for unity, and to build bridges of understanding. May the fruit of love overflow in my life, reflecting the heart of Christ in every interaction. (Colossians 3:14; Ephesians 4:3)

Father, I commit to spiritual growth. I want to be intentional about growing spiritually. Give me a deeper hunger for Your Word and help me grow in grace and in the knowledge of my Lord Jesus Christ. I declare that I am like a tree planted by streams of water, bearing fruit in every season and prospering in all I do. Holy Spirit, transform me from the inside out and shape me to reflect the image of Jesus Christ more and more each day. (1 Peter 2:2; Psalm 1:3)

Holy Spirit, I invite You to take complete control of my life. Lead me, guide me, and empower me to walk boldly in obedience, love, and grace. I reject every distraction, every hindrance, and every work of the enemy that would try to pull me away from Your presence. Strengthen me to persevere and remain steadfast, knowing that Your plans for me are good and that Your power is at work within me. (Ephesians 3:20)

I seal this prayer with faith, declaring that I will walk in the Spirit and fulfill the purpose You have for my life. I believe I receive this prayer, and I release my most holy faith to bring it to pass. In the mighty name of Jesus, amen.

Hearing and Following God's Voice

Heavenly Father, In the name of Jesus, I come before You with a grateful and submitted heart, thanking You for the privilege of hearing Your voice and being led by Your Spirit. I declare that I am Your sheep, and I know Your voice. I hear Your voice clearly. I recognize Your voice without confusion, and I am acquainted with it. When You speak, I discern Your motives, intentions, and heart with accuracy.

My ears are anointed to hear, not only Your voice, but also the voices of those You send as messengers to speak on Your behalf. I follow where You lead, and I do not follow the voice of a stranger. I yield only to voices that are submitted to Your leadership, timing, will, and way.

Thank You for the gentle whisper that speaks peace to my heart, even in the midst of the storm. Your voice carries the weight of glory, and my entire being responds to You in full surrender and joyful obedience.

Just as You guided Elijah with a still, small voice, I ask You to guide me today with clarity and precision. Holy Spirit, Spirit of Truth, lead me into all truth. Show me the way I should go. I ask for wisdom, and I receive it by faith, trusting that You give it generously and without finding fault.

Open my ears to hear Your Word. Soften my heart to receive what you are speaking in this season. Direct my steps so I walk in perfect alignment with Your will. I choose to trust You with all my heart and lean not on my own understanding. As I acknowledge You in all my ways, I thank You for making my path straight before me.

I will be still and know that You are God. I rest confidently in Your ability to guide me through every decision, every door, every challenge, and every assignment. I stand on Your Word in Jeremiah

33:3 and call on You, believing that You will show me great and mighty things I do not yet know.

Keep my heart tender and obedient as I listen for Your voice. I will walk boldly into the plans You've prepared for me. Jesus, I hear You knocking, and I open the door of my heart. Come in and fellowship with me. Let Your peace rule in my heart, and may I never return to foolish or fruitless ways.

I declare that I am led by the Spirit of God. I walk in divine wisdom, and I hear Your voice clearly today and every day. I believe I receive this prayer, and I release my most holy faith to bring it to pass. In the mighty name of Jesus, Amen.

Faith Confessions: Hearing and Following God's Voice
1. I declare that I am God's sheep, and I hear His voice clearly. I will not follow the voice of a stranger. (John 10:27)
2. I trust in the Lord with all my heart and lean not on my own understanding. He directs my paths in every decision I make. (Proverbs 3:5-6)
3. The Spirit of truth leads me into all truth and shows me the way I should go. (John 16:13)
4. I am still before the Lord, and I know that He is God. His peace fills my heart and mind. (Psalm 46:10)
5. My ears are open to hear the gentle whisper of God's voice, guiding me in every circumstance. (1 Kings 19:11-12)
6. I listen carefully to voice of the Lord my God, and His words bring peace to my heart. (Psalm 85:8)
7. I do not harden my heart when I hear God's voice. I respond in obedience and faith. (Hebrews 3:7-8)
8. When I call on the Lord, He answers me and shows me great and mighty things I do not yet know. (Jeremiah 33:3)
9. The Lord stands at the door of my heart and knocks, and I welcome Him into every area of my life. (Revelation 3:20)
10. I ask God for wisdom, and He gives it to me generously. I walk in divine understanding and clarity. (James 1:5)

11. I hear a voice behind me saying, "This is the way; walk in it," and I follow the leading of the Holy Spirit. (Isaiah 30:21)
12. I declare that no evil will come near me, and the Lord protects and leads me in all my ways. (Psalm 91:10-13)

Divine Release of the Anointing on Your Life

Heavenly Father, I come before Your throne of grace in the name of Jesus, covered by the power of His blood. I enter into Your presence with thanksgiving and praise, declaring that You alone are holy, mighty, and worthy of all honor. Father, I thank You that through Jesus Christ, I have access to the fullness of Your Spirit and the anointing that empowers me to walk in victory, authority, and purpose.

Your Word declares in Isaiah 61:1, *"The Spirit of the Sovereign Lord is upon me, for the Lord has anointed me to bring good news to the poor. He has sent me to comfort the brokenhearted and to proclaim that captives will be released and prisoners will be freed."* Father, I stand on this promise, and I ask for a fresh outpouring of Your anointing upon my life right now. Release Your anointing to break every yoke, destroy every chain, and remove every burden that has tried to hinder me from walking in the fullness of Your calling for my life.

Holy Spirit, saturate my mind, heart, and spirit with Your power. Anoint my eyes to see with spiritual clarity, my ears to hear Your voice with precision, and my heart to discern Your will. Let the anointing of wisdom, knowledge, and understanding flow through me as I walk in alignment with Your divine purpose. According to 1 John 2:27, *"The anointing You have given me abides within me and teaches me all things."* I receive that anointing now, guiding me, empowering me, and positioning me to fulfill my Kingdom assignment without fear or hesitation.

Father, I declare that the same anointing that rested upon Jesus now rests upon me. As it is written in Acts 10:38, *"God anointed Jesus of Nazareth with the Holy Spirit and with power, and He went about doing good and healing all who were oppressed by the devil, for God was with Him."* I declare that this same anointing is released in my life today, empowering me to bring healing to the sick, freedom to the oppressed, and hope to the hopeless. I decree that I walk in supernatural boldness, releasing signs, wonders, and miracles as evidence of Your presence within me.

Let the oil of Your anointing flow over every area of my life, my family, health, relationships, finances, ministry, and career. Let it bring unprecedented favor, supernatural increase, and divine acceleration. I refuse to be limited by fear, doubt, or past failures. Your anointing destroys every limitation, making the impossible possible and the unseen manifest. I take authority over every hindrance and declare that nothing can stop me from fulfilling my God-ordained destiny.

Father, I receive this fresh anointing with faith and expectation. I believe that as I step forward, doors are opening, mountains are moving, and breakthroughs are manifesting. I seal this prayer in the name of Jesus, declaring that I believe I receive it, and I release my most holy faith to bring it to pass. In the name of Jesus, I seal this prayer and say, amen.

The Lord is My Shepherd

Father, in the mighty name of Jesus, I lift my heart in gratitude and declare with full assurance, You are my Shepherd! You are the One who leads me, guides me, provides for me, and protects me. You are the Keeper of my soul, the Watchman over my life, and the Overseer of my destiny.

Because You are my Shepherd, I shall not want. I lack nothing. You supply every need I have according to Your riches in glory by Christ Jesus. You lead me beside still waters and restore my weary soul. You make me lie down in green pastures, places of provision, joy, peace, and rest. Even when I walk through the darkest valleys, I will fear no evil, because You are with me. Your rod and Your staff, they comfort me.

Father, I declare that Your voice I hear, and the voice of a stranger I will not follow. You go before me and make the way clear. You anoint my head with oil, and my cup runs over. Surely, goodness and mercy are chasing me down every day of my life, and I will dwell in Your house forever.

I reject the voice of fear, doubt, and confusion. I reject the lies of lack and limitation. I decree that my Shepherd leads me into abundance, into safety, into divine appointments, and into fulfilled purpose. You fight for me. You defend me. You cover me. You sustain me.

Father, I thank You that You are not a distant Shepherd, You are near to me. You are intimately involved in every detail of my life. You lead me step by step. You correct me in love. You rescue me when I stray. You rejoice over me with singing. You see me, You know me, and You have called me by name.

Today, I fully trust Your leadership. I fully trust Your timing. I fully trust Your provision. I release every burden, every care, and every unanswered question into Your capable hands. I surrender to Your will. I follow Your voice. I move at Your pace and timing. I stand on Your promises.

The Lord is my Shepherd, and I shall not be moved! I believe I receive this prayer and release my most holy faith to bring it to pass. In Jesus' mighty and matchless name, I pray, amen.

Hungering and Thirsting After Righteousness

Father, in the mighty name of Jesus, I come before Your throne of grace through and by the blood of Jesus, humbled, yet expectant, longing for more of You.

Lord, I declare that You alone can satisfy the deep cravings of my heart. You are my Source, my Strength, and my Sustainer. Just as You promised, my soul longs for You the way deer pants for water (Psalm 42:1). Today, I cry out with hunger. My cry is, "I need more of You!"

Father, I refuse to be satisfied with yesterday's manna. You promised that those who hunger and thirst for righteousness will be filled (Matthew 5:6). I boldly declare that I am hungry for You. I am thirsty for Your presence. Lord, fill me until I overflow. Let every dry and barren place in my life be saturated with Your living water.

Holy Spirit, ignite a fresh fire within me. Burn away anything that is not like You. Remove distractions, idols, and anything that dulls my hunger. You said that when I seek first the Kingdom and Your righteousness, everything I need will be added to me (Matthew 6:33). So today, I seek Your face, Your will, and Your Kingdom above all else.

Lord, I cry out for Your presence and Your glory to be revealed in me and through me. You promised that rivers of living water would flow from within those who believe (John 7:38). Let that river flow. Let Your power break every chain, destroy every yoke, and release freedom, restoration, and peace in my life. Rekindle the fire in my heart for more of You. Fan the flame that's already within me until it consumes everything that's not of You.

I come against every spirit of complacency, lukewarmness, and spiritual dryness in Jesus' name. I declare that I am on fire for You! Your Word is like fire shut up in my bones (Jeremiah 20:9), and I refuse to hold it back. Let that fire be released in my prayer life, in my worship, and in my pursuit of a holy lifestyle.

I will not settle for less than Your best. You said that when I seek You early, my soul would be satisfied in dry and weary places (Psalm 63:1). So, I come after You, Lord. Satisfy my soul with Your presence. Let Your glory fill my life, my home, and every space I walk into.

Father, I cry out, "More of You, Lord." Let the Holy Spirit lead me into deeper places of intimacy with You. Let Your anointing fall fresh on me, equipping me, empowering me, and enabling me to walk in the fullness of Your will. I surrender completely, my heart, my mind, my desires, I give them all to You.

Lord, I believe that as I hunger and thirst for righteousness, You are filling me. You are releasing fresh revelation, fresh anointing, and fresh power in my life. I declare that I am a person of fire, bold, courageous, and filled with the presence of the Holy Ghost.

I seal this prayer in faith, believing that You are answering me even now. I release my most holy faith to bring this to pass. I declare it is done, and I thank You for the overflow.

In the mighty, matchless, and powerful name of Jesus Christ, I pray, amen and amen.

Prayer to Forgive and Release Bitterness

Heavenly Father, I come before You in the name of Jesus, humbled by Your mercy and grace. Your Word commands me to forgive others, just as You have forgiven me. I confess that holding on to unforgiveness and bitterness has weighed me down, and I no longer want these burdens in my heart. I release every hurt, offense, and grievance into Your hands, trusting You to heal and restore my soul.

Father, Your Word says to "get rid of all bitterness, rage, and anger" (Ephesians 4:31). I choose to release these emotions now, letting go of every grudge and offense. I declare that I am free from the spirit of unforgiveness, and I receive Your peace in its place. Lord, help me to walk in kindness and compassion, just as You have shown kindness and compassion to me.

Holy Spirit, empower me to forgive, even when it feels difficult. I know that forgiveness is not a feeling but an act of obedience to Your Word. I trust that as I forgive, You will heal my heart and restore my peace. Your Word says that if I forgive others, You will forgive me (Matthew 6:14-15). I choose forgiveness today and declare that bitterness and resentment have no place in my life.

Lord, I clothe myself with compassion, kindness, humility, gentleness, and patience, as Your Word instructs (Colossians 3:12-13). I ask that Your love fills my heart and bind me to others in perfect unity. As I release every offense and forgive from my heart, I thank You for setting me free from the chains of bitterness. I declare that I am walking in Your love and Your peace reigns in my heart.

Father, I believe that I receive this prayer and release most holy faith to bring it to pass. In Jesus' mighty name, amen!

Chapter 3: Prayers for Protection and Spiritual Warfare

Protection and Spiritual Warfare

This is the chapter where the remnant rises up. The committed ones, those who understand that this walk with God is a call to war in the Spirit and we must stand watch over what belongs to the Kingdom. There are some things in life that won't shift until you learn how to fight spiritually, with the authority you've been given by Heaven.

This isn't about sensationalism or fear tactics, this is about warfare strategy. It's about taking your seat in the Spirit and enforcing what Jesus already accomplished at the cross for you. According to Colossians 2:15 (NLT) – *"In this way, He disarmed the spiritual rulers and authorities. He shamed them publicly by His victory over them on the cross."* We are not trying to get the victory. We are enforcing the victory that was already won by Jesus Christ.

When you step into warfare prayers, you step into your God-given jurisdiction. You put on the whole armor of God (Ephesians 6), not just to protect yourself, but to take ground, overthrow demonic forces and systems, and push back darkness with Holy Ghost power.

There is a battle for your mind. There is a battle for your family. There is a battle for your health, your destiny, your city, and the next generation.

God is calling us not just to react, but to respond with spiritual intelligence, to pray offensively, and to command our Kingdom rights and authority in this earth.

In this chapter, you'll be guided to:

- Declare Psalm 91 not as poetry, but as a covenant of protection
- Plead the blood of Jesus with understanding and intentionality
- Bind and loose with prophetic boldness
- Take dominion over spiritual atmospheres

- Call forth angelic assistance, divine covering, and supernatural enforcement
- Renounce fear, confusion, witchcraft, and every demonic foothold
- Release the Word of God like a sword into situations that demand supernatural turnaround

You'll be reminded that your fight is not with people. The battle is never about personalities, it's about principalities. But the weapons in your mouth, when aligned with the Word and charged by the Spirit, are devastating to the enemy's plans.

This is where the warrior in you is refined. This is where your mantle as an intercessor is sharpened. You'll find that as you war from a place of righteousness, God's glory becomes your shield, and His angels go on assignment responding to the faith-filled words you speak.

According to Isaiah 54:17 (KJV) – *"No weapon that is formed against thee shall prosper; and every tongue that shall rise against thee in judgment thou shalt condemn. This is the heritage of the servants of the Lord, and their righteousness is of me, saith the Lord."* You don't have to fear warfare when you understand your heritage.

This chapter is about spiritual ownership. It's about refusing to let the enemy run rampant through your territory while you remain silent. It's about using your voice, your authority, your faith and your discernment to set boundaries in the Spirit and declare, "NO MORE!"

So, rise up, prayer warrior.
Put on your spiritual armor.
Take out your sword.
And release the decrees of Heaven.
You are protected, you are equipped, and you are dangerous to the kingdom of darkness. Let's war for what we have a right to!

Putting On the Whole Armor of God

Father, in the name of Jesus, I come before You today with boldness and full confidence in Your Word. I step into this day fully armed and fully dressed in the armor that You have given me. I do not enter this day unprepared. I come ready, equipped, and standing in the power of Your might!

I put on the **Belt of Truth**. I declare that I am grounded in Your truth today. Lies, deception, and confusion, I cast them down right now. I will not be moved by opinions, circumstances, or negative emotions. I am anchored in the truth of Your Word!

I put on the **Breastplate of Righteousness**. Thank You, Lord, that I am the righteousness of God in Christ Jesus. My heart is covered, my emotions are guarded, and I am protected by the finished work of the cross. No fiery dart of condemnation or guilt can penetrate my armor today!

I put on the **Shoes of the Gospel of Peace**. I walk in the peace of God that surpasses all understanding. I carry peace everywhere I go today. My steps are ordered by You, Lord, and I trample over every serpent, scorpion, and power of the enemy. Wherever I step, victory is established!

I take up the **Shield of Faith**. I declare that every flaming arrow of the wicked one is quenched by my shield of faith. Doubt, fear, and anxiety, you have no place here! My faith is alive, my faith is active, and my faith is working for me right now!

I put on the **Helmet of Salvation**. My mind is covered and guarded by the blood of Jesus. I declare that I have the mind of Christ. My thoughts are filled with the promises of God. I think on things above and not beneath. I refuse every lie of the enemy, and I receive divine clarity, understanding, knowledge, wisdom, and focus.

Lord, I take up the **Sword of the Spirit**, which is the Word of God. I speak the Word boldly over every situation in my life. I declare that no weapon formed against me shall prosper. Your Word is my weapon, and I use it today to cut down every attack of the enemy!

Father, I stand fully dressed and fully armed, knowing that victory belongs to me. I am covered from the crown of my head to the soles of my feet. I plead the blood of Jesus over my life, over my family, over my home, over my finances, over my calling, and over my destiny.

I stand in full authority today, declaring that I am more than a conqueror through Christ who loves me. I enforce my victory, and I will not back down. I will not retreat. I will not be moved!

I believe I receive this prayer, and I release my most holy faith to bring it to pass. In Jesus' name, Amen!

Psalm 91 Declaration

I declare and decree the promises of Psalm 91 over my life, my family, and all that concerns me. I stand in faith, knowing that God's Word is true and His promises are unshakable. I decree and declare that Psalm 91 is my covenant promise. I am covered, protected, and victorious through the power of God's Word. I will not fear, for the Lord is my refuge, my fortress, and my deliverer. No weapon formed against me shall prosper, and I am hidden in the shadow of the Almighty. In Jesus' name, Amen!

- I dwell in the secret place of the Most High, and I abide under the shadow of the Almighty. I declare that I am covered by the presence and power of God, where no harm can reach me. (Psalm 91:1)
- I say of the Lord, "He is my refuge and my fortress, my God, in whom I trust." I decree that the Lord is my protector and my safe place. My trust is in Him alone. (Psalm 91:2)
- Surely, He will deliver me from the snare of the fowler and from the deadly pestilence. I declare that I am delivered from every trap of the enemy and protected from sickness, disease, and harm. (Psalm 91:3)
- He will cover me with His feathers, and under His wings, I will find refuge; His truth is my shield and buckler. I decree that I am shielded by God's truth, and His faithfulness surrounds me like a fortress. (Psalm 91:4)
- I will not fear the terror of the night, nor the arrow that flies by day. I declare that fear has no place in my life. I am bold and courageous because the Lord is my protector. (Psalm 91:5)
- Nor the pestilence that stalks in darkness, nor the destruction that lays waste at noonday. I decree that no sickness, plague, or calamity can touch me or my household. (Psalm 91:6)
- A thousand may fall at my side, ten thousand at my right hand, but it will not come near me. I declare that I am surrounded by divine protection, and no harm will come near me. (Psalm 91:7)

- I will only observe with my eyes and see the punishment of the wicked. I decree that I will see the victory of the Lord over every adversary. (Psalm 91:8)
- Because I have made the Lord my dwelling place, the Most High, who is my refuge, no harm will overtake me, no disaster will come near my home. I declare that my home, my family, and everything I possess are covered by the blood of Jesus Christ and safe in His hands. (Psalm 91:9-10)
- He will command His angels concerning me to guard me in all my ways. I decree that angels are assigned to me, going before me, surrounding me, and protecting me from every hurt, harm, and danger. (Psalm 91:11)
- They will lift me up in their hands so that I will not strike my foot against a stone. I declare that the Angels of God are guiding my steps and ensuring my safety. (Psalm 91:12)
- I will tread upon the lion and the cobra; I will trample the great lion and the serpent. I decree that I have victory over every scheme of the enemy, and I walk in authority over all wickedness and darkness. (Psalm 91:13)
- Because I love the Lord, He will rescue me; He will protect me, for I acknowledge His name. I declare that my love and faith in the Lord activate His divine rescue and protection over my life. (Psalm 91:14)
- I will call on the Lord, and He will answer me; He will be with me in trouble. He will deliver me and honor me. I decree that when I pray, God hears and answers. He is my deliverer and the One who lifts me up. (Psalm 91:15)
- With long life, He will satisfy me and show me His salvation. I declare that I will live a long, healthy, and abundant life, experiencing the fullness of God's salvation and blessings. (Psalm 91:16)

Protection and Pleading the Blood of Jesus

Heavenly Father, I come boldly before Your throne of grace in the name of Jesus, thanking You for the power of His blood. I plead the blood of Jesus over every area of my life, declaring that no weapon formed against me shall prosper (Isaiah 54:17). Father, I thank You that the blood of Jesus speaks a better word over me, words of redemption, protection, and victory (Hebrews 12:24).

Lord, I plead the blood of Jesus over my mind. Let every thought align with Your truth. I cast down every lie of the enemy that tries to take root (2 Corinthians 10:5). Protect my mind from fear, doubt, and confusion, and fill me with peace that surpasses all understanding (Philippians 4:7).

I plead the blood of Jesus over my physical body, declaring divine health and healing. Sickness, disease, and infirmity must bow to the name of Jesus Christ. Your Word declares that by His stripes, I am healed (Isaiah 53:5). Let every system, organ, cell, tissue, and function in my body come into alignment with Your perfect design.

Father, I plead the blood of Jesus over my home. I declare it a sanctuary of peace and safety. I cast out every evil assignment and unclean spirit now, in the name of Jesus Christ. Your Word says no evil shall befall me, and no plague will come near my dwelling (Psalm 91:10). Let Your angels encamp around me, standing guard at every door and window, pushing back the forces of darkness.

I plead the blood of Jesus over my family. Cover my children, my spouse, and my loved ones with Your divine protection. Shield them from harm, danger, and every attack of the enemy. I declare that my family is marked by the blood of the Lamb, and the destroyer must pass over (Exodus 12:23). Surround them with godly influences and hedge them in with Your grace and mercy.

I plead the blood of Jesus over my finances. I declare that every seed I sow will be blessed and multiplied for Your glory. Cancel every assignment of lack and poverty, and release provision and abundance according to Your riches in glory (Philippians 4:19).

Thank You, Father, for giving Your angels charge over me to guard me in all my ways (Psalm 91:11). I declare that they are ministering spirits sent to serve and protect me (Hebrews 1:14). Let them stand watch over me and war on my behalf.

Lord, I push back the forces of darkness in the mighty name of Jesus. Every plan, plot, and scheme of the enemy is nullified by the power of the blood of Jesus Christ. I declare that darkness cannot stand in the light of Your glory. I command every stronghold to be broken and every chain to be loosed (2 Corinthians 10:4).

I declare that the blood of Jesus surrounds me like a shield of protection. It guards and protects my going out and coming in from this time forth and forevermore (Psalm 121:8). Thank You, Father, for safety, security, and supernatural protection. I trust in You as my refuge and fortress, and I dwell under the shadow of Your wings (Psalm 91:1–2). I am divinely protected in all things.

I believe I receive this protection and safety and I release my most holy faith to bring it to pass. In the mighty and matchless name of Jesus Christ, I pray. Amen and Amen.

Binding and Loosing on Earth as it is in Heaven

Heavenly Father, I come before You in the mighty name of Jesus Christ, armed with the authority You have given me as a believer. Your Word declares in Matthew 16:19 that whatever I bind on earth will be bound in heaven, and whatever I loose on earth will be loosed in heaven. I stand on that promise today, empowered by the fire of the Holy Ghost, to exercise my authority in prayer.

Father, in the name of Jesus, I bind every spirit of wickedness, every plan of the enemy, and every stronghold that seeks to exalt itself against the knowledge of Christ (2 Corinthians 10:4–5). I bind the spirit of fear, confusion, lack, sickness, and oppression. I command every demonic force, every lying spirit, and every weapon formed against me to be cast out and rendered powerless by the blood of Jesus. By the authority of Your Word, I declare that they have no place in my life, in my family, in my home, or in my community.

Now, Father, I loose the promises of Your Word into every area of my life. I loose peace that surpasses all understanding (Philippians 4:7). I loose divine healing and wholeness, because by Your stripes, I am healed (Isaiah 53:5). I loose prosperity and provision, for You promised to supply all my needs according to Your riches in glory in Christ Jesus (Philippians 4:19). I loose joy, restoration, and the power of the Holy Spirit to flow freely in and through my life.

Holy Spirit, ignite a fresh fire within me. Let the consuming fire of Your presence burn away anything not of You and empower me to walk in boldness and victory. I declare that heaven's agenda is established in my life today. No weapon formed against me shall prosper, and every tongue that rises against me in judgment is condemned (Isaiah 54:17).

I seal this prayer in the name of Jesus, fully believing that it is done on earth as it is in heaven. In the mighty, matchless name of Jesus, I pray. Amen and Amen

Believers' Scriptural Authority to War Against Principalities

Heavenly Father, I come boldly before Your throne of grace, in the mighty and matchless name of Jesus Christ, my Savior, and my King. I thank You, Lord, that You have given me authority over all the power of the enemy, and nothing shall by any means harm me (Luke 10:19). Today, I stand in my God-given authority, clothed in the full armor of God, ready to war in the Spirit against every principality, power, ruler of darkness, and spiritual wickedness in high places (Ephesians 6:12).

Father, I declare that I am seated with Christ in heavenly places, far above every power and dominion, and every name that is named, not only in this age but also in the one to come (Ephesians 1:21). I take my rightful position in Christ Jesus, and I decree and declare that no weapon formed against me shall prosper, and every tongue that rises against me in judgment, I shall condemn (Isaiah 54:17).

In the name of Jesus, I take authority over every demonic assignment, every stronghold, and every scheme of the enemy. I cancel and nullify every plot, plan, and strategy of hell that has been set against me, my family, my ministry, and every area of our lives.

I bind every spirit of fear, doubt, confusion, division and oppression. I command every unclean spirit operating in darkness to be exposed and brought into the light of God's truth. By the blood of Jesus Christ, I dismantle and destroy every generational curse, every word curse, and every demonic altar erected against my destiny and purpose.

Father, let Your warring angels be released on assignment right now, fighting on my behalf in the heavenly realms. Let the fire of God consume every demonic blockade, every hindrance, and every resistance in the spirit. I declare that the enemy's plans are overturned, overruled, dismantled, and rendered powerless in the name of Jesus!

I decree and declare that I am more than a conqueror through Christ Jesus who loves me (Romans 8:37). I walk in victory, I stand in power, and I move in divine authority. The enemy is under my feet, and every high thing that has exalted itself against the knowledge of God must bow to the name of Jesus.

Lord, teach my hands to war and my fingers to fight (Psalm 144:1). Fill me with boldness, discernment, and supernatural insight to recognize the enemy's tactics and counter them with the truth of Your Word.

I release the Word of God as a two-edged sword against every demonic force. I declare, the Lord is my refuge and fortress; I will not fear (Psalm 91:2). I declare, greater is He that is in me than he that is in the world (1 John 4:4). I declare, the battle is not mine, but the Lord's (2 Chronicles 20:15).

Father, I seal this prayer in the blood of Jesus Christ. I thank You that every declaration is established, every stronghold is broken, and every chain is destroyed. I walk in the victory and authority that Christ purchased for me on the cross.

I believe I receive this prayer and release most holy faith to bring it to pass. In the mighty, matchless, and all-powerful name of Jesus Christ, I pray.

Amen and Amen!

Breakthroughs in Stubborn Situations and Strongholds

Heavenly Father, in the mighty name of Jesus, I come before You as a warrior in the Spirit, ready to stand firm in the authority You have given me through Jesus Christ. I thank You that You are the Lord, strong and mighty in battle, and that nothing is too hard for You. Today, I take authority over every stubborn situation and every stronghold that has sought to exalt itself against the knowledge and power of Christ Jesus.

Father, Your Word declares that You frustrate the plans of the crafty and thwart their schemes. I decree and declare that every plan of the enemy against my life is canceled and rendered powerless. No weapon formed against me shall prosper, and every tongue that rises against me in judgment is condemned in the name of Jesus Christ!

Lord, I stand on Your promises in Isaiah 49:24-26, that You will contend with those who contend with me, you will fight with those who fight with me, and You will deliver me from every stronghold. I plead the blood of Jesus over my mind, family, finances, and destiny, and I declare that I overcome by the blood of the Lamb and the word of my testimony.

Father, let every mountain in my life be brought low, and let every valley be raised up by Your power. I declare that stubborn situations melt like wax in Your presence. Let God arise and let His enemies be scattered! I bind every demonic force assigned to hinder my progress, and I loose the power and glory of God to bring breakthroughs in every area of my life.

Holy Spirit, I invite You to strengthen me with Your might in my inner man. Empower me to stand firm, to resist the enemy, and to walk in the victory You have already won for me. I declare that the God of peace is crushing Satan under my feet and I walk in the authority given to me by Jesus Christ.

Lord, I thank You that no enchantment, divination, or curse can stand against me because I am blessed and empowered with victory in Christ Jesus and I enforce that victory right now. Your angels surround me, guarding me in all my ways, and Your everlasting arms uphold me. I trust in Your Word, Lord, and I declare that every stubborn situation and stronghold is breaking NOW in the name of Jesus Christ.

Father, I seal this prayer in faith, declaring that breakthroughs, victories, and miracles are manifesting in my life today. I believe I receive this prayer and release my most holy faith to bring it to pass. In Jesus' mighty name, Amen!

Faith Confessions for Warfare Against Stubborn Situations and Strongholds

1. I declare that God frustrates the plans of the wicked, and their schemes will not succeed against me. (Job 5:12)
2. I decree that no weapon formed against me shall prosper, and every tongue that rises against me in judgment is condemned. (Isaiah 54:17)
3. The Lord has delivered me from every stronghold, and my captors are defeated by His mighty hand. (Isaiah 49:24-26)
4. I overcome by the blood of the Lamb and the word of my testimony, and I will not be defeated. (Revelation 12:11)
5. The Lord is my helper, and I will not be disgraced. I set my face like a flint, and I know I will not be put to shame. (Isaiah 50:7-9)
6. I bind every force that gathers against me, and I declare that it will not prevail, for God is with me. (Isaiah 54:15)
7. Every evil counsel spoken against me is shattered and brought to nothing by the mighty hand of God. (Isaiah 8:9-10)
8. The Lord is with me, delivering me from every adversary and preserving me from harm. (Jeremiah 1:8, Jeremiah 1:19)

9. I declare that my feet are secure, and my strength will equal my days. The eternal God is my refuge, and His everlasting arms uphold me. (Deuteronomy 33:25-27)
10. Let God arise and let His enemies be scattered. Every stubborn situation and stronghold melts like wax in my presence because God is with me. (Psalm 68:1-2)
11. No stronghold of pride or deception can stand against me, for the Lord brings it low. (Obadiah 1:3-4)
12. Every mountain in my life is made a plain by the power of God. (Zechariah 4:7)
13. The God of peace crushes Satan under my feet, and I walk in victory today. (Romans 16:20)
14. The Lord rescues me from every evil attack and brings me safely into His heavenly kingdom. (2 Timothy 4:18)
15. Whatever I bind on earth is bound in heaven, and whatever I loose on earth is loosed in heaven. (Matthew 18:18)
16. I have authority to trample on snakes and scorpions, and over all the power of the enemy, and nothing shall harm me. (Luke 10:19)
17. A thousand may fall at my side and ten thousand at my right hand, but it will not come near me. (Psalm 91:7)
18. No disaster will strike me, and I am protected by the angels of God wherever I go. (Psalm 91:10-13)
19. As I meditate on God's Word and walk in obedience, I am strong, courageous, and prosperous. (Joshua 1:5-8)
20. There is no divination or enchantment against me, for I walk in the blessing of God. (Numbers 23:23)
21. I prosper in all things and remain in good health, just as my soul prospers. (3 John 1:2)

Declaring the Mind of Christ and Breaking the Enemy's Influence

Heavenly Father, I come boldly before Your throne in the name of Jesus, declaring that I have the mind of Christ. My thoughts, my desires, and my decisions are fully submitted to You. I take every thought captive and make it obedient to Jesus Christ. No deception, no confusion, no compromise will take root in my heart, mind and soul. I reject every lie of the enemy and align my mind with Your truth. Your Word is my foundation, my anchor, and my guide. I walk in divine wisdom, discernment, and clarity.

I bind the spirit of compromise, deception, and unrepentance. Every scheme of the enemy sent to dull my sensitivity to Your voice is exposed and dismantled. I will not be led astray by the world's distractions, false doctrines, or enticing words. I set my affections on things above, not on things beneath. I renounce anything that does not align with Your righteousness, and I choose to walk in purity and holiness before You.

I resist the spirit of lust and perversion in every form. Every ungodly desire, every impure thought, every unclean influence is cast down now in the name of Jesus. I declare that my body is the temple of the Holy Spirit, set apart for Your glory. No stronghold of sin, addiction, or compromise will have dominion over me. I walk in self-control, purity, and a renewed mind, and I will not be ensnared by the temptations of the flesh.

I take authority over every demonic influence that seeks to infiltrate my life, my home, my relationships, and my atmosphere. I plead the blood of Jesus over my mind, my emotions, and my spirit. Every spirit of confusion, manipulation, and oppression must flee from me. The light of God's Word shines in me, and darkness cannot overpower it.

Lord, I yield completely to You. Let the fire of Your presence purify my heart and refine my thoughts. Let Your truth be the standard by which I live. I put on the whole armor of God, standing firm against every attack of the enemy. My mind is girded with truth, my heart is covered in righteousness, my steps are ordered in peace, and my faith is unshakable.

I declare that I will walk in power, in purity, and in divine authority. The devil has no access to me, no claim over me, and no foothold in my life. I belong to You, Lord, and I will walk in victory all the days of my life.

I believe I receive this prayer and release most holy faith to bring it to pass. In Jesus' name, Amen.

A Prayer for Angelic Intervention and Victory

Heavenly Father, in the mighty name of Jesus, I come before You with faith and authority, standing on the power of Your Word. You are the Lord of Hosts, the Commander of Heaven's armies, and I declare that Your angelic forces are moving on behalf of Your people right now in the name of Jesus.

Your Word declares in Psalm 34:7, "The angel of the Lord encamps around those who fear Him, and He delivers them." Father, I thank You that even now, angels are encamping around me, around my family, around everything You have assigned to my hands. No weapon formed against us shall prosper, and every tongue that rises against us in judgment is condemned.

I summon angelic reinforcements according to Hebrews 1:14, for Your angels are ministering spirits sent to assist those who inherit salvation. I call forth divine assistance in every battle, divine protection over every step, and supernatural intervention in every challenge. Let the hosts of Heaven war against every opposition, push back every force of darkness, and establish Your Kingdom purposes in my life.

According to Exodus 14:19-20, just as the angel of God stood between Israel and their enemies, I declare that angelic warriors are standing between me and every adversary, blocking every attack, confusing the enemy's camp, and securing my victory. No scheme of the wicked shall prevail, for the Lord of Hosts fights for me.

Lord, You have commanded in Psalm 91:11-12 that Your angels guard us in all our ways. I decree that my path is shielded, my steps are ordered, and every stumbling block is removed. Angels of acceleration, bring divine opportunities! Angels of breakthrough, open doors that no man can shut! Angels of provision, release what has been held up! I align with Heaven's divine timing and walk in supernatural favor.

I bind the spirit of fear, doubt, and resistance that tries to hinder the move of God in my life. I declare according to Isaiah 54:17 that no attack, no delay, no obstacle can stand against the power of the Living God. Every barrier is shattered, every mountain is moved, and every stronghold is broken in Jesus' name!

Father, let the wind of Your Spirit carry me into new realms of victory. Victory that doesn't just benefit me, but victory that transforms the lives of everyone connected to me. Let supernatural assistance be evident in my life, so that the testimony of Your faithfulness will be undeniable. I decree divine protection, supernatural direction, and angelic intervention over my home, my finances, my purpose, my destiny, and my family.

I believe I receive this prayer, and I release my most holy faith to bring it to pass. Lord, let it be established according to Your Word, and let Your name be glorified in my life! In Jesus' mighty name, Amen!

Declaring Psalm 91 & Putting On the Whole Armor of God

Father, in the mighty name of Jesus, I come humbly before Your throne of grace. I come under the covering of the blood of Jesus Christ, standing on the power of Your Word, and declaring that no weapon formed against me shall prosper. I thank You for divine protection, supernatural shielding, and angelic assistance in every area of my life.

I decree and declare Psalm 91 over my life right now:

I dwell in the secret place of the Most High, and I abide under the shadow of the Almighty. I say of the Lord, You are my refuge and my fortress, my God, in You I trust. Father, I thank You that no trap of the enemy can hold me! You deliver me out of every scheme, every snare, and every deadly attack. You cover me, protect me, and keep me safe under the shadow of Your wings!

Lord, Your truth is my unshakable defense, my shield and my covering! I refuse to walk in fear. I will not flinch at the terror of the night or the attacks that come in the day. Disease, destruction, and disaster may be all around me, but I am covered! Though a thousand fall at my side and ten thousand at my right hand, it will not touch me. I will stand firm and see with my own eyes how You deal with the wicked. I dwell in the secret place, and I am protected by the Most High!

Because I have made the Lord my refuge, even the Most High, my dwelling place, no evil shall befall me, neither shall any plague come near my dwelling. You give Your angels charge over me to keep me in all my ways.

The angels of the Lord have charge over me, lifting me up so I won't trip, stumble, or fall into any hidden trap. I crush every spiritual threat and demonic tactic under my feet. I trample over the enemy's lies, toxic relationships, demonic delays, manipulation, fear, and sabotage. Every plot, every plan, and every setup are rendered powerless against me. Because I have set my love on the Lord and I cling to His name, He delivers me, promotes me, and positions me for victory. I know His name, and because of that, I walk in power, favor, and divine protection!

I call upon You, and You answer. You are with me in trouble. You deliver me and honor me. With long life You satisfy me and show me Your salvation.

Now, Lord, I do not step into this day uncovered, I put on the whole armor of God. I gird my loins with the **belt of truth**, I am rooted in Your Word and led by Your Spirit.

I put on the **Breastplate of Righteousness**, I am in right standing with You, and no condemnation can hold me. My feet are shod with the preparation of the **Gospel of Peace**, I walk in authority, unity, and purpose everywhere I go.

I lift up the **Shield of Faith**, quenching every fiery dart of doubt, fear, sickness, and lack. I put on the **Helmet of Salvation**, my mind is renewed, my thoughts are covered, and I walk in divine clarity. I wield the **Sword of the Spirit**, the living, active Word of God. I speak it, I declare it, and I war with it until I see manifestation.

I decree today that I am covered, I am protected, and I am equipped. No accident, no sickness, no attack, no sabotage, no delay, no weapon, and no spirit of fear shall have any place in my life. I cancel every assignment of the enemy and release the angels of God to go before me, make every crooked place straight, and establish divine victory. I will not fear. I will not fall. I will not faint, because the Lord my God is with me everywhere I go.

And now I declare with bold faith, I believe I receive this prayer, and I release my most holy faith to bring it to pass.

In Jesus' name, Amen.

Resisting the Devil & Drawing Close to God

Heavenly Father, I come before You in the name of Jesus, standing in my God-given authority! I submit myself fully to You, O Lord, my heart, my spirit, my mind, my soul, and my body belong to You! You are my refuge, my strong tower, and my ever-present help in times of need. I declare that I am hidden in Christ Jesus, covered by the blood of Jesus, and filled with the fire of the Holy Spirit.

As Your Word declares in James 4:7-8, I submit myself to God, I resist the devil, and he must flee from me. I take my stand today against every work of the enemy, every demonic assignment, and every scheme of the adversary. Satan, I serve you notice, YOU HAVE NO PLACE in my life! I rebuke every lie, every attack, and every weapon formed against me. They are rendered powerless by the authority of Jesus Christ.

I draw near to You, Lord! I press into Your presence, and I welcome You to rule and reign in my life. Purify my heart, cleanse my hands, and align me with Your perfect will. I break every ungodly attachment, silence every lying voice, and cast down every demonic stronghold that would try to rise against me. I declare and enforce my victory over every demonic work. The devil, demonic forces nor wicked people will not distract me, discourage me, or derail me, for I am rooted in You O Most High.

I put on the full armor of God. I take up the shield of faith and quench every fiery dart of the enemy. I wield the sword of the Spirit, which is the living Word of God, and I declare that no weapon formed against me shall prosper. I wear the helmet of salvation and my mind is guarded in Christ Jesus.

My feet are planted in peace, and I tread upon serpents and scorpions with authority. Devil, I command you to flee from me NOW! I resist your temptations, I reject your deceptions, and I stand firm in the truth of God's Word. Every attack against my mind, my body, my family, my finances, and my destiny is destroyed and rendered powerless in the name of Jesus.

Father, I hunger for You! Draw me closer, Lord, saturate me with Your presence, fill me with Your wisdom, and ignite a fresh fire within me. I will walk in righteousness, I will abide in truth, and I will move forward in victory. I declare that I am unshakable, immovable, and unstoppable in Christ.

I decree and declare, the enemy has fled, the chains are broken, and the victory is mine! I am fully submitted to God, and I will walk in power, authority, and divine purpose.

I believe I receive this prayer and release most holy faith to bring it to pass. In Jesus' name, Amen.

Chapter 4: Prayers for Financial Breakthrough and Kingdom Wealth

Financial Breakthrough and Kingdom Wealth

God delights in the prosperity of His servants. Psalm 35:27 (KJV) says, *"Let them shout for joy, and be glad, that favor my righteous cause: yea, let them say continually, Let the Lord be magnified, which hath pleasure in the prosperity of his servant."* There is nothing wrong with being blessed. There is nothing unholy about walking in abundance.

He is a covenant-keeping God and His covenant includes wealth, increase, and overflow, not just for our own benefit, but so we can advance His Kingdom, help the poor, fund ministry, and leave a legacy.

As believers, we must shift our mindset and stop tolerating lack as if it were holy. Poverty is not a fruit of the Spirit. Lack is not God's ultimate plan for you. Struggle is not your portion. The truth is, wealth is your right as a covenant child of God. Deuteronomy 8:18 (KJV) says, *"But thou shalt remember the Lord thy God: for it is he that giveth thee power to get wealth, that he may establish his covenant which he swore unto thy fathers, as it is this day."*

Let that verse settle into your spirit. God has given us the power, the authority, strategy, ability, and favor to get wealth. That means it's not just about hustle or hard work. It's about walking in divine alignment, receiving downloads from Heaven, and managing resources under the anointing. He gives you power to produce. Power to build. Power to prosper. Power to multiply. Wealth isn't the goal, obedience is. But obedience will always lead you into provision.

In this chapter, we are not just praying for breakthrough, we are commanding it. We are releasing prophetic decrees that calls forth the harvest. We are declaring debt cancellation, financial miracles, business expansion, divine favor, supernatural contracts, and open doors.

Some of you have been faithful tithers and givers, but you haven't always known how to boldly speak to your finances. Now is the time to release your voice over your money. Call forth resources from the north, south, east, and west. Prophesy to the dry bones of your bank account. Decree that money is finding you. Assign your dollars an assignment. Give your wealth a calling. This is not hype. This is biblical authority.

Proverbs 10:22 (KJV) says, *"The blessing of the Lord, it maketh rich, and he addeth no sorrow with it."* The blessing carries weight. It is empowerment and enablement from Heaven to thrive without toil. That is what you carry. That is what you have inherited. You are a citizen of the Kingdom, and your provision flows from a different economy. It flows from the economy of Heaven.

So, let's break cycles of lack, poverty and limitation. Let's silence the lies of the enemy that tell you it's not for you. Let's come out of survival mode and walk boldly in overflow. This is your season to flourish.

Get ready to speak life over your money, your business, your resources, and your legacy. We are releasing the anointing for financial dominion and commanding wealth to locate us. Let's pray with authority and expectation, knowing that we were born to prosper for the glory of God.

Financial Increase Faith Confession

Heavenly Father, I come to your throne of Grace through and by the blood of Jesus Christ. I ask you to receive my words and requests for financial increase in my life. I ask for your anointing to be upon my lips as I speak forth in faith these prayers and decrees. Let the authority that you have given me be established as I speak today.

Father, in the name of Jesus, I confess your will over my finances this day, that I have given the tithes of my increase and claim the windows of heaven blessings for my life. Thank You Father, my mind is alert, and my ears hear Your voice and the voice of the stranger I will not follow. I thank you Father that I receive new doors of opportunity opening for me and my family. Father, I have given to those that are in need, therefore I will never lack. I will always have all sufficiency in all things as you are raising up others to use their power, their ability and their influence to help me to accomplish your will and plan for my life.

I expect daily, for the Spirit of God to speak to men and women concerning giving to me. In the name of Jesus, those to whom the Spirit of God has designated are free to obey and give to me good measure, pressed down, shaken together, and running over. In the name of Jesus, every need is met with heaven's best. I have given for the support of the work of God and those who teach His Word. You promised that You would supply all my need according to your riches in glory by Christ Jesus. So, I thank You Father, I live the best and enjoy the best in every area of my life.

Father, Your Word says, I can decree a thing because of my covenant vow with you for the Kingdom of God in the earth. Now this is my decree, I decree and declare that I am out of debt and my needs are met, I have plenty more to put in store. I owe no man nothing but to love them. I decree and declare that my struggles with finances are OVER! The grace of God is manifesting in my life and finances NOW! My money is increasing daily. Unexpected income is coming to me NOW! I thank You Father for wisdom and insight to bring it to pass. You give me and my family richly all things to enjoy. Now, Satan, I bind your activity in my life and finances, and I loose the angels of God, the ministering spirits of God to minister for me and bring in the necessary finances so that I may continue to finance the Kingdom of God. Father Your Word declares that my giving increases the fruits of my righteousness. I thank You Father, I have the abundance of peace and the abundance of goodness. The maximum return on my giving is mine because I give to promote the Name of Jesus and the gospel in the earth.

In the name of Jesus Christ, the King of Kings and Lord of Lords. I believe I receive this and release most holy faith to bring it to pass.

Declarations of Success, Prosperity, Abundance, & God's Goodness

- **I decree and declare** that the blessing of the Lord makes me rich, and He adds no sorrow with it. I am walking in divine prosperity and abundance today! (*Proverbs 10:22*)
- **I decree and declare** that everything I set my hands to do will prosper, for the Lord my God is causing me to succeed and excel in all my endeavors. (*Psalm 1:3*)
- **I decree and declare** that God is supplying all my needs according to His riches in glory by Christ Jesus. Lack and limitation are far from me! (*Philippians 4:19*)
- **I decree and declare** that I will lend to many nations and not borrow, for the Lord has made me the head and not the tail, above only and not beneath. (*Deuteronomy 28:12-13*)
- **I decree and declare** that I am experiencing the overflow of God's abundance in every area of my life. My cup is running over! (*Psalm 23:5*)
- **I decree and declare** that the favor of God surrounds me like a shield, opening doors that no one can shut and bringing divine opportunities my way. (*Psalm 5:12*)
- **I decree and declare** that wealth and riches are in my house, and the righteousness of God is firmly established in my life. (*Psalm 112:3*)
- **I decree and declare** that God's goodness and mercy are following me all the days of my life, and I dwell in the abundance of His presence. (*Psalm 23:6*)
- **I decree and declare** that I am walking in divine health, prosperity, and success because God's Word is alive and active in my life. (*3 John 1:2*)
- **I decree and declare** that no weapon formed against my finances, family, or future will prosper. The Lord is my defense, and He ensures my victory. (*Isaiah 54:17*)
- **I decree and declare** that the windows of heaven are open over me, pouring out blessings so abundant that I don't have room enough to receive them! (*Malachi 3:10*)
- **I decree and declare** that the Lord is giving me the power to create wealth, and my success is a testimony of His covenant promises. (*Deuteronomy 8:18*)

- **I decree and declare** that my paths are directed by the Lord, and He is establishing every step I take. I walk in divine order. (*Proverbs 16:9*)
- **I boldly declare** that I'm walking in overflow! My bank accounts, investments, and storehouses are full and fresh resources are flowing into my hands. God is releasing supernatural provision, and I have more than enough to bless others and advance the Kingdom of God in the earth! (*Proverbs 3:9-10*)
- **I decree and declare** that the glory of God is resting upon me, and His goodness is manifesting in every area of my life. I am blessed to be a blessing! (*2 Corinthians 9:8*)
- **I decree and declare** that my labor is not in vain, and I will reap a bountiful harvest in due season. (*Galatians 6:9*)
- **I decree and declare** that I am walking in the abundance of God's peace, joy, and provision. (*John 10:10*)
- **I decree and declare** that every resource I need is being released, and divine connections are aligning for my success. (*Isaiah 45:3*)
- **I decree and declare** that the goodness of the Lord is evident in my life, and His favor is opening doors I could not open on my own. (*Psalm 27:13*)
- **I decree and declare** that I am flourishing like a tree planted by streams of water, yielding fruit in every season. (*Psalm 92:12-13*)
- **I decree and declare** that I walk in the supernatural favor of God, and His blessings chase me down and overtake me. (*Deuteronomy 28:2*)
- **I decree and declare** that God is making all grace abound toward me, giving me sufficiency in all things so I may abound in every good work. (*2 Corinthians 9:8*)
- **I decree and declare** that every delay is being turned into divine acceleration, and every obstacle into a stepping stone for my victory. (*Amos 9:13*)
- **I decree and declare** that I am walking in the fullness of God's covenant promises, and His hand is guiding me into prosperity and success. (*Joshua 1:8*)
- **I decree and declare** that my life reflects the goodness and faithfulness of God, and my testimony brings glory to His name. (*Psalm 34:8*)

Faith Confession of Abundance

Heavenly Father, I come to your throne of Grace through and by the blood of Jesus Christ. I ask you to receive my words and requests for favor and financial increase in my life. I ask for your anointing to be upon my lips as I speak forth in faith these declarations and decrees. Let the authority that you have given me be established as I speak today.

- God is about to do something in my life that I have never seen before.
- God is about to take me where I couldn't go on my own.
- God is about to show me favor in a way I have never imagined. It is going to be unprecedented. Out of the norm. Unlike anything that I have ever seen before.
- God is about to show me abundance like I have never seen before. He is about to increase me to where there is overflow in my life.
- This is a set time of favor in my life.
- There will be moments of favor that will catapult me to the next level and thrust me into generational abundance and legacy wealth.
- God is showering me with his goodness and mercy which follow me everywhere I go, all the days of my life.
- I am living in a place of more than enough and lack is a thing of my past.
- I am experiencing new opportunities for advancement, promotion, and increase.
- I am hearing God's voice more than I have ever heard before.
- I am moving to new places in prayer and worship.
- I am walking in the gifts and talents that God has given me.
- I am experiencing love, joy, and peace in abundance.

In the name of Jesus Christ I pray amen. I believe and I receive this and release most holy faith to bring it to pass.

Releasing Money Miracles and Supernatural Breakthrough

Father, I thank You that I am a covenant child, and Your Word declares that You delight in the prosperity of Your servants. I am blessed, highly favored, and walking in supernatural abundance. The wealth of the wicked is laid up for me, and I receive divine transfers now in the name of Jesus. I decree and declare that money comes to me swiftly, easily, and consistently. Unexpected income, supernatural provision, and financial miracles are locating me now. My hands are anointed to prosper, and everything I touch multiplies. I walk in divine opportunities, open doors, and the manifestation of Your promises. There is no lack in my life, only increase, overflow, and supernatural supply. In Jesus' name, I believe, I receive it.

Father, in the mighty name of Jesus, I step into my covenant rights as a kingdom citizen and command the blessing upon my life. Your Word declares in Deuteronomy 28:8 that You command the blessing on my storehouses and in all that I set my hands to do. So, I call forth the commanded blessing now! Let supernatural increase be released over my life. I speak to every financial hindrance, every delay, and every blockage, be removed in Jesus' name!

I declare breakthrough over my finances, breakthrough over my business, breakthrough over every financial seed I have sown. I call forth divine provision from the north, south, east, and west. Lord, You are Jehovah Jireh, my provider, and I decree that all my needs are met according to Your riches in glory by Christ Jesus (Philippians 4:19).

I release the angels of prosperity to go forth and bring in the financial harvest that belongs to me. I command money to come NOW! Debts to be canceled! Favor to surround me like a shield! I decree that supernatural ideas, divine connections, and unexpected resources are locating me now. The wealth of the wicked is transferring into the hands of the righteous (Proverbs 13:22), and I am a recipient of kingdom wealth.

I take authority over lack, struggle, and financial hardship. I bind the spirit of poverty and loose the power of divine overflow. Lord, You said in Malachi 3:10 that You would open the windows of heaven and pour me out a blessing I don't have room enough to receive. I stand on that promise! Let the floodgates open! Let supernatural provision flow! I call forth multiple streams of income and unexpected deposits.

I declare that I am a lender and not a borrower, the head and not the tail, above only and never beneath (Deuteronomy 28:12-13). I walk in financial dominion, wealth, and kingdom prosperity. Money is not my master, I rule over money, and it serves my God-given purpose. My wealth is a tool for kingdom impact, and I give freely as You lead. I seal this prayer with faith, believing I receive every promise spoken. Lord, let the supernatural manifest speedily. In Jesus' name, I believe I receive this prayer and release most holy faith to bring it to pass. Amen.

Debt Cancelation Accelerator Affirmation

Instructions
You must make a list of all your debtors and the amount you owe. You will say this affirmation over your debts while releasing your faith for supernatural debt cancelation. I encourage you to say the affirmation daily until you are 100% debt free. Now don't go out and get more debt. It's important to use the wisdom of God and as the bible says to owe no man nothing but to love him. I hope you catch that.

Debt Cancelation Accelerator Affirmation
Repeat aloud and say it with conviction in your heart:
Heavenly Father, you are the great deliverer and you said that if I call upon you, that you would deliver me. I ask that you deliver me out of my debt. I ask that you cause unexpected income to come and financial miracles to come. I ask that I have debt removing favor on my life from this day forward.

I speak to this mountain of debt and I command it to be removed and cast into the sea. I experience divine favor with my debtor _____ and my debtor of $_____ is release and canceled now. The spirit of debt and lack no longer control my life and I am no longer a slave to my lender. I experience supernatural debt cancelation and favor. I command this balance to decrease to zero now. I am out of debt, my needs are met, and have plenty of money in my checking, savings, retirement, and investment accounts. I no longer use debt as a way to live above my means. I am debt free NOW. I release my faith to make debt freedom a reality for me.

I believe I receive this and release most holy faith to bring it to pass. In Jesus name, I am debt free.

Financial Breakthrough and Money Miracles

Heavenly Father, in the mighty name of Jesus, I enter Your courts with thanksgiving and Your gates with praise. I honor You as Jehovah Jireh, my Provider, the Source of every good and perfect gift. I exalt Your name and declare Your sovereignty over every area of my life, including my finances.

Right now, by the authority of the name of Jesus and the power of His blood, I take dominion over every demonic force assigned to hinder my financial prosperity. I bind every spirit of lack, poverty, and debt in the name of Jesus, and I command you to loose your grip off my finances and flee. I dismantle every plot and scheme of the enemy to devour my resources, and I declare that no weapon formed against my finances shall prosper. I speak to the north, south, east, and west, and I command resources, opportunities, and blessings to come forth. I decree that supernatural doors are opening, debts are being canceled, and the heavens are releasing divine provision over my life.

Father, I thank You that angels are moving on my behalf, bringing answers to my prayers and orchestrating financial miracles. Lord, Your Word declares that You have given me the power to get wealth. I ask for divine strategies, creative ideas, and wisdom for stewardship. Anoint my hands to prosper and bless the work that I do. I declare that everything I touch multiplies and increases according to Your will.

Father, I consecrate my finances to You. Let the finances and resources I receive be used to glorify Your name and advance Your Kingdom. Let my testimony of breakthrough inspire others to trust in Your unfailing promises.

I stand in faith, unshaken and unwavering. I declare victory over my finances and proclaim that breakthrough is here. I thank You in advance for unexpected income, supernatural favor, and overflowing abundance. I call it done in the mighty name of Jesus. Amen and Amen.

Prayer to Pronounce Blessings and Favor Over Finances

Heavenly Father, In the mighty name of Jesus, I lift my hands and my heart in faith, declaring that You are Jehovah Jireh, the Lord my Provider. You are my Source. You are the Giver of every good and perfect gift. I declare right now, I am blessed, highly favored, and walking under an open Heaven.

I pronounce supernatural blessing over my finances. I decree that lack has no place in my life. The assignment of poverty on my bloodline is disrupted and canceled by the redemptive power of the blood of Jesus Christ. Poverty is no longer effective in my life. Poverty is broken off now. My bloodline is full of favor and overflowing with blessings from this point and forever more. I command the grip of financial stress to loose its hold. I thank You, Lord, that Your Word says in Deuteronomy 28:12 that You will bless all the work of my hands and open the heavens to pour out rain in due season. My due season is now.

Father, let favor rest on my business, my career, my investments, and every seed I sow. Let divine opportunities locate me in season and out of season. Let unexpected provision find me. Let doors open that no man can shut. Let the windows of Heaven overflow in my direction bringing strategy, resources, and increase.

I declare that I am a faithful steward over all the resources that are given to me. I honor You with the first fruits of my increase. Because I obey You, Proverbs 3:10 says, my barns will be filled with plenty and my vats will overflow with new wine. I receive abundance now, not for greed, but for Kingdom purpose.

Father, I speak blessing over my bank accounts, my cash flow, and my contracts. I call in promotions, raises, favor with decision-makers, and supernatural returns on every good seed. Let wealth be attracted to me, not because of who I am, but because of who You are in me.

I bind every spirit of financial sabotage, lack, delay, and confusion. I loose wisdom, clarity, multiplication, and favor. I will not fear inflation, recession, or limitation. My economy is Heaven's economy. I live under supernatural provision. I live under an open heaven.

I believe I receive this prayer, and I release my most holy faith to bring it to pass. In Jesus' name, Amen

Prayer for Growth, Expansion, Increase, and Abundance

Heavenly Father, in the mighty name of Jesus, I come boldly before Your throne of grace, lifting my heart and voice in faith, declaring that You are the God of growth, expansion, increase, and abundance! I exalt You as the source of every good and perfect gift. There is no lack in You, no limitation in Your power, and no boundary to what You can do.

Lord, Your Word declares in Isaiah 54:2-3, "Enlarge the place of your tent, stretch your tent curtains wide, do not hold back; lengthen your cords, strengthen your stakes. For you will spread out to the right and to the left." Today, I stand on this promise and decree that the anointing for growth and expansion is being released upon me right now in the name of Jesus!

I break every limitation, every barrier, and every stronghold that has tried to hold me back. I declare that doors of opportunity are opening, territories are enlarging, and divine connections are being established. The power of God is moving, shifting, and realigning things in my favor.

Father, You are the God of increase! Your Word says in Psalm 115:14, "May the Lord give you increase more and more, you and your children." I declare supernatural increase over my life—spiritual growth, financial increase, business expansion, and abundant opportunities. I am blessed to be a blessing, and overflow is my portion.

Today, I release my faith toward heaven, believing that as I pray, the anointing is flowing, yokes are breaking, and burdens are being lifted. I speak life over every dry place, and I command it to grow and flourish. I call forth abundance from the north, south, east, and west. I declare that promotions are being released, businesses are expanding, and divine strategies are being downloaded.

Holy Spirit, pour out fresh oil upon me. Let the anointing to prosper, to advance, and to multiply rest upon my life. According to Deuteronomy 28:12, "The Lord will open to you His good treasure, the heavens, to give the rain to your land in its season and to bless all the work of your hand." I declare that this is my season of rain! The heavens are open and the blessings of the Lord are overtaking us.

I am experiencing growth and divine acceleration. I am expanding and increasing in ways that I could never imagine. Abundance is my covenant right and I receive abundance in my life now. I will not settle for less than God's best because the blessing of the Lord makes us rich and adds no sorrow with it (Proverbs 10:22).

Father, I thank You that as I pray, Your power is being released, Your glory is being revealed, and Your promises are manifesting right before my eyes.

I believe, I receive this prayer, and I release our most holy faith to bring it to pass. In Jesus' mighty name, Amen!

Biblical Generosity and Spirit-Led Giving

Heavenly Father, I come before You today with a heart full of thanksgiving, acknowledging that every good and perfect gift comes from You. You are Jehovah Jireh, my Provider, and I thank You for Your faithfulness and provision.

Lord, Your Word teaches us in 2 Corinthians 9:6-7 that whoever sows sparingly will also reap sparingly and whoever sows generously will also reap generously. Today, I ask You to give me a heart that is generous, joyful, and willing to give according to Your leadership.

Father, remove every root of greed, fear, and self-centeredness from my heart. Break the chains of a poverty and scarcity mindset and replace them with faith, trust, and boldness to give freely. I declare that I will not hold back what belongs to You but will honor You with my tithes, offerings, and gifts.

Your Word declares in Malachi 3:10 that if I bring my tithes into the storehouse, You will open the floodgates of heaven and pour out blessings I cannot contain. Father, I stand on this promise today, trusting that as I obey, You will provide exceedingly and abundantly above all I can ask or think. You are providing beyond my highest thoughts and dreams.

Holy Spirit, lead me in my giving. Direct my heart and mind to opportunities where my generosity can make an eternal kingdom impact. Whether it's in our churches, our communities, or in the lives of those in need, may I give with discernment, love, and purpose.

Lord, Your Word says in Luke 6:38 that as I give, it will be given back to me, good measure, pressed down, shaken together, and running over. I declare that my giving will not only meet immediate needs but will also overflow to bring transformation and restoration to others.

Father, I pray for financial wisdom and stewardship. Teach me to manage my resources in honor to you, to save with purpose, to invest with wisdom, and to give with open heart. May my finances always reflect my trust in You and my commitment to Your Kingdom.

I speak blessings over every giver, every seed sown, and every act of obedience. Multiply the financial seeds they sow and may they never lack anything because they take care of your kingdom. May Your favor rest upon our homes, our families, our businesses, and our ministries.

Lord, let our lives be a testimony of Your faithfulness and love. May our generosity bring glory to Your name, draw others to Your love, and serve as an instrument to advance Your Kingdom on earth.

I declare that I am blessed to be a blessing, and I walk in radical generosity, spirit-led giving, and divine provision. I believe I receive this prayer, and I release most holy faith to bring it to pass. In the mighty and matchless name of Jesus Christ, I pray. Amen and Amen!

Building Kingdom Wealth, Entrepreneurship, and Legacy Income

Heavenly Father, I come before You today, fully aware that You are Jehovah Jireh, our Provider, and the One who gives us the power to create wealth. Lord, I thank You for every resource, opportunity, and talent You have entrusted to me.

Father, according to Deuteronomy 8:18, I declare that You have given me the ability to produce wealth. Let every idea, strategy, and opportunity You have assigned to me manifest in its fullness. Teach me to operate in wisdom, integrity, and diligence as I build wealth and a legacy that honors You.

Lord, as written in Proverbs 13:22, I commit to leaving an inheritance not just for my children, but for my children's children. Help me to build and steward wealth that will impact generations for Your glory.

Father, I stand on Philippians 4:19, believing that You will meet every need according to Your glorious riches in Christ Jesus. Lack, poverty, and financial strain are not my portion. I declare supernatural abundance is flowing into my life, home, and businesses.

Lord, I declare Psalm 35:27 over my life, that You delight in the prosperity of Your servants. Let me experience divine favor, open doors, and supernatural provision as I faithfully pursue my Kingdom assignment.

Father, I thank You for the promise of Proverbs 10:22, that Your blessing makes rich, and You add no sorrow with it. I declare that every financial breakthrough I receive will be accompanied by peace, joy, and gratitude.

Lord, ignite entrepreneurial vision in Your people. Release creative business ideas, strategies for wealth creation, and the courage to execute bold plans. Let Your people rise as Kingdom entrepreneurs, using their influence to glorify You and uplift others.

I rebuke lack, poverty, and poor money management. I cancel every assignment of debt and financial oppression in Jesus' name. I declare financial freedom, prosperity, and abundance is flowing into every area of our lives.

Father, align my heart with Your Kingdom purposes. Allow me to see money not as an end, but as a tool to fund Kingdom work, bless others, and bring glory to Your name. Raise up men and women of faith who will steward financial resources with integrity and generosity. Let our lives be marked by faith-filled giving, wise investing, and impactful legacy-building. Father, I declare that our finances are covered by the blood of Jesus. No weapon formed against our financial well-being will prosper.

I thank You, Lord, that resources are being released, doors are opening, and miracles are happening in our finances even now. I trust You to guide me, empower me, and use me for Your glory. I believe I receive this prayer, and I release most holy faith to bring it to pass. In the mighty and matchless name of Jesus Christ, I pray. Amen and Amen!

Declaring Blessings Over the Economy and God's People

Father, in the mighty name of Jesus, I come boldly before Your throne of grace today. I stand in full authority as Your son/daughter, and I declare right now that You are Jehovah Jireh, our provider. You are the God who supplies all my needs according to Your riches in glory by Christ Jesus!

I pronounce blessings over the local, national and world economy today. Father, I speak life into every system, every market, every business, and every place of commerce. I declare that the economy is not my source. You are my source. I take my eyes off what I see in the natural, and I fix my eyes on the faithfulness of my God.

I decree and declare that Your goodness is running over in the lives of Your people. Father, I thank You that I am not moved by headlines, I am not moved by reports, and I am not moved by what I see with my natural eyes. I am moved only by Your Word! Your Word says the righteous will never be forsaken, nor their seed begging bread. I declare today that provision is flowing into the hands of Your people!

Father, in the name of Jesus, I push back every demonic force and every wicked agenda that is working to disrupt the flow of Your provision. I cancel every assignment of shortage, of lack, of inflation, of recession, of manipulation, and of economic oppression. I break its power in the name of Jesus!

I declare that wealth is being transferred into the hands of the righteous. I decree open doors, open contracts, divine connections, favor in the marketplace, and opportunities that supersede natural understanding. Angels of provision, go forth and minister for the heirs of salvation! Resources are being released now!

Father, I thank You that Your people are flourishing in the midst of famine. Your Word says in Psalm 37:19, "They will not be disgraced in hard times; even in famine they will have more than enough." So, I declare more than enough! Overflow! Increase! Abundance!

I declare supernatural provision over families, over businesses, over ministries, and over communities. I decree that the economy of Heaven overrides every earthly limitation. I declare that I live under open heavens!

Father, I release this prayer in full faith, and I decree that I will see the manifestation of Your goodness in the land of the living. I believe I receive it, and I release our most holy faith to bring it to pass. In Jesus' name, Amen!

Financial Resources for Churches, Ministers, & Missionaries

Heavenly Father, I come before You today with a grateful heart, acknowledging You as Jehovah Jireh, our Provider, the one who sees our needs and provides. You own the cattle on a thousand hills, and nothing is too hard for You.

Lord, according to Philippians 4:19, You promise to meet every need according to Your glorious riches in Christ Jesus. Today, I stand on that promise and declare that every ministry, church, and missionary called by Your name will lack nothing.

Father, I stand in agreement with 2 Corinthians 9:8 and declare abundance over every Kingdom work that is established in the earth. Let every church, outreach effort, and missionary experience financial overflow. May they abound in every good work You've assigned to them.

Lord, I stand on Malachi 3:10, asking that You open the floodgates of Heaven and pour out blessings upon Your people who are faithfully stewarding Your resources. Release supernatural provision, resources, and finances to fuel Kingdom work across the globe.

Father, I declare Luke 6:38 over every giver in the Body of Christ. Stir hearts to give willingly, cheerfully, and obediently. Let every gift multiply and return in abundance, pressed down, shaken together, and running over.

Lord, according to Proverbs 3:9-10, we honor You with our wealth and the first fruits of our increase. Teach Your people to steward resources with wisdom, integrity, and a Kingdom mindset. Let savings, investments and financial storehouses be filled to overflowing, and let every financial seed sown produce an abundant harvest.

Father, I pray for supernatural debt cancellation for churches, ministries, and missionaries. Break the chains of financial burdens that hinder Kingdom progress. Let buildings be paid off, resources be multiplied, and every financial barrier be removed in Jesus' name.

Lord, send destiny helpers to support and uplift every Kingdom assignment. Release skilled laborers, generous givers, and influential partners who will stand alongside churches, ministries and missionaries to see Your will accomplished on the earth.

Father, I declare that no vision from You will die due to lack of resources. Every God-ordained project will grow and flourish. Every Kingdom initiative will thrive. Every missionary called by you will be equipped. Every ordained spirit led church will overflow with resources to bless their communities and fulfill the Great Commission.

I rebuke the devourer in the name of Jesus. Every spirit of lack, delay, and financial stagnation is broken right now in the name of Jesus. The wealth of the wicked is being transferred into the hands of the righteous for Kingdom purposes.

Lord, raise up faithful stewards who will manage resources with excellence, generosity, and wisdom. Let every resource be used for Your glory and the advancement of Your Kingdom.

Father, I thank You for financial breakthroughs, debt freedom, and supernatural increase being released right now. I give You all the glory, honor, and praise for what You are doing and what You will continue to do. I believe I receive this prayer, and I release our most holy faith to bring it to pass. In the mighty and matchless name of Jesus Christ, I pray. Amen and Amen!

Global and National Economy

Heavenly Father, I come boldly before Your throne of grace, standing in the authority of Your Word and calling upon You as Jehovah Jireh, my Provider. You are the God who owns the cattle on a thousand hills, and nothing is too hard for You.

Lord, I lift up the global and national economies before You. In a world filled with financial instability, economic downturns, and unjust systems, I declare that You are still sovereign over every financial structure, policy, and institution.

Your Word says in Philippians 4:19 that You will supply all my needs according to Your riches in glory through Christ Jesus. Today, I declare supernatural provision over nations, communities, families, and individuals.

Lord, grant wisdom, discernment, and integrity to financial leaders, policymakers, and government officials who make decisions that affect economies. Remove selfish ambition, greed, and corruption from leadership and replace it with righteousness, accountability, and compassion.

I declare Deuteronomy 8:18 over the global economy, You are the Lord my God, and it is You who gives me the power to get wealth. Father, release strategies, innovation, and creative ideas to spark economic growth, employment opportunities, and financial stability.

I plead the blood of Jesus over financial systems, markets, businesses, and every economic institution. I break the spirit of lack, poverty, and financial oppression. Every cycle of debt, generational poverty, and financial bondage is broken now in the name of Jesus.

Lord, let wealth be distributed righteously. Protect the vulnerable from exploitation, and let policies be enacted that uplift the poor, support small businesses, and provide opportunities for sustainable growth.

I declare Malachi 3:10 over my life, I bring all the tithes into the storehouse, and You promised to open the windows of heaven and pour out a blessing so great there will not be room enough to receive it. Father, I align my financial habits with Your Word. Teach me to steward resources with wisdom, integrity, and purpose.

Lord, I intercede for families experiencing financial hardship. Provide jobs for the unemployed, resources for the underprivileged, and hope for the discouraged. Open doors that no man can shut and release financial miracles that testify of Your goodness. Father, I ask for protection over global economies from catastrophic events, economic crashes, and manipulations that lead to mass suffering. Place Your hedge of protection over nations that are vulnerable to financial collapse.

I pray for a revival of generosity among Your people. Let Your church rise up as a beacon of hope, a storehouse of provision, and a refuge for those in need. Let ministries be funded, missionaries be supported, and communities be transformed by financial blessings.

Father, let righteous policies and laws be enacted that protect families, uplift communities, and honor You. Guide leaders to make decisions that prioritize justice, equity, and compassion.

I declare Proverbs 3:9-10 over every household and ministry connected to me, we will honor the Lord with our wealth and the best part of all we produce, and God will cause our banking, saving, and investment accounts to overflow, our resources to multiply, and our capacity to expand. We will not run out and we will overflow financially.

Father, I thank You in advance for breakthroughs, testimonies, financial miracles, and supernatural debt cancellations. I thank You for new opportunities, unexpected blessings, and open doors. I declare that the wealth of the wicked is laid up for the righteous (Proverbs 13:22), and resources are being transferred for Kingdom purposes.

I believe I receive this prayer, and I release most holy faith to bring it to pass. In the mighty and matchless name of Jesus Christ, I pray. Amen.

Divine Connections, Destiny Helpers, and Supernatural Favor

Heavenly Father, in the name of Jesus, I come before You with boldness, standing on the authority of Your Word! You are the God of divine alignment, the Master Orchestrator of purpose, and the One who orders my steps. Today, I call forth divine connections and destiny helpers from the four corners of the earth! Let those whom You have assigned to bless, assist, and propel me forward, locate me now, in Jesus' name!

Your Word declares in Isaiah 43:5-6, "Do not be afraid, for I am with you; I will bring your children from the east and gather you from the west. I will say to the north, 'Give them up!' and to the south, 'Do not hold them back.'" So, I decree and declare that every divine connection, every kingdom relationship, every assigned helper must come forth NOW! Let the north give them up! Let the south release them! Let the east and the west bring them speedily into my life, for we are in alignment with Your perfect will!

Father, I bind and break every demonic delay, every spirit of resistance, and every blockade the enemy has set up to keep me from divine appointments! According to Isaiah 45:2-3, You go before me and make the crooked places straight! Every gate of brass is shattered and every iron bar is cut asunder! I declare that no barrier, no hindrance, and no obstacle shall stand in the way of the divine helpers You have assigned to my life!

I declare that doors of favor, opportunity, and supernatural provision are opening right now! Just as You raised up Boaz for Ruth, Pharaoh's cupbearer for Joseph, and Jonathan for David, You are raising up the right people to support, uplift, and propel me into my next season. Divine partnerships, strategic relationships, and kingdom alignments are forming even now!

Lord, Your Word says in Psalm 5:12, "Surely, Lord, you bless the righteous; you surround them with your favor as with a shield." I declare that I am clothed in divine favor! I am shielded by favor! I walk in favor! Everywhere I go, favor goes before me! I am called, chosen, and set apart for such a time as this, and no good thing shall be withheld from me!

Father, I thank You for supernatural acceleration! What should take years, You will accomplish in days! What man says is impossible, You make possible! I align my life with Your divine timetable and declare that my destiny helpers will recognize me, seek me out, and be moved to bless and assist me, in Jesus' name!

I believe I receive this prayer, and I release my most holy faith to bring it to pass! Thank You, Father, for Your faithfulness! It is done, it is sealed, and it shall manifest, in Jesus' mighty name! Amen!

Chapter 5 – Prayers for Healing and Deliverance

Healing and Deliverance

Healing is not a maybe, it is a covenant promise. Jesus didn't just die for our salvation; He was wounded for our healing. Every stripe on His back, every drop of blood poured out, paid the price for our spiritual, physical, emotional, and mental healing. God's desire is not for you to live sick, stuck, or suffering. He wants you whole, restored, free, and walking in divine health.

Isaiah 53:5 (KJV) says, *"But he was wounded for our transgressions, he was bruised for our iniquities: the chastisement of our peace was upon him; and with his stripes we are healed."*

There is nothing too hard for God. No diagnosis is too difficult. No sickness is beyond His reach and His power. No trauma is too old to be healed. God has given you power over it all, cancer, diabetes, arthritis, migraines, autoimmune disease, anxiety, PTSD, depression, and generational infirmity. That power is available to you and I. Healing is the children's bread (Matthew 15:26), and I refuse to let you settle for less than what Jesus already purchased.

In this chapter, I want you to stir your faith again. Maybe the doctors gave up. Maybe the symptoms seem worse. Maybe you've learned to "live with it." But I speak life over you today. You don't have to cope with sickness and infirmity, you can be made whole.

Jeremiah 30:17 (KJV) says, *"For I will restore health unto thee, and I will heal thee of thy wounds, saith the Lord..."* God is a healer, a restorer, and a deliverer. He heals broken bodies, shattered emotions, bruised spirits, and tormented minds. I'm believing right now that as you read this, healing is filling the atmosphere around you and restoring your faith for healing.

You may have come from a family line of sickness or bondage, but in the name of Jesus, I declare that the cycle is broken NOW. That infirmity stops with you. You are the healed of the Lord, and you're walking out of this chapter with a new declaration: **"I shall live and not die, and declare the works of the Lord"** (Psalm 118:17).

This chapter doesn't just focus on physical healing, but also deliverance, freedom from torment, addiction, oppression, soul ties, and demonic influence. You were never created to live in chains. You were born to be free. Free from fear. Free from mental torment. Free from oppression. Free from spiritual bondage. Free from cycles of affliction. John 8:36 (KJV) says, *"If the Son therefore shall make you free, ye shall be free indeed."*

Now is the time to renounce anything that's held you bound and receive the power of the Holy Spirit to live free. This chapter includes powerful prayers and declarations to command healing in every part of your life: your body, mind, heart, emotions, and spirit. There's also a focus on breaking generational sickness, breaking soul ties, and walking in daily freedom.

This chapter is a divine appointment for breakthrough. It's time to receive your miracle by faith. As you go through each prayer and confession, speak boldly. Lay hands on yourself. Call out specific illnesses. Rebuke the spirit of infirmity. Take authority over pain. Expect the presence of God to meet you right there.

Let the healer, Jehovah Rapha, come in. Let the Deliverer arise. Whom the Son sets free is free indeed.

Healing Miracles and Manifestations

Heavenly Father, I come before Your throne of grace, standing on the authority of Your Word and the finished works of Jesus Christ. Lord, You are Jehovah Rapha, my Healer, and I thank You that Your healing power is still active and alive today. Your healing power is working in me.

Father, I remember the healing miracles recorded in the Book of Acts, where the lame walked, sick people were healed, and the demonically oppressed were set free. Today, I ask for the same boldness, faith, and supernatural manifestations of Your healing power in my life and in my community.

Lord, just as Peter declared in Acts 3:6, "In the name of Jesus Christ of Nazareth, rise up and walk," I declare healing over every sickness, every disease, and every physical ailment. Let the lame walk, the blind see, and the deaf hear. Father, I stand in agreement with Acts 4:30, I ask You to stretch out Your right hand with healing power. Let signs, wonders and miracles be evident in our lives, in the name of Jesus. I declare that every chain of infirmity is broken. I cancel every negative report and declare there is a divine reset bringing healing now in Jesus' name. Bring complete restoration to broken and sick bodies. Father, bring restoration to weary souls in the name of Jesus.

Holy Spirit, let the same power that raised Christ Jesus from the dead flow through every sick and diseased body right now. Let fevers break by the fire of the Holy Ghost. Let tumors disappear. Let organs regenerate and be fully restored in the perfection in which you created them. Let bodies be healed at the root and pain be removed in the name of Jesus.

I stand on James 5:14-15, and I pray with unwavering faith. I declare that healing flows like a river, washing away every disease, affliction, and trace of infirmity. I bind the spirit of infirmity and command you to be removed right now in Jesus' name. You have no right or authority to take residence in our bodies. Lord, I ask for supernatural healing encounters to become common in my life and among those connected to me. Just as in Acts 9:34, when Peter spoke and Aeneas was instantly healed, I declare instant and undeniable healing miracles are taking place in our lives and all around us.

Father, let Your healing power fill our bodies, homes, hospitals, and every place where Your name is lifted. Just as Your healing presence was strong in Luke 5:17, let Your presence overshadow me now. Let those who encounter me experience the touch of Your healing hand.

Lord, I release every burden, every worry, and every fear regarding sickness and disease into Your capable hands. I trust You, Lord, and I stand on the unshakable foundation of Your Word. I declare healing over my mind, my heart, and my emotions. Heal past wounds, traumas, and broken places. Bring wholeness, peace, and restoration to every area of my life.

Father, let these miracles serve as testimonies that draw others to Your love and power. May those who witness these healings come running to the cross declaring, "Surely the Lord is in this place."

I refuse to settle for anything less than Your best. I expect miracles to manifest all around me. I expect and believe for breakthroughs. I give You all the glory and honor for every healing manifestation now.

I believe I receive this prayer, and I release my most holy faith to bring it to pass. In the powerful and matchless name of Jesus, I pray. Amen and Amen.

Prayer to Command Healing and Rebuke Specific Sicknesses

Heavenly Father, in the mighty name of Jesus, I come before You as Your child, boldly standing on the authority You've given me through the finished work of the cross. I declare that Jesus Christ is Lord over my life, my family, and every member of the (_____). I give You glory for being our Healer, Deliverer, and Redeemer.

Father, right now, I take authority over every sickness and disease that is attacking our bodies, minds, and spirits. I stand on the truth of Your Word, which declares that by the stripes of Jesus Christ, we are healed (Isaiah 53:5). I come against every work of the enemy, Satan, and every demonic force, and I command healing to manifest in the name of Jesus Christ.

I rebuke and resist:

- **Cancer:** I curse cancer of any kind at its root, commanding every tumor and abnormal cell to shrivel up and die. I declare that our bodies are free from cancer, and I speak life, health, and wholeness into every organ, cell, and tissue.
- **Diabetes:** I command our blood sugar levels to normalize and pancreas function to be fully restored. I declare healing over every metabolic disorder, in Jesus' name.
- **High Blood Pressure and Heart Disease**: I speak to our cardiovascular systems, commanding hearts to beat with strength and rhythm, arteries to be clear, and blood pressure to stabilize and normal, in Jesus' name.
- **Arthritis and Chronic Pain**: I rebuke every form of inflammation, stiffness, and pain in our joints and muscles. I declare full mobility and freedom from any and all discomfort, in the name of Jesus.
- **Respiratory Issues**: I speak healing to our lungs, airways, and breathing capacity. Asthma, COPD, and all forms of respiratory distress must bow to the name of Jesus and the power of healing.
- **Mental Illness**: Anxiety, depression, bipolar disorder, PTSD, and every other affliction of the mind, I rebuke you in the name of

Jesus. I declare that our minds are sound, peaceful, and guarded by the Spirit of God.

- **Autoimmune Disorders**: I command our immune systems to be recalibrated and to function in the perfection of God's design and purpose. Lupus, rheumatoid arthritis, and all autoimmune diseases, you are defeated!
- **Neurological Conditions**: I speak healing over migraines, seizures, nerve damage, and every form of neurological impairment. I declare that brain functions and nervous systems are restored in Jesus' name.
- **Digestive Issues**: I command healing to digestive systems. IBS, Crohn's disease, ulcers, and all gastrointestinal conditions, you must go now in Jesus' name.
- **Reproductive Health**: I speak life and restoration to our reproductive systems. Barrenness, endometriosis, fibroids, and every dysfunction are healed by the power of Jesus.
- **COVID-19 and Viruses**: I take authority over every virus and infection. I declare that our bodies are covered by the blood of Jesus Christ and no plague shall come near our dwelling (Psalm 91:10).

I rebuke the spirit of infirmity! You have no authority over me, my family, or the members of _____. I declare that every stronghold of sickness is broken, every chain is loosed, and our bodies are set free from sickness in the name of Jesus.

Heavenly Father, I declare:

- Complete restoration of every cell, tissue, and organ in our bodies.
- Divine strength and energy flowing through us.
- Renewed vitality and perfect health as You originally intended.

Lord, I thank You that Your healing power is flowing right now. I declare that I will walk in divine health and wholeness. Testimonies are being birthed at this very moment and I give You all the glory for miraculous healings taking place.

I believe I receive this prayer, and I release our most holy faith to bring it to pass. I declare that it is done in Jesus' name! Amen and Amen!

Daily Prayer for Deliverance and Freedom from Bondage

Heavenly Father, I come boldly before Your throne of grace, standing in the gap for my family members, loved ones, friends, and the lost in this world. Lord, You said in John 8:36 that whom the Son sets free is free indeed. So today, I declare freedom over every life bound by sin, addiction, fear, and oppression.

By the authority of Your Word in 2 Corinthians 10:4–5, I pull down every stronghold and rebuke every high thing that exalts itself against the knowledge of God. I cast down every argument, every deceptive demonic influence, and every lie of the enemy that has held my loved ones captive.

Lord, let Your anointing destroy every yoke of bondage holding them captive in their mind, will, and emotions. Break every chain of addiction, every generational curse, and every destructive pattern that has kept them bound. Let the chains fall by the fire of the Holy Ghost and let Your people walk free. I declare that they are free now in the name of Jesus. I rebuke every satanic and demonic force that has held them captive and I command those spirits to loose them and let them go now in the name of Jesus.

Father, I thank You that they are coming out of darkness, out of deception, and out of the lies of the enemy. I decree that they will receive Jesus Christ as Lord over their lives. They will respond to the wooing power of the Holy Spirit and open their hearts to receive the glory and grace that has been made available through Christ. They are cleansed, made whole, and complete in Him.

Holy Spirit, I ask You to fill every empty place in their hearts. Where darkness once lived, let Your light shine brightly. Let every void be filled with Your presence, Your peace, Your joy, and Your power.

I declare that my family, my loved ones, and those I'm interceding for will not be controlled by the flesh but will live Spirit-controlled lives. According to Romans 8:2, the law of the Spirit of life in Christ Jesus has made them free from the law of sin and death.

I decree they are more than conquerors through Christ who loves them, just as You promised in Romans 8:37. They will not be overcome by evil, but they will overcome evil with good. They will wear the full armor of God and resist every scheme and lie of the enemy. I declare they are submitted to God and the enemy must flee from them (James 4:7–8).

Father, I ask You to heal every wound caused by bondage and traumatic situations in their lives. Heal their minds. Heal their emotions. Heal their spirits. Restore everything the enemy has tried to steal, kill, or destroy. Let the peace of God guard their hearts and minds in Christ Jesus.

I proclaim that they will walk in the freedom You have provided. They will not return to chains, but will stand firm in the liberty where Christ has made them free (Galatians 5:1). I ask You to lead them to the right church, the right tribe, and the right community of believers that will help them grow, be discipled, and live a life that honors You.

I declare that the Spirit of the Lord is upon them and where the Spirit of the Lord is, there is liberty (2 Corinthians 3:17). I believe that even now, chains are breaking, hearts are softening, and Your Spirit is moving mightily. Let Your freedom reign in our home, in our family, and in every part of our lives.

I thank You for speedy results. I believe and I receive this prayer. I release my most holy faith to bring it to pass. In the mighty and matchless name of Jesus, I pray. Amen and Amen

Divine Cures and Breakthroughs

Heavenly Father, I come boldly before Your throne of grace through and by the blood of Jesus, lifting up scientists, researchers, medical professionals, and all those working to discover cures and treatments for diseases that plague this world. You are Jehovah Rapha, the God who heals. I know that You hold the keys to every mystery, every cure, and every solution hidden within creation.

Your Word says in James 1:5 that if anyone lacks wisdom, they can ask and You will give it freely. So today, I cry out on behalf of every researcher, scientist, doctor, and innovator. Lord, release supernatural wisdom, divine insight, and strategies straight from Heaven. Illuminate hidden pathways, reveal what has not been seen, and bring clarity where confusion has slowed progress. You said in Daniel 2:22 that You reveal deep and secret things, and You know what is in the darkness. So, I ask You now shine Your light into laboratories, research centers, hospitals, and operating rooms. Expose every overlooked detail. Reveal hidden solutions. Unlock every healing breakthrough waiting to be discovered.

I take authority over every spirit of pride, greed, and dishonesty that would try to manipulate or hinder progress in research. I bind confusion, fear, and political agendas that slow down the release of life-saving treatments. I declare that integrity, transparency, and righteousness will govern every discovery and every breakthrough. I plead the blood of Jesus over medical professionals, researchers, and their families. Protect their minds, their hands, and their hearts from fatigue, fear, and error. Shield them from attacks of the enemy and surround them with divine protection and peace.

Lord, I call forth cures for cancer, diabetes, heart disease, neurological disorders, autoimmune diseases, rare illnesses, and every affliction that has brought pain and loss. Let the knowledge of Your healing power manifest both supernaturally and through the hands of those You've equipped. I declare that every breakthrough will be accessible to those who need it. Greed will not hoard life-saving answers, medicines, and treatments in Jesus' name. I decree that You are breaking every barrier of financial restriction, geographical limitation, and racial inequality. Let healing flow to the ends of the earth.

Father, open financial floodgates and pour out resources on ethical researchers, nonprofit institutions, and initiatives devoted to compassion and healing. Send funding to support the work of healing through both science and spirit. Your Word says in Psalm 107:20 that You sent Your Word and healed them, delivering them from destruction. I stand on that promise. Let Your Word go forth in power. Let healing manifest in hospitals, in clinics, in homes, and in within our bodies.

Holy Spirit, move through every facility where research and treatment are being done. Fill the atmosphere with Your presence. Guide the hands of surgeons, inspire the minds of scientists and nurses, and bring divine insight into every trial and process. Let the impossible become possible. I declare that every discovery will point back to You. Let doctors and scientists stand in awe of Your wisdom. Let testimonies rise that glorify Your name.

Father, I thank You in advance for cures being released, for diseases being eradicated, and for healing flowing across nations. I believe nothing is too hard for You.

I believe I receive this prayer, and I release my most holy faith to bring it to pass. In the powerful and matchless name of Jesus Christ, I pray. Amen and Amen.

Freedom from Addiction and Destructive Habits

Heavenly Father, I come boldly before Your throne of grace, lifting up every area of my life and every person connected to me who is bound by addiction or destructive habits. Your Word declares in John 8:36 that whom the son sets free is free indeed. Today, I stand on that promise and declare complete freedom over every stronghold of addiction in the mighty name of Jesus.

Father, I pull down every mental, emotional, and spiritual stronghold by the authority of 2 Corinthians 10:4–5. I demolish every argument, every lie, and every thought pattern that has kept me or my loved ones in cycles of bondage. We will not allow the enemy to deceive or keep us trapped in shame, guilt, or fear.

Lord, let Your anointing destroy every yoke of addiction and every destructive habit in our lives. Break the chains of substance abuse, sexual sin, pornography, gambling, toxic relationships, stealing, lying, and anything else that has taken root. By the power of the Holy Ghost, I declare that those chains are falling now. Chains fall now in the name of Jesus. Power of the Holy Ghost, break the chains of addiction and self-destructive habits that have hindered us from walking in the abundant life Jesus came to give.

I declare that sin no longer has dominion over me or those I'm praying for, because I are under the freedom of God's grace, just as Romans 6:14 says. Where there was weakness, I declare strength is rising. Where there was hopelessness, I declare faith is igniting. We are strong in the Lord and in the power of His might. Addiction and destructive habits have no authority over our lives.

Holy Spirit, I ask You to dry up every root cause with the fire and healing power of the Holy Ghost. Heal our hearts from trauma, rejection, fear, and brokenness. Fill every void with Yourself. Fill us with Your peace, joy, and perfect love. Let the renewing power of Your Word transform our minds and reshape our desires to align with Your will. Replace the desires of our hearts with the desires that please You.

Father, Your Word says in 1 Corinthians 10:13 that You always provide a way of escape. Open our eyes to the way out that You've already made available. Strengthen us to say no to destructive behavior and choices and yes to the disciplines and wisdom that bring freedom and life.

Lord, I ask for divine connections. Order our footsteps and align me and those I love with godly mentors, accountability partners, and believers who will speak life, hope, and truth. Raise up a community around us that will always points us back to You.

I declare that every cycle of defeat and failure is broken and our victory is secured in Christ Jesus. We will not return to chains but will stand firm in the liberty where Christ has made us free, just as You declared in Galatians 5:1. Let Your grace empower us to live Holy Spirit-controlled lives. Set our souls on fire with fresh zeal and passion for Your presence. Let our testimonies shine as a beacon of hope for others still trapped in darkness. I declare that our stories will pull others into Your marvelous light.

Father, I thank You in advance for speedy results. I believe that even now, chains are breaking, hearts are healing, and lives are being transformed including mine. I believe I receive this prayer, and I release my most holy faith to bring it to pass. In the mighty and matchless name of Jesus I pray, Amen and Amen.

Prayer for Healing for the Brokenhearted

Heavenly Father, I come before You today with a humble heart, lifting up to You every place in my life where my heart has been broken and my spirit wounded. You are the God who sees me, who knows me, and who fully restores. Your Word declares in Psalm 34:18 that You are close to the brokenhearted and You rescue those whose spirits are crushed. Today, I stand on that promise and ask You to draw near to me and to those I love who carry the weight of emotional pain.

Lord, I plead the blood of Jesus over my heart and mind, over every area that has been shattered by loss, betrayal, rejection, and disappointment. Let the healing and cleansing power of the blood of Jesus wash away bitterness, resentment, and grief. May it bring the refreshing and restoration that only You can give.

Father, I declare Isaiah 61:1 over my life today: The Spirit of the Lord is upon me, and You are comforting my broken heart. Holy Spirit, comfort me in the places where I'm mourning, soothe the areas that are aching, and bind up the wounds that still feel raw and tender.

Lord, where I have carried the pain of rejection, remind me that You have accepted me, chosen me, and called me Your own. Replace every feeling of abandonment with the truth of Your eternal love. Fill every empty place in me and make me whole in You.

I bring before You the grief of my losses, whether of loved ones, relationships, opportunities, or unfulfilled dreams. You said in Matthew 11:28–29 that when I come to You, You will give me rest. Father, let me feel the tangibleness of Your presence and Your embrace today. Wrap me in Your peace and give me the deep rest that only You can provide. Heal, Jesus, heal me.

Lord, I rebuke every spirit of heaviness, hopelessness, and despair. I bind every lie of the enemy that says healing isn't possible. I declare freedom over my heart and mind. I am not hopeless; I am healed and whole in You.

Father, pour out Your peace like a river. According to John 14:27, You have given me a supernatural peace, not as the world gives, but the kind that surpasses my natural understanding. Let your divine peace flood every hurting place in me today.

I ask You for restoration. Where trust has been broken, where love has grown cold, and where relationships have been strained, breathe new life. Restore what was lost. Heal what was torn. Renew what seems irreparable. Heal, Jesus, heal.

I pray for emotional strength and resilience. Lord, teach me to cast all my cares upon You, because You care for me deeply (1 Peter 5:7). Even when I walk through valleys of pain, remind me that I am never alone; You are walking with me, step by step. Heal, Jesus, heal.

And for every moment when I have felt forgotten or invisible, whisper into my soul, "I will never leave you nor forsake you" (Hebrews 13:5). Let me know deep within that I am seen, heard, known, and loved by You.

I ask that forgiveness would flow in every broken place. Soften every hardened heart; mine and those of others. Release every lingering offense and let grace triumph over pride and anger. Rebuild what was broken with compassion, patience, and love.

Lord, let Your presence fill every empty space in my heart. Replace fear with faith. Replace sorrow with joy. Replace brokenness with Your supernatural wholeness. Let Your love be the balm that heals every wound.

Father, I thank You because I know You are faithful to Your Word. You are healing the emotional scars. You are lifting the burdens. You are restoring my joy. I receive it by faith today.

I believe I receive this prayer, and I release my most holy faith to bring it to pass. In the mighty and matchless name of Jesus, I pray. Amen and Amen.

Prayer for Healing in Mental Health

Heavenly Father, I come boldly before Your throne of grace, standing in faith for emotional and mental healing. You are Jehovah Rapha, the God who heals, and I declare that You are Lord over my mind, will, emotions, and every thought pattern within me.

Father, Your Word says in Philippians 4:6–7 that I should be anxious for nothing, but in everything by prayer and supplication, I can make my requests known to You. So today, I bring You every burden, worry, fear, and oppressive thought. I lay them at Your feet. I exchange anxiety for peace, despair for joy, and confusion for divine clarity and understanding.

Lord, I plead the blood of Jesus over my mind; over every thought, emotion, lie, fear, and every area where torment has tried to reside. Let the blood of Jesus wash over me with renewing, cleansing, and restoring power. Break every stronghold of depression, suicidal thoughts, anxiety, and hopelessness.

Father, I declare the truth of 2 Timothy 1:7 over myself. You have not given me a spirit of fear, but of power, love, and a sound mind. I rebuke the spirit of fear and every lying voice of the enemy that tries to whisper defeat, worthlessness, and failure into my soul. Holy Spirit, saturate my heart and mind with Your peace. Replace restlessness with stillness, worry with trust, and darkness with Your marvelous light. Let the peace of God that surpasses all understanding guard my heart and my mind in Christ Jesus.

I ask You, Lord, to heal every emotional wound. Heal the scars of past trauma. Break the chains of generational cycles of mental illness. Restore what was broken and breathe strength and resilience into every weary place in me. I speak healing over myself and those I'm standing in the gap for; healing from anxiety, depression, PTSD, bipolar disorder, schizophrenia, and every other mental health condition. I declare stability in our minds, souls and spirits. I declare emotional wholeness. I declare wholeness in the name of Jesus.

Father, renew my thought life. Just as Romans 12:2 instructs, transform me by the renewing of my mind. Let every toxic, negative, or self-defeating thought be replaced with Your truth. Your Word tells me I am loved, chosen, victorious, and more than a conqueror through Christ Jesus.

I declare Isaiah 26:3 over my mind. You will keep me in perfect peace because my mind is stayed on You. Help me to fix my focus on You, Lord, and silence every distracting, fearful, or negative voice trying to cloud my thinking. When I feel weary or hopeless, remind me of Your promise in Psalm 34:18 that You are close to the brokenhearted and that You rescue those whose spirits are crushed. Let me feel Your nearness. Let me be comforted by Your presence.

I declare that the anointing of the Holy Spirit is bringing deliverance and clarity over my mind. I bind the spirit of torment, and I declare that I walk in a sound mind, filled with peace and divine insight. Lord, restore my rest. Let me sleep peacefully, free from nightmares, insomnia, or anxious racing thoughts. Let my mind be refreshed and my soul renewed every morning.

Breathe fresh life into me, Holy Spirit. Fill me with joy where there was sorrow. Let laughter and light return. Replace heaviness with hope and despair with delight in Your presence.

I also lift up every counselor, therapist, pastor, and mental health professional serving on the frontlines. Strengthen them, anoint them, and give them supernatural wisdom and discernment as they minister to others. Raise up godly, spirit-filled professionals to walk with Your people through their healing journey.

Father, I thank You for victory over every mental health battle. I declare freedom. I declare peace. I declare wholeness in my heart and in my mind. I believe I receive this prayer, and I release my most holy faith to bring it to pass. In the mighty and matchless name of Jesus Christ, I pray. Amen and Amen.

Holy Spirit and Supernatural Healing

Father, in the mighty name of Jesus, I boldly enter Your throne of grace, covered by the blood of the Lamb. I come with confidence and full assurance, standing on Your Word and declaring that You are Jehovah-Rapha, the Lord who heals me! Hallelujah! I thank You that Your healing power is flowing in my life right now through the presence of the Holy Spirit, bringing restoration, deliverance, and wholeness to every part of me.

Holy Spirit, I invite You to saturate this atmosphere with Your glory. Let Your power move like a mighty rushing wind, breaking every chain of sickness, disease, and infirmity. I decree and declare that no sickness, no pain, and no disorder can stand in the presence of Almighty God. Right now, I prophesy the release of the anointing that destroys every yoke. In the presence of Jesus, tumors dissolve, blood pressure is regulated, hearts are strengthened, organs are made whole, joints are restored, and immune systems are supercharged with divine health and the life of God.

I take authority over every spirit of illness and infirmity, and I bind and rebuke them in the name of Jesus. I command healing to manifest in my body right now. I declare healing now in the name of Jesus. Every chronic illness, pain, fatigue, and hidden ailment affecting my body, be gone in the name of Jesus Christ. I am healed! I speak life into every cell, every tissue, and every organ in my body. My lungs breathe freely, my heart beats strong, and my mind is renewed with peace and clarity. The same Spirit that raised Christ Jesus from the dead is quickening my mortal body right now, infusing me with strength, vitality, and perfect health.

Holy Spirit, flow like a river of living water, saturating my heart, my body, and my emotions. Just as Jesus laid hands on the sick and they recovered, I release that same healing power to flow through me. I declare creative miracles are taking place, organs are being revitalized, bones are being strengthened, and damaged nerves are being restored. Depression, anxiety, and fear must bow to the name of Jesus Christ. I declare that peace, which surpasses all understanding, is flooding my mind and emotions, bringing freedom and joy.

Father, I thank You that You are the same yesterday, today, and forever. I stand in agreement with Heaven, declaring that testimonies of miraculous healing are breaking forth now. My body is being fully restored from the crown of my head to the souls of my feet. Pain is leaving my body, right now in the name of Jesus. Wholeness is taking root. My strength is being restored. I decree that doctors will be amazed and medical reports will confirm what You have already done!

And now, I seal this prayer by faith, declaring with bold confidence, I believe I receive total and complete healing, and I release my most holy faith to bring it to pass. In the mighty and matchless name of Jesus, Amen!

Personal Deliverance and Walking in Freedom

Heavenly Father, I come boldly before Your throne of grace today, lifting my voice in gratitude for the freedom You have given me through Jesus Christ. Your Word declares in John 8:36 that whom the Son Jesus Christ sets free is free indeed, and today I stand on that truth and promise.

Father, I acknowledge the strongholds, sins, and habits that have tried to keep me bound. I repent for every area where I have knowingly or unknowingly given the enemy access to my life. According to Your Word in 2 Corinthians 10:4-5, I pull down every stronghold, every high thing that exalts itself against the knowledge of God, and I take every thought captive to the obedience of Christ.

Thank You, Lord, that sin no longer has dominion over me. According to Romans 6:14, I am not a slave to sin, fear, or shame. I am empowered by Your grace to walk in holiness, righteousness, and victory.

Holy Spirit, I invite You to shine Your light into every hidden area of my heart. Reveal the roots of bondage, every cycle of sin, and every destructive habit that needs to be uprooted. I surrender them at the foot of the cross, and I ask for Your strength to replace them with disciplines and desires that honor You.

Father, Your Word says in Isaiah 61:1 that You came to set the captives free and open the prison doors for those who are bound. Today, I declare freedom over my mind, emotions, and spirit. Every chain is broken. Every shackle is destroyed. Every lie of the enemy is silenced in the name of Jesus.

I put on the full armor of God, and I stand firm against every scheme and strategy of the enemy. I resist temptation, I reject shame, and I rebuke the voice of condemnation. I declare that I am an overcomer by the blood of the Lamb and the word of my testimony.

You promised in Psalm 34:17 that You hear my cry and deliver me from all my troubles. So today, I cry out to You for complete deliverance, healing, and restoration. Let Your peace flood my heart and let Your joy rise up as my strength.

I will not return to cycles of bondage, fear, or defeat. I choose to walk boldly in the freedom that Jesus purchased for me at Calvary. I am free, and I walk in the freedom Christ died to give me.

I believe I receive deliverance and freedom, and I release my most holy faith to bring it to pass. In the mighty and matchless name of Jesus, I pray. Amen and amen.

Strength to Overcome Sickness and Walk in Divine Health

Heavenly Father, I come boldly before Your throne of grace, standing on the promises of Your Word and declaring health, strength, and vitality over my life. You are Jehovah Rapha, the Lord who heals me, and I thank You for Your healing power that flows through my entire body even now.

Your Word says in Isaiah 40:31 that those who trust in You will renew their strength. I declare that my strength is being renewed right now in the name of Jesus. I receive supernatural strength in my body, clarity in my mind, and peace in my spirit. Forgive me, Lord, for the times I have not properly cared for my body. I honor this temple of the Holy Ghost, and I know Your grace is sufficient for me. In every area of weakness, Your strength is being perfected.

I plead the blood of Jesus over every lingering symptom and chronic condition. By the Your stripes, I am healed (Isaiah 53:5). I command sickness to leave my body now in the name of Jesus. The fire of the Holy Ghost is burning away disease and disorder. Every organ, cell, tissue, and system is being made whole. Healing is flowing, and I receive it now in Jesus' name.

I speak to every diagnosis; cancer, diabetes, heart disease, high blood pressure, autoimmune disorders, inflammation, and neurological issues, you have no power. The blood of Jesus is against you. The spirit of infirmity will not prevail over me. I am free, healed, and whole in Jesus' name.

Lord, restore what sickness tried to steal in Jesus' name. Renew my energy. Bring clarity to my thoughts. Let divine vitality surge through me. I declare Jeremiah 33:6 over my life. You are healing every wound and releasing true peace into my heart and mind. Peace, peace, divine peace is flooding my entire being now in the name of Jesus.

Father, thank You that You heal all my diseases (Psalm 103:3). Let Your healing power flow through every part of me. Help me walk in wisdom concerning my health. Teach me to care for my body with discipline and purpose. I choose to honor You through rest, nourishment, and movement.

I rebuke every assignment of sickness and every spirit of infirmity. I declare that my immune system is strong, my body is resilient, and I am covered under the shadow of the Almighty (Psalm 91:1).

I thank You, Lord, for supernatural recovery. I thank You for testimonies that will bring You glory. I have renewed strength to fulfill my purpose and walk boldly in everything You've called me to do. I speak 3 John 1:2 over my life, I prosper and I am in good health, even as my soul prospers.

I believe I receive this prayer, and I release my most holy faith to bring it to pass. In the powerful and matchless name of Jesus Christ, I pray. Amen and Amen.

Prayer to Set Captives Free

Heavenly Father, in the mighty and matchless name of Jesus, I come boldly before Your throne of grace. I thank You that You are still the God who sets captives free! You are the chain breaker, the opener of prison doors, the deliverer of all who cry out to You in truth!

Lord, I thank You that when the body of Christ prays in faith, prison doors open, chains are broken, angels are dispatched, and miracles happen right before our eyes. So today, I stand in faith, releasing heaven's authority over every area of bondage and captivity. I lift up every person who is trapped, physically, mentally, emotionally, spiritually, or financially and I declare, **BE FREE NOW!!! BE FREE NOW in Jesus' name!**

I take authority over every demonic force that has tried to hold Your people hostage, every spirit of addiction, depression, fear, lack, perversion, confusion, rebellion, witchcraft, and heaviness, I bind you and command you to loose your hold now! I release the Word of deliverance. I plead the blood of Jesus over every physical and spiritual captive. I speak divine escape routes in the name of Jesus. I speak angelic intervention to open the doors, break the gates of iron, and cut the bars NOW! I declare archangels are setting captives free.

Father, I declare that prison gates are opening! Hidden traps are being exposed. What was binding their feet is breaking off NOW in the name of Jesus. What once held their minds hostage is losing its grip NOW. Generational chains are being shattered. Cycles of dysfunction are being STOPPED by the power of God. Right now, Lord, shine Your light into every dark place and bring supernatural release!

I pray for sons and daughters to be loosed. For marriages to be freed from oppression and division. For minds to be set free from torment. For finances to be delivered from restriction. For gifts and callings to be unlocked. I prophesy divine turnaround and total deliverance!

Thank You, Lord, that You've anointed us to proclaim liberty to the captives. So, I am proclaiming freedom NOW! I say, "Come out of the tomb! Be free! Be restored!" I release Your fire over every household, Hallelujah. I release your power over every bloodline and every region that's been in captivity. Father, let a fresh wind of freedom sweep through our families, our cities, and this nation.

Father, I believe I receive this prayer and I release my most holy faith to see it come to pass. Chains are breaking NOW. Doors are opening NOW. Angels are moving. Freedom is here. In the powerful name of Jesus I pray, Amen and Amen!

Chapter 6 – Prayers for Family, Marriage and Relationships

Family, Marriage, and Relationships

Family is God's idea. Marriage is His covenant. Relationships are His design. When we invite Him into the center of it all, His peace, unity, and love begin to flood every corner of our lives. This chapter is dedicated to aligning our families with heaven's blueprint; breaking curses, releasing blessings, and declaring the promises of God over our entire bloodline.

We are not powerless bystanders just allowing life to happen to us. We are spiritual gatekeepers, called to stand in the gap for our families, to war in the spirit for our marriages, and to intercede for our children, siblings, parents, spouses, and loved ones. We carry the authority of Jesus Christ to declare salvation, deliverance, healing, restoration, and breakthrough into every relationship we're connected to.

Acts 16:31 (KJV) – *"And they said, believe on the Lord Jesus Christ, and thou shalt be saved, and thy house."*

I believe families are being restored in this hour. Marriages are being reconciled. Prodigals are coming home in the name of Jesus. Children are being rescued from the traps of the enemy. Generational curses of divorce, poverty, abuse, addiction, infidelity, and brokenness are being dismantled by the power of the blood of Jesus. It's time to draw a line in the sand and say, **"It stops with me!"** A new bloodline starts now, one of righteousness, peace, joy, unity, and generational blessing.

Joshua 24:15 (KJV) – *"And if it seem evil unto you to serve the Lord, choose you this day whom ye will serve; whether the gods which your fathers served that were on the other side of the flood, or the gods of the Amorites, in whose land ye dwell:* **but as for me and my house, we will serve the Lord.**"

In this chapter, we'll pray over every aspect of family life; daily protection, marriages, singlehood, children, teens, friendships, and more. Whether you're believing for healing from betrayal, strength in your singleness, peace in your household, or unity in your marriage, there is a prayer for you here.

Psalm 133:1 (KJV) – *"Behold, how good and how pleasant it is for brethren to dwell together in unity!"*

Family is not just blood. Family is also covenant. God places people in your life to help sharpen you, love you, and walk with you. That's why we're also covering divine connections; relationships ordained by God and protected by His Spirit. This is your time to speak life into your relationships, forgive where there's been offense, and stand in faith for full restoration.

If the enemy has fought your family, your marriage, your children, or your relationships, it's because there's something powerful attached to your bloodline. But today we war for what's ours. We declare peace in our homes, restoration in our marriages, protection over our children, and clarity in our relationships.

God is healing families. He's restoring what was broken. He's binding hearts back together and He's covering your entire household under the shadow of His wings.

Psalm 91:1-2 (KJV) – *"He that dwelleth in the secret place of the most High shall abide under the shadow of the Almighty. I will say of the Lord, He is my refuge and my fortress: my God; in him will I trust."*

Prepare your heart. Call out every name. Speak over your marriage. Intercede for your children. Forgive the past. Invite the Holy Spirit into your household and let heaven reign in your home.

Let's pray for family like never before.

Daily Prayer Over My Family
(To be spoken aloud each morning)

Heavenly Father, in the mighty and matchless name of Jesus, I come before You this day, covering my family in prayer. I thank You for the gift of family; for every loved one You've entrusted to me. Today, I declare that we are blessed and highly favored. The blood of Jesus covers and protects us.

Lord, I plead the blood of Jesus over our minds, bodies, hearts, and spirits. No weapon formed against us shall prosper. I cancel every assignment of the enemy and declare that every hidden trap is exposed and dismantled.

Father, I speak divine protection over my household. Keep us safe from harm, danger, sickness, and all evil. Let Your angels be stationed around us, at our doors, in our vehicles, in our schools, in our workplaces and everywhere I go.

I declare that our home is filled with peace, joy, love, and the presence of God. No strife, division, or confusion are welcome here. I rebuke you now in the name of Jesus. I declare unity, understanding, patience, and honor among every family member.

Father, I speak blessings over our finances. I declare increase, abundance, and overflow is our portion all the days of our lives. I thank You that every need is supplied and more than enough is coming into our hands to bless others and advance Your Kingdom. I operate in supernatural wisdom in all that I do and God's wisdom leads us into paths of peace and plenty.

I call forth health and healing in our bodies. I declare strength, wholeness, and supernatural energy. Every generational illness is broken. Every diagnosis must bow to the name of Jesus. We walk in divine health and healing daily.

I speak purpose and progress over my family. Every child, every spouse, every loved one, they will fulfill the destiny You have placed on their lives. I declare clarity, direction, and favor over their steps. They are leaders, world-changers, and Kingdom builders.

Lord, teach us to walk in love and truth. Let forgiveness and grace flow freely in our homes. Help us to honor one another and serve each other with compassion. May our homes reflect Your love and kindness.

I declare that this day is blessed. Good news floods our ears. Doors are opening. Miracles are manifesting and the favor of God surrounds us like a shield. We will experience testimony, after testimony.

I believe I receive this prayer and release my most holy faith to bring it to pass. In Jesus' mighty name I pray, amen.

Strengthening Marriages, Family Unity, and Restoration

Heavenly Father, I come boldly before Your throne of grace today, standing in the gap for my marriage, my family, and every relationship connected to me. Father, I honor You as the author of marriage and the foundation of the family. Your Word declares in Matthew 19:6 that what You have joined together, no one should separate.

Today, I plead the blood of Jesus over my marriage, over my spouse, over my children, and over my entire household. Let the blood of Jesus cover every conversation, every decision, and every doorway in my home. I declare that no weapon formed against us will prosper. Every plot, plan, and scheme of the enemy is canceled by the authority of Jesus Christ.

Lord, I pray for divine protection over the covenant of marriages in my life and those around me. Guard us from infidelity, distrust, pride, and selfishness. Rekindle love where it has grown cold. Let humility replace stubbornness and restore intimacy, trust, and connection in our marriage.

I declare Colossians 3:13-14 over my home. Let forgiveness flow freely. I pull down the spirit of offense, pride, and bitterness that seeks to divide us. Soften our hearts, break down every wall, and heal emotional wounds that have lingered for too long.

Father, restore communication between every husband and wife, parent and child, and sibling. Let our words be seasoned with grace and love. Break every cycle of harmful language, anger, and misunderstanding that has taken root.

I declare that unity, peace, and restoration are flowing through my family right now in the name of Jesus. Holy Spirit, hover over my home. Let you glory fill our home. Saturate our home with Your presence. Fill every room with Your peace and every heart with worship.

I come against every generational curse and cycle of dysfunction. I plead the blood of Jesus over past wounds, childhood trauma, and broken patterns. Let every stronghold be broken off everyone family member in the name of Jesus.

I speak restoration over every broken relationship connected to me. Father, let the prodigals return home. Heal the hearts of parents and children who have been estranged. Heal marriages on the edge of separation and bring supernatural reconciliation.

Lord, I thank You for single parents in my family and community. Strengthen them, encourage them, and provide for every need they face. Be their guide, their helper, and their peace.

I declare Psalm 91 over my family. No evil will come near our dwelling. No harm will overtake my loved ones. I release angelic protection over every doorway, every vehicle, every school, and every workplace.

I decree and declare that my family is strong in the Lord and in the power of His might (Ephesians 6:10). As for me and my house, we will serve the Lord (Joshua 24:15). Let revival begin in my home. Let our marriage reflect Your love. Let our family reflect Your glory. Use us to be a beacon of light in the world around us.

I thank You, Father, because You are faithful to Your Word. You are healing, restoring, and protecting right now. I believe I receive this prayer, and I release my most holy faith to bring it to pass. In the mighty and matchless name of Jesus I pray, Amen and Amen.

Healing and Restoration in Families and Relationships

Heavenly Father, I come before You today standing in the gap for my family and the relationships connected to my life that may be broken, strained, or distant. You are the God of restoration, the Healer of hearts, and the One who mends what has been torn. Your Word says in Psalm 147:3 that You heal the brokenhearted and bind up their wounds. So today, Lord, I ask You to release Your healing power into my family.

I plead the blood of Jesus over my home, marriage, relationship with my children, siblings, and every connection You have placed in my life. Let Your cleansing blood wash away all bitterness, resentment, and unforgiveness. Heal every generational wound and break every toxic cycle by the power of the blood of Jesus Christ.

Lord, I declare Malachi 4:6 over my family that You are turning the hearts of parents to their children and the hearts of children to their parents. Where there's been distance or estrangement, I ask for divine reconciliation. Heal the pain of absent fathers, distant mothers, and relationships wounded by anger, pride, or misunderstandings.

I rebuke division, offense, and discord that has tried to take root in my family. I bind every work of the enemy that seeks to destroy the unity You desire for us. Let every hidden plot of the enemy be exposed and dismantled in the name of Jesus.

Holy Spirit, soften every hardened heart. Let forgiveness flow freely in my family. Teach me to forgive as You have forgiven me. Remove pride and stubbornness, and release grace, humility, and compassion in their place.

Father, where trust has been broken, I ask You to restore it. Heal the wounds caused by betrayal, neglect, and hurtful words. Where there has been dishonesty, let truth reign. Where there has been silence, let love-filled communication be restored.

I lift up families suffering from addiction, abuse, and trauma. Shine Your healing light into the darkest places. Break every chain of addiction. Destroy strongholds of fear, shame, and despair. Bring wholeness where there has been deep brokenness.

I declare Ephesians 4:31-32 over my family that bitterness, rage, and anger are being removed, and kindness, tenderness, and forgiveness are rising up as You have shown through Christ Jesus.

I break every generational curse and every unhealthy cycle that has followed my bloodline. Let Your truth set me and my family free from every lie that has kept us bound.

I declare peace and unity in my family. I speak love into every relationship. Let siblings support one another. Let parents uplift their children. Let spouses walk in honor and unity.

For those in my family experiencing loss, grief, or separation, Lord, bring deep comfort. Wrap them in Your love. Let them feel Your nearness as You promise in Your Word that You are close to the brokenhearted.

Father, let my home be a place of worship, a place of prayer, and a sanctuary of peace. Let faith arise. Let love flow freely. Let healing be evident in our family.

I declare that love wins in my home. Love wins in my entire family. Peace will reign, and forgiveness will flow. I believe I receive this prayer, and I release my most holy faith to bring it to pass. In the mighty and matchless name of Jesus, I pray. Amen and Amen.

Prayer for Family (People) based on Ephesians

Heavenly Father, I come before You with a humble heart, just as Paul did when he prayed for the church at Ephesus. Today, I lift up my family to You, asking that they be strengthened with power through Your Spirit in their inner being. Lord, I pray that Christ will dwell in their hearts through faith and that they will be rooted and grounded in Your love. Let them fully know and experience the depth, height, and width of Your grace and mercy.

Father, I ask that their lives be completely transformed as they submit to Your will and walk in Your ways. Open the eyes of their understanding so they may know the hope to which You have called them, and the riches of Your glorious inheritance. I declare that they are growing in wisdom, knowledge, and revelation of who You are. They are walking in the fullness of Your love and truth.

Lord, empower them to live lives that reflect Your glory and grace. Let them be filled with the fullness of Your Spirit, walking worthy of their calling, growing strong in faith, and becoming steadfast in their devotion to You. I believe that Your mighty power is at work within them, accomplishing immeasurably more than they could ever ask or think.

Father, I cover my family in prayer, believing that their hearts are fully yielded to You. I trust that they are led by your Holy Spirit in every decision, every action, and every word. May they grow deeper in their relationship with You, walking in love, faith, and unity with other believers.

I believe I receive this prayer and release my most holy faith to bring it to pass. In the mighty name of Jesus, Amen.

Prayer for Children to Walking in Purpose

Heavenly Father, I come boldly before Your throne today, standing in the gap for my children. You are their Creator and the Author of their lives, and You have set them apart for your divine purpose. Just as You said in Jeremiah 1:5, before they were formed, You knew them and appointed them. Today, I plead the blood of Jesus over every child connected to me.

Father, I declare Psalm 91:11–12 over them. Let Your angels encamp around them. Protect them from harm, danger, accidents, abuse, and every evil scheme of the enemy. Keep them safe in their homes, schools, workplaces and every environment they enter.

Lord, stir up in them a hunger for Your Word. Let their hearts burn with passion for prayer, worship, and a deep personal relationship with You. Make them like David, young, bold, and after Your own heart. Let them walk in integrity, humility, and strength.

I break every generational curse, every chain of addiction, rebellion, and destructive behavior in the name of Jesus. I cancel every assignment of the enemy against their lives, and I declare that no weapon formed against them will prosper.

Holy Spirit, guide their steps. Give them wisdom beyond their years and sharpen their discernment in every decision. Surround them with godly friends and remove every influence that does not honor You.

Father, I rebuke fear, anxiety, and low self-worth from their hearts and minds. Remind them that they are fearfully and wonderfully made. Let them walk in confidence, fully knowing who they are in Christ, sons and daughters of the Most High God.

I declare that my children will excel in every area of life, academically, spiritually, emotionally, socially and financial. They are leaders, visionaries, and world changers for their generation.

I speak peace over their minds, purity over their hearts, and strength over their spirits. They will not give in to peer pressure, and they will not compromise their faith. They will stand boldly for righteousness and shine as light in a dark world.

Father, place godly mentors, teachers, and role models in their lives who will speak life, wisdom, and encouragement into them. Remove every toxic relationship and replace it with divine connections rooted in truth, love, and Christ-like values.

For those who have strayed away, I call them back now in the name of Jesus. Let Your love pull them out of darkness and draw them back into alignment with Your perfect will.

I declare that every child and teenager connected to me will fulfill their God-ordained purpose. They will dream big, live boldly, pray with power, and walk in supernatural favor all the days of their lives.

Father, I cover every school they attend, every teacher, administrator, and peer, with the blood of Jesus. Let those spaces be filled with Your protection, wisdom, and influence.

Thank You, Lord, that You are faithful to Your Word. I trust that You are watching over these young lives, guiding them, and keeping them in the center of Your will.

I believe I receive this prayer, and I release my most holy faith to bring it to pass. In the mighty and matchless name of Jesus, I pray. Amen and Amen.

Psalm 91 Declaration Over Our Children and Youth

Father, in the name of Jesus, I come boldly to Your throne of grace on behalf of every child, every son and daughter, every young person connected to us. I stand in the gap today, declaring the whole of Psalm 91 over their lives!

Lord, I declare that our children dwell in the secret place of the Most High and abide under the shadow of the Almighty. I speak it with authority, no matter where they go, no matter what they face, they are covered by the blood of Jesus, they are protected, they are shielded by the power of Your presence!

I declare, the Lord is their refuge and fortress. He is their safe place. He is their security. He is their protection from the snares of the enemy and from every deadly disease. I call out every hidden danger and every attack of the enemy, and I cancel it now in the name of Jesus.

Father, I speak that Your angels are on assignment, surrounding our children, lifting them up, shielding and keeping them from harm. No weapon formed against them shall prosper. No evil will befall them, and no plague will come near their dwelling!

I plead the blood of Jesus over their schools, over their friendships, over their environments. Lord, let Your angels guard their coming and their going. Let them rise with wisdom beyond their years, with discernment in their choices, and with boldness in their faith.

Father, I decree right now, our children will not be lost to this world. They will not be deceived by the lies of the enemy. They will not be snatched from their destiny. They are rooted and grounded in Your truth. Their identity is found in Christ alone.

I declare long life over them. I declare divine purpose is fulfilled. I declare that every gift and every calling inside of them will rise and manifest in its time and season. I call forth leaders, history-makers, game-changers, and glory-carriers!

Father, let Psalm 91 not just be words, let it be a living hedge of protection around our children and youth. Shield them from violence, from sickness, from accidents, from every form of evil. Hide them under the shadow of Your wings. Be their defense, be their fortress, and be their mighty deliverer!

And Father, I seal this prayer in faith. I release most holy faith to bring it to pass, and I declare it is so, it is settled, it is done, in the mighty and matchless name of Jesus. Amen and Amen!

Prayer of Purpose and Wholeness in Singleness

Heavenly Father, I come before Your throne of grace by the blood of Jesus, standing in faith for myself and every single person connected to me. You are El Roi, the God who sees me, knows me, and loves me deeply. Your Word says in Jeremiah 29:11 that You have good plans for me, plans to prosper me and not to harm me, plans to give me hope and a future.

Father, I plead the blood of Jesus over my life. Cover me with Your protection. Guard my heart from discouragement and shield my mind and heart from every lie of worthlessness, inadequacy, or loneliness.

Lord, remind me of who I am in You. Help me to see myself as You see me, fearfully and wonderfully made. Let my identity be firmly rooted in Christ alone, not in my relationship status. Holy Spirit, fill every empty place in my heart with Your presence. Replace loneliness with joy, insecurity with confidence, and fear with unshakable faith. You are my greatest companion, and Your love is always more than enough.

Father, I ask for clarity and direction concerning my purpose. Guide me to walk boldly in every assignment You have entrusted to me. Let my life be a testimony of Your goodness and faithfulness.

I reject and rebuke every lie of the enemy that tries to whisper that I am forgotten, overlooked, or unloved. Your Word promises that You are close to the brokenhearted, and I rest in the assurance that Your plans for me are perfect and right on time.

Lord, fill my life with meaningful friendships, godly community, and mentors who challenge me to grow spiritually. Surround me with people who speak life, faith, and hope into every season I walk through.

I pray for emotional healing from every heartbreak, disappointment, or betrayal I have experienced. Heal every wound. Restore every broken place. Let joy return to the places where sorrow tried to take root.

Let this season of singleness be marked by purpose, fruitfulness, and deeper intimacy with You. Teach me to enjoy this time of serving You with joy, and to trust that You are orchestrating every detail of my life with care and intentionality.

Father, I surrender my heart and desire for marriage to you. Prepare me for the spouse You have ordained for me. Equip me with wisdom, patience, and discernment while I wait. Help me not to settle for less than Your best and align me divinely with the one You have chosen. Let us meet at the right time and in the right place. May our relationship bring You glory, be rooted in righteousness, and hidden in You.

I declare Matthew 6:33 over my life, I will seek first the Kingdom of God, and everything else will be added to me in due time. I thank You, Father, for peace that surpasses all understanding. I trust that Your plans are unfolding perfectly in my life.

I believe I receive this prayer, and I release my most holy faith to bring it to pass. In the mighty and matchless name of Jesus, I pray. Amen and Amen.

Healthy God-ordained Friendships

Heavenly Father, I come before You with a heart open and fully surrendered, lifting up the friendships You've placed in my life. You are a God of relationship, and You created me for connection, designed to walk with others in love, support, and community.

Father, I thank You for the gift of friendship. Your Word in Proverbs 17:17 says, "A friend is always loyal, and a brother is born to help in time of need." Let my friendships reflect that truth. Fill my relationships with loyalty, trust, support, and compassion.

I plead the blood of Jesus over every friendship in my life. Let the blood of Jesus purify my motives, heal past wounds, and cover each relationship with Your grace and divine protection. Father, remove every toxic connection from my life, any relationship that is rooted in manipulation, deceit, jealousy, or emotional harm. Open my eyes to see what no longer serves my growth or my walk with You, and give me the courage to release those connections in love and in peace.

Align me with divine friendships, people who will challenge me, uplift me, pray with me, and walk alongside me in righteousness. Let my inner circle be filled with people who sharpen me spiritually and help me become more like You. Teach me, Lord, to set healthy boundaries in my friendships. Help me to love selflessly without compromising the well-being of my heart and soul. Keep me free from unhealthy attachments, and let my relationships be balanced, pure, and life-giving.

For the times I have felt alone or isolated, I ask You to bring godly friends into my life. Break the spirit of loneliness from my emotions and fill my heart with renewed hope and joyful expectation for meaningful, Spirit-led connections. I ask for healing in the friendships that have been strained or broken, where trust was lost, where hurtful words were exchanged, or where distance grew over time. If it's Your will, Father, restore those relationships. Remove pride, remove ego, and let the love of Christ take its place. Let my friendships reflect Your love, Father. Help me to be a selfless, kind, and forgiving friend, just as You have been with me. Let these relationships glorify You and draw us closer to Your heart.

I declare Ecclesiastes 4:9-10 over my life, "Two are better than one, for they can help each other succeed. If one falls, the other can reach out and help." Let me be that kind of friend, one who shows up, lifts others, and celebrates their wins with joy.

Holy Spirit, be at the center of every friendship in my life. Guide our conversations, our times of laughter, our shared prayers, and even our vulnerable moments. Let Your presence be evident in every connection You ordain. I also ask for discernment, Lord. Help me recognize who belongs in my inner circle. Give me wisdom about who I allow to speak into my life and who I entrust with my heart.

I thank You in advance for the divine friendships You are sending, those who will sharpen me as iron sharpens iron, and walk with me as I grow in faith. I declare that my friendships are healthy, joyful, Spirit-led, and centered in Christ. Every toxic connection is broken, every root of bitterness is uprooted, and every divine connection is established and flourishing.

I believe I receive this prayer, and I release my most holy faith to bring it to pass. In the mighty and matchless name of Jesus, I pray. Amen and Amen.

Chapter 7 – Prayers for Purpose, Destiny and Calling

Purpose, Destiny, and Calling

There is a divine assignment on your life. You were created with purpose, on purpose, and for purpose. God did not make a mistake when He made you. I don't care what anyone has told you. Before you were formed in your mother's womb, He knew you and called you (Jeremiah 1:5). It is time to rise up and walk boldly in what He has destined for you to do.

This chapter is for every person who has ever wondered, "Why am I here?" It is for those who are hungry to live beyond survival and step into significance. If you feel like you've missed it, delayed it, or dismissed it, God's purpose for your life still stands. The call is still active. The gifts and callings of God are without repentance (Romans 11:29), which means He hasn't changed His mind about you. You are valuable to God. Your life has meaning and purpose.

Walking in purpose is not about striving; it's about surrender. It's about seeking the face of God, yielding to His Spirit, and following the path He lays out. While the road may not always be easy, it will always be worth it. Purpose will require faith. Destiny will demand your yes. But when you walk in alignment with Heaven, the impact of your obedience will touch generations. It's called leaving a legacy of faith.

In this chapter, we will pray bold prayers to stir up your dreams and vision, activate gifts, and bring clarity to your calling. We will cancel the lies of the enemy that try to keep us bound by fear, shame, or comparison. We will break cycles of delay and distraction and call forth divine alignment and acceleration.

This is your moment to get in agreement with Heaven concerning your purpose. Get in agreement with your destiny! Don't let your calling lie dormant another day. Stir it up. Speak it out. Write the vision and make it plain (Habakkuk 2:2). You were born for such a time as this.

Let's pray and declare God's purpose will manifest in our lives with boldness, clarity, and supernatural confirmation. This is not the season to shrink back. This is the season to rise, walk in Kingdom authority, and fulfill your assignment with power and grace.

Living a Life of Kingdom Purpose

Heavenly Father, I come to Your throne of grace through and by the blood of Jesus. I humbly approach your presence today, fully surrendered to Your will and confident in Your divine plan for my life. You are the Master Architect, and every detail of my life is in Your hands. Thank You for calling me, equipping me, and preparing me for divine assignments that bring glory to Your name.

Today, I align myself with Matthew 6:33. I choose to seek first Your Kingdom and Your righteousness, trusting that everything else will be added as I walk in alignment with Your plan. Teach me to prioritize Your will above my own desires, ambitions, and preferences. Where there has been slack, delay, or procrastination in my life, replace it with a deep passion and urgency to pursue Your assignment with focus and faith.

Lord, I declare that my life is not random but intentional. According to Ephesians 2:10, I am Your handiwork, created in Christ Jesus for good works You prepared in advance for me to walk in. Let every step I take lead me closer to the fulfillment of what You've ordained for me.

I refuse to settle. I reject complacency, mediocrity, and half-hearted obedience. I declare that I will not fall short of what You've promised. Proverbs 19:21 reminds me that though I may make many plans, it is Your purpose that will prevail. Align every area of my life with Your divine blueprint.

Father, I release my faith for the full manifestation of every promise You've spoken over me. Just as Romans 8:28 declares, I know You are working all things together for my good because I am called according to Your purpose. I won't settle for glimpses, I declare that I will walk in the fullness of what You have spoken.

Lord, give me clarity for every assignment You've entrusted to me. Remove all confusion, fear, and doubt. Help me to walk boldly in my calling, refusing to compare or measure myself against others. I am uniquely called, and I embrace the path You've laid out for me.

I take authority over every hindrance, distraction, and delay. Every barrier blocking the manifestation of Your promise must fall now, in the name of Jesus!

Your Word in Psalm 138:8 declares that You will fulfill Your purpose for me, and Your faithful love endures forever. I thank You that not one promise will return void. Everything You've spoken will come to pass.

Father, release favor over my Kingdom assignments. Open doors that no man can shut. Connect me with divine relationships, mentors, and partnerships that accelerate Your purpose and align with Your will.

I declare that I will live a purpose-driven life. I will walk in confidence, fully submitted to Your Spirit, and I will see the fruit of my obedience. I will not settle for anything less than Your perfect will.

Let my life reflect Your glory. Let my obedience inspire others to rise up and pursue You with passion. May generations be transformed by my faithfulness and surrender.

I believe I receive this prayer, and I release my most holy faith to bring it to pass. In the mighty and matchless name of Jesus Christ, I pray. Amen and Amen.

Prayer for Building a Legacy of Faith

Heavenly Father, I come before You with a heart full of gratitude for the gift of faith You've placed in me. You are the Author and Finisher of my faith, and I honor You for the legacy of grace and truth You've entrusted to me.

Today, I stand on Psalm 78:4, declaring that I will not hide Your praiseworthy deeds, Your power, or the wonders You've done. I will boldly share my testimony and speak of Your goodness to the generations that follow me.

Father, help me live a life that reflects Your glory. Let my actions, words, and attitudes consistently point to You. May I be a living example of unwavering faith, humility, and obedience to Your Word. As Proverbs 13:22 declares, let me leave an inheritance of faith, wisdom, and godly principles for my children and my children's children. I pray that the seeds I plant will bear fruit for generations to come.

Lord, as You commanded in Deuteronomy 6:6-7, may Your Word remain close to my heart. Teach me to impress Your truth upon the hearts of my children and my children's children. Let every conversation, every moment at home, and every opportunity I have be used to point the next generation toward You, in the name of Jesus.

Father, I pray for every parent, guardian, and mentor, including myself. Strengthen us with wisdom, patience, and love as I raise and influence the next generation. May I not grow weary in teaching, guiding, and nurturing those You've entrusted to us.

Lord, I stand on 2 Timothy 1:5 and declare that generational faith is rising in my family line. May the faith that lived in my godly forefathers continue to grow and flourish in me, my children, and everyone I am called to impact. Let my life make a mark that echoes beyond my years.

Empower me, Lord, to let my light shine brightly, just as You said in Matthew 5:16. Let my life be a testimony of Your faithfulness so that others may see my good works and glorify You.

I come against every scheme of the enemy designed to hinder the faith of the next generation. I declare that my family, my children, my grandchildren, and every future generation will not be overtaken by deception, confusion, compromise, or spiritual complacency. They will rise as bold, faith-filled believers who will carry the gospel of Christ into every area of society.

Let revival break out in my home, my church, my community, and everywhere You've given me influence. Stir hearts to pursue You with passion. Let a love and passion for you spread like wildfire, lighting up dark places and drawing many into Your Kingdom. I commit to living a life that honors You, not just for today, but for eternity. I will pass down a legacy of worship, prayer, and devotion to You.

Thank You, Father, that my faith will not end with me, but will be carried forward by those I have impacted. I believe that every seed I have sown, every prayer I have lifted, and every act of faith will bring forth a harvest of righteousness.

I believe I receive this prayer, and I release my most holy faith to bring it to pass. In the mighty and matchless name of Jesus Christ, I pray. Amen and Amen.

Prayer for a Purpose-Driven Life

Heavenly Father, I come before You with a surrendered heart, acknowledging that You are the Author and Finisher of my faith. You have designed me with intention, called me with purpose, and equipped me with everything I need to fulfill Your plan for my life.

Lord, Your Word in Jeremiah 29:11 assures me that You know the plans You have for me, plans to prosper me and not to harm me, plans to give me hope and a future. Today, I stand on that promise, trusting that every detail of my life is safely in Your hands.

Father, reveal Your purpose to me. Open my spiritual eyes and ears to recognize the unique calling You have placed on my life. Speak clearly, Lord, and guide me in the paths You've prepared for me. Remove all confusion, doubt, and fear, and replace them with faith, boldness, confidence, and clarity.

As it says in Ephesians 2:10, I am Your handiwork, created in Christ Jesus for good works that You prepared beforehand. Help me to walk in those works with confidence, knowing that I am fulfilling divine assignments.

Father, I surrender my plans, ambitions, and timelines to You. Your Word declares in Proverbs 19:21 that many are the plans in a person's heart, but it is Your purpose that prevails. Align my desires with Your will and help me to trust Your perfect timing. Let me never be satisfied outside of Your will.

Lord, break every chain of fear, insecurity, and comparison that tries to hold me back. Silence the voices of doubt and discouragement. Help me to stay focused on the race You've set before me, running with perseverance and unwavering faith.

I declare Romans 8:28 over my life, that all things are working together for my good because I am called according to Your purpose.

Even in challenges and setbacks, I trust that You are working behind the scenes to fulfill Your promises.

Let my life bear fruit for Your Kingdom, Father. May my purpose impact my family, my community, and the nations for Your glory. Teach me to steward my gifts, talents, and resources wisely, using them to build and advance Your Kingdom here on earth.

I find joy in serving You, Lord, knowing that my life is not my own but fully surrendered to Your will. As Psalm 138:8 declares, fulfill Your purpose for me. Let nothing be left undone that You have destined for me to accomplish. I ask for divine connections and destiny helpers to come alongside me as I pursue Your plan. Surround me with godly counsel, mentors, and accountability partners.

Ignite a fire within me to live boldly, passionately, and purposefully for You. May every step I take, every word I speak, and every decision I make bring glory and honor to Your holy name.

I declare that I will not live passively or aimlessly, but I will rise up in faith, walking boldly in the calling You've placed upon my life. I believe I receive this prayer, and I release my most holy faith to bring it to pass. In the mighty and matchless name of Jesus Christ, I pray. Amen and Amen.

Declare the Will of God Being Done on Earth as It Is in Heaven

Heavenly Father, in the mighty name of Jesus, I come before You in agreement with Heaven, declaring that Your will is being done in my life on earth as it is in heaven. Lord, I honor You as my Father and Shepherd, the One who leads me, provides for me, and sustains me. I exalt Your holy name and declare Your sovereignty over every area of my life.

My Father who is in heaven, hallowed be Your name. Your kingdom come, Your will be done in my life on earth as it is in heaven. I align my heart, mind, and actions with Your perfect will. Let Your plans prevail in my home, my family, my community, and in every decision I make. Let heaven invade every part of my life, filling it with Your peace, Your order, and Your power.

Give me this day my daily bread. I thank You for meeting my needs today. I trust You to provide for me spiritually, emotionally, physically, and financially. You are Jehovah Jireh, the God who supplies all my needs according to Your riches in glory by Christ Jesus.

Forgive me my debts as I forgive my debtors. Father, cleanse me from every sin, every hindrance, and every wrong thought or action. Teach me to walk in love and forgiveness, releasing others as You have so graciously released me. Let nothing block the flow of Your will in my life.

Lead me not into temptation, but deliver me from evil. Lord, guide me away from every snare, distraction, and deception of the enemy. Keep my feet firmly planted on the path You have set before me, and deliver me from every scheme and attack of the wicked one.

For Yours is the kingdom, the power, and the glory forever. Amen. I declare that Your kingdom reigns over every part of my life. Your power is at work within me, and Your glory will be revealed through me. I magnify You, King of kings and Lord of lords.

The Lord is my Shepherd; I shall not want. Father, I thank You for being my Shepherd, the One who leads me with wisdom and care. Because You are with me, I lack nothing. You guide me into green pastures and beside still waters. You restore my soul and give me peace.

You lead me in the paths of righteousness for Your name's sake. I declare that I walk in alignment with Your Word and Your purpose. Order every step I take as I fulfill the divine assignments You have placed on my life.

Even though I walk through the valley of the shadow of death, I will fear no evil. You are with me. Your rod and Your staff, they comfort me. I declare that no challenge, no adversity, and no weapon formed against me will prosper. You are with me, protecting and guiding me through every trial and difficulty. I will not be shaken, because You are my strength and my shield.

You prepare a table before me in the presence of my enemies. You anoint my head with oil, and my cup runs over. I thank You, Lord, for Your abundant blessings even in the midst of opposition. My cup overflows with Your goodness, favor, and provision.

Surely goodness and mercy follow me all the days of my life, and I dwell in the house of the Lord forever. I declare that Your goodness and mercy are chasing me down, and I will remain in Your presence and in Your will every day of my life.

Father, I decree that Your will is being done in my life just as it is in heaven. I believe it. I receive it and I release my most holy faith to see it come to pass. In the mighty and matchless name of Jesus, I pray, Amen and Amen.

Operating in the Gifts of the Spirit and Releasing His Power

Heavenly Father, in the mighty name of Jesus, I come before You with a heart surrendered, and a spirit yielded to Your will. I thank You that You have called me, anointed me, and filled me with the Holy Spirit. I declare that I will not operate in my own strength or wisdom, but in the power of Your Spirit moving through me.

Lord, Your Word says in 1 Corinthians 12:7 that the manifestation of the Spirit is given to each one for the common good. I receive the gifts You have placed within me, and I choose to stir them up and walk in them with boldness. I refuse to shrink back, and I refuse to let fear or doubt silence what You have placed inside of me. I declare that I am a vessel, consecrated for Your glory, and I will release Your power in the earth.

Holy Spirit, flow through me. Speak through me. Move through me. I yield my mind, my hands, my voice, and my heart to You. Let words of wisdom and words of knowledge flow freely. Let faith rise within me to believe for the impossible. Let the gifts of healing be released through my hands. Let the working of miracles be evident in my life. Let prophecy, discernment, tongues, and interpretation be activated and flow according to Your will. I am available, and I am ready to be used for Your Kingdom.

Father, I thank You that Your power is alive in me. I am not weak, I am not powerless, and I am not ordinary. I have been filled with resurrection power, the same power that raised Jesus from the dead (Romans 8:11). I step into that power today. I release it over my life, my family, my ministry, my business, and every assignment You have given me. Let signs, wonders, and miracles follow me as I walk in obedience.

I take authority over every distraction, every spirit of fear, and every lie of the enemy that would try to hinder the gifts from flowing in my life. I declare that I will not suppress what You have placed inside of me. I will not quench the Spirit, but I will fan the flame of the gift of God that is within me (2 Timothy 1:6-7).

Father, let my life be a demonstration of Your power. Let me operate in the gifts, not for my own glory, but so that Your name may be exalted. Use me to be a blessing, to minister life to others, and to expand Your Kingdom on the earth. I believe I receive this prayer, and I release my most holy faith to bring it to pass. In Jesus' name I pray, Amen.

Faith Confessions for Operating in the Gifts of the Spirit
- I am filled with the Holy Spirit, and I walk in His power. (Acts 1:8)
- The gifts of the Spirit are active and operating in my life. (1 Corinthians 12:7-11)
- I stir up the gift of God within me and refuse to let fear hold me back. (2 Timothy 1:6-7)
- The same Spirit that raised Jesus from the dead dwells in me. (Romans 8:11)
- I release healing, miracles, and break through as the Holy Spirit moves through me. (Mark 16:17-18)
- I have the mind of Christ, and I discern by the Holy Spirit of God. (1 Corinthians 2:16)
- I walk in supernatural wisdom, knowledge, and faith. (1 Corinthians 12:8-9)
- I prophesy and speak the Word of the Lord with boldness and authority. (Acts 2:17-18)
- I refuse to quench the Spirit and I allow Him to flow through me freely. (1 Thessalonians 5:19)
- Signs, wonders, and miracles follow me because I believe. (Mark 16:20)

I believe I receive what I have declared, and I release my most holy faith to bring it to pass. In Jesus' name I pray, Amen.

Perseverance and Boldness to Act on Your Vision

(Repeat these out loud in faith)

1. I am empowered by God to persevere through every challenge and delay. I will not grow weary, for in due season, I will reap a harvest of blessings as I remain steadfast in faith. (Galatians 6:9)
2. God has equipped me with strength, courage, and boldness. I will rise up and act on the vision He has given me, knowing that He is with me every step of the way. (Joshua 1:9)
3. Delays do not mean denial. I trust God's perfect timing, and I declare that His plans for me will unfold exactly as He has purposed. (Habakkuk 2:3)
4. I walk by faith and not by sight. I refuse to be discouraged by temporary obstacles because I know God is working all things together for my good. (2 Corinthians 5:7; Romans 8:28)
5. I am bold and courageous, acting in faith on the vision God has given me. I will not fear, for the Lord is my helper, my strength, and my shield. (Psalm 27:1)
6. I declare that every challenge I face is preparing me for the fulfillment of my vision. I embrace God's refining process and trust His wisdom. (James 1:2-4)
7. The Holy Spirit guides me into all truth and provides clarity for my vision. I walk in divine alignment with God's will and purpose for my life. (John 16:13)
8. I will not quit or shrink back in fear. I press on toward the goal, confident that God's grace is sufficient for me. (Philippians 3:13-14; 2 Corinthians 12:9)
9. I am strong and courageous because the Lord is with me. His Spirit empowers me to move forward boldly, knowing He has gone before me. (Deuteronomy 31:6)
10. God's Word is a lamp to my feet and a light to my path. I trust Him to guide me as I take bold steps of faith toward the vision He has given me. (Psalm 119:105)

Walking in Prophetic Insight

Heavenly Father, I come boldly before Your throne of grace through and by the blood of Jesus. I thank You that the blood of Jesus gives me access to divine wisdom, supernatural insight, and hidden mysteries that only Your Spirit can reveal. You are the God who sits high and looks low, the One who knows the end from the beginning. Nothing is hidden from You, and because I am in You, I declare that nothing shall be hidden from me.

Lord, I ask for an increase in the Spirit of Discernment. Sharpen my ability to perceive what is of You and what is not. Let every veil be removed and let my eyes be enlightened. Give me prophetic insight to see beyond the natural, to discern the times and seasons, and to navigate with divine precision.

Father, I refuse to be led by my emotions, by what I see with my natural eyes, or by the deceptions of the enemy. I bind every spirit of confusion, manipulation, and distraction that seeks to cloud my vision. I loose divine clarity, supernatural wisdom, and insight in Jesus' name. My mind is alert, my spirit is sharp, and my ears are tuned to the frequency of Heaven.

Holy Spirit, I yield completely to You. Activate my spiritual senses. Make me like the sons of Issachar, help me to understand the times and know what to do. Give me eyes to see, ears to hear, and the wisdom to apply what You reveal. I declare that I am not ignorant of the enemy's devices. I will not be deceived, tricked, or manipulated. Every hidden agenda, every false voice, and every lying spirit is exposed and dismantled now in the name of Jesus.

Father, open the heavens over my life. Let prophetic clarity flow freely in my life. Let the spirit of wisdom and revelation rest upon me. I declare that I will not miss divine opportunities and I will not fall into the traps of the enemy. I am led by the Spirit of God in all that I do. I walk in alignment with Heaven's agenda.

I take authority over every false vision, false prophecy, and counterfeit assignment that seeks to misdirect me. I silence the voice of the stranger, and I declare that I will only follow the voice of my Shepherd, Jesus Christ. My discernment is increasing daily, and I move with precision, wisdom, and boldness in every decision.

Lord, I thank You that I am marked for Your purpose and anointed to see, hear, and discern with clarity. I believe I receive this prayer, and I release my most holy faith to bring it to pass. In the mighty name of Jesus I pray. Amen and Amen.

Chapter 8 – Prayers for Favor, Blessings and Miracles

Favor, Blessings, and Miracles

When we walk in Kingdom authority, we must boldly declare the promises of God over our lives. This chapter is not about hype or wishful thinking. It's about walking in the confidence of who we are in Christ. As believers, we are blessed, highly favored, and chosen. The favor of God is not something we chase. It surrounds us as a shield.

We don't have to beg for miracles. Jesus has already made a way for us to access Heaven's abundance. The same God who parted the Red Sea and fed the multitude is still working today. He delights in blessing His children. His goodness is not seasonal, it's constant. His favor is not limited, it is overflowing.

This chapter is an invitation to speak life and abundance. To speak blessing. To decree and declare favor over your life with faith and authority. You'll find prayers that declare God's goodness over your week, your work, your family, and every assignment on your life. There are faith confessions for divine connections, open doors, supernatural provision, and miraculous breakthrough. YESSSS, speak by faith over your life child of God!

You are not waiting on favor. Favor is already working on your behalf. The blessing of the Lord makes rich and adds no sorrow. You are surrounded with favor like a shield. Open your mouth and declare it. Speak blessing over your day. Speak favor over your children. Declare miracles, signs, and wonders to break forth.

You are not average. You are a covenant child of God. You are an heir to every promise in His Word. Lift your head. Speak the Word. Walk in the supernatural flow of God's favor. Your mouth is a weapon. Use it. Your confession is a seed. Plant it and expect the harvest.

Declaration of Blessing Over Our Lives

Heavenly Father, in the mighty and matchless name of Jesus, I come before You with a heart full of gratitude, expectation, and faith. I thank You that the blessing of the Lord makes rich and adds no sorrow. I declare today that Your hand is upon my life, and I speak the blessing over every area of my life.

I declare the blessing over my spirit. I am strong in the Lord and in the power of His might. I am filled with the Holy Spirit, led by His voice, and anchored in truth. I walk in discernment, wisdom, and supernatural insight.

I declare the blessing over my mind. I have the mind of Christ. Every thought is aligned with the Word of God and the will of God. Confusion is broken. Fear is dismantled. I walk in clarity, focus, peace, and divine understanding.

I declare the blessing over my body. By the stripes of Jesus, I am healed. Every organ, cell, tissue, and system functions according to God's original design. I have energy, vitality, and strength for the assignment and calling on my life.

I declare the blessing over my relationships. I walk in love, forgiveness, and unity. God is restoring what was broken. Divine connections and covenant friendships are being released into my life. My family is covered, healed, and walking in purpose together.

I declare the blessing over my finances. The windows of heaven are open over my life. I am a faithful steward, a generous giver, and I walk in overflow. Every bill is paid, every debt is paid in full, and unexpected provision is chasing me down and running me over.

I declare the blessing over my work and assignments. I am called, appointed, and anointed for good works ordained by God. God is opening doors for me that no man can shut. I walk in favor, excellence, and supernatural results. Everything I set my hands to do prospers.

I declare the blessing over my future. My steps are ordered by the Lord. I walk in kingdom purpose and divine alignment. No weapon formed against me will prosper. I will not be delayed, denied, or defeated. I go from glory to glory and victory to victory.

Father, I thank You for Your blessing, Your presence, and Your power. I believe I receive this prayer and I release my most holy faith to bring it to pass. In Jesus' mighty name I pray, Amen.

Commanding Favor and Declaring Grace

Father, in the name of Jesus, I come before You today as Your child, blood-washed, blood-covered, and fully persuaded that Your favor surrounds me like a shield. I rise in faith and authority, commanding this day to align with Your perfect will and plans for my life.

I declare that favor is going before me today. Favor is opening doors no one can shut. Favor is shifting policies, unlocking resources, reversing decisions, and making ways in the wilderness for me and those connected to me. I decree supernatural favor over my home, my family, my business, my career, my ministry, and every God-ordained assignment on my life.

I command every barrier to break and shatter now in the name of Jesus. Every demonic blockage be removed! Every invisible wall, every chain of limitation, every generational resistance be destroyed by the fire of God. Father, release Your warring angels on assignment to tear down every hindrance and to go before me to prepare the way.

I declare that grace is being loosed into my life right now, divine grace to finish what I started, grace to recover lost time, grace to walk through open doors, grace to show up with strength, wisdom, and excellence. I receive the grace to thrive under pressure, to prosper in dry places, and to stand strong in the face of adversity.

Let there be grace for breakthrough. Grace for elevation. Grace for visibility. Grace to build. Grace to lead. Grace to rest. Grace to rise. Let unmerited, undeniable, unstoppable grace be released over my life now.

I speak to every obstacle in my path and say, "Be removed and cast into the sea." I command systems to shift in my favor. I call forth contracts, approvals, opportunities, and unexpected blessings to be loosed and released today. What was delayed is being released NOW. What was held up is coming forth NOW. I decree favor in the courtroom, favor in the boardroom, favor in the marketplace, and favor with all of my relationships. Favor that brings divine connections and destiny helpers into my life.

Father, I thank You that Your grace is sufficient for me. Your favor is flowing freely in my life and Your power is moving mightily in my life. I walk boldly in what You've called me to do, knowing You've gone before me and made every crooked path straight. I declare that favor surrounds me as a shield. Everyone I come into contact with today will recognize Your hand of favor upon my life. Unprecedented favor is mine.

I believe I receive this prayer and I release my most holy faith to bring it to pass. In the mighty and matchless name of Jesus I pray, Amen.

Walking in the Favor of God

Heavenly Father, I thank You today that I am covered, clothed, and crowned with Your favor! Your Word declares in Psalm 5:12 (NLT) – "For you bless the godly, O Lord; you surround them with your shield of love and favor." Father, I declare that Your favor is surrounding me right now like a mighty shield. It goes before me, it stands behind me, and it rests upon me.

I decree and declare that I am not limited by circumstances, not confined by opinions, and not blocked by obstacles, because Your favor is working for me in realms seen and unseen! Romans 8:31 reminds me, "If God is for us, who can ever be against us?" No weapon formed against me prospers because Your favor opens doors that no man can shut.

Father, I prophesy over my day and my destiny. Doors that were once closed are swinging open wide! Opportunities that were out of reach are now within my grasp! I do not chase after blessings, Your Word says in Deuteronomy 28:2 (NLT) – "You will experience all these blessings if you obey the Lord your God: Your blessings will overtake you!" I thank You, Lord, that Your favor causes blessings to pursue me and overtake me. Chasing me and overtaking me.

I walk in divine appointments, supernatural provision, and uncommon opportunities, because the hand of the Lord is mighty upon my life. Like Joseph, even in tight places, I rise to the top. Genesis 39:21 (NLT) declares, "But the Lord was with Joseph in the prison and showed him His faithful love. And the Lord made Joseph a favorite with the prison warden." Father, Your favor promotes me beyond natural circumstances. Your favor on my life is bringing elevation to levels that I could not accomplish on my own.

Like Esther, I am positioned for such a time as this! (Esther 4:14) I embrace my divine assignment with boldness and confidence.

Like David, I am anointed and recognized by heaven and earth. Your anointing upon my life opens doors of recognition and elevation.

Because of Your shield of favor on my life, I lack nothing! (Psalm 34:10) My hands are blessed, my name is being mentioned in rooms I have not yet entered, and my steps are divinely ordered by You according to Psalm 37:23, The Lord directs the steps my steps and he delights in every detail of my life.

The right people are drawn to me and wrong connections are removed by Your hand. I am established in every good work, and I declare God is causing all things to work together for my good because I love him and I am called according to his purpose. (Romans 8:28)

Father, I stand in unwavering faith today, believing that this is my season of unprecedented favor! I declare favor over my home, my family, my business, my ministry, my finances, and my future.

I believe I receive this prayer, and I release my most holy faith to bring it to pass. In Jesus' name I pray, Amen!

Divine Connections & Open Doors

Father, in the mighty name of Jesus, I enter into Your presence, covered by the blood of Jesus Christ. I stand on Your word and I am in expectation for a supernatural breakthrough. Lord, I thank You for being the God who opens doors that no man can shut. I declare that doors are thrusting wide open for me, and supernatural opportunities leading to overflow and abundance are coming into my life.

Go before me, Lord. Make every crooked path straight and every rough place smooth. I ask in the name of Jesus that You align me with the right people at the right time. The blessing of Abraham is drawing the right relationships and divine opportunities to me now. Divine alignment is manifesting right now in the name of Jesus.

I declare that divine connections are being released to me. I am being connected to relationships filled with favor, wisdom, strategy, and supernatural opportunity. I'm aligned with people who help carry the vision You have given me, who open new doors, and who speak my name in rooms filled with influence and abundance. I cancel every assignment of the enemy that has been sent to delay me, distract me, or confuse me, and I decree divine access! Access to what has been ordained for me.

Your Word says in Revelation 3:8 that You have opened a door that no man can close. I walk through it by faith. According to Isaiah 45:2–3, I thank You that You are going before me, breaking down barriers and revealing hidden treasures, resources, and provision meant for this season, this year, and this decade. I declare divine setups, unexpected blessings, and unprecedented favor are locating me now!

The right doors are opening. The right calls are coming in. The right partnerships are forming. I declare supernatural alignment with purpose and destiny. I will not miss my moment or forfeit my timing.

I refuse to settle for anything less than what You have ordained for my life.

Father, I thank You that promotion does not come from people, it comes from You. So, I release my faith and expectation for divine promotion. Promotion comes to me now today, in Jesus' name. You are speaking my name to those who will propel my life into overflow, influence, and generational impact.

Blow my mind with what only You can do. Release contracts, overflow, clients, sponsors, grants, divine help, and angelic assistance. Let Kingdom connections be made that impact lives and generations to come.

I invoke the power of the Holy Ghost to saturate every area of my life and every household connected to me. Let a fresh wave of favor hit my life this day, this week, this month, this season, this year, this decade, and this century. What's been held up is being released now. What's been closed is swinging wide open!

I seal this prayer with bold faith. I believe I receive it, and I release my most holy faith to bring it to pass. In Jesus' mighty and matchless name, I pray, Amen and Amen.

Divine Connections, Destiny Helpers, and Supernatural Favor

Heavenly Father, in the name of Jesus, I come before You with expectation standing on the authority of Your Word! You are the God of divine alignment, the master orchestrator of purpose, and the One who orders my steps. Today, I call forth divine connections and destiny helpers from the four corners of the earth. Let those whom You have assigned to bless, assist, and propel me forward locate me now, in Jesus' name!

Your Word declares in Isaiah 43:5-6, "Do not be afraid, for I am with you; I will bring your children from the east and gather you from the west. I will say to the north, 'Give them up!' and to the south, 'Do not hold them back.'" So, I decree and declare that every divine connection, every kingdom relationship, every assigned helper must come forth NOW! Let the north give them up! Let the south release them! Let the east and the west bring them speedily into my life, for I am in alignment with Your perfect will!

Father, I bind and break every demonic delay, every spirit of resistance, and every blockage the enemy has set up to keep me from divine appointments! According to Isaiah 45:2-3, You go before me and make the crooked places straight! Every gate of brass is shattered, and every iron bar is cut asunder! I declare that no barrier, no hindrance, no obstacle shall stand in the way of the divine helpers You have assigned to my life!

I declare that doors of favor, opportunity, and supernatural provision are opening right now! Just as You raised up Boaz for Ruth, Pharaoh's cupbearer for Joseph, and Jonathan for David, You are raising up the right people to support, uplift, and propel me into my next season. Divine partnerships, strategic relationships, and kingdom alignments are forming even now!

Lord, Your Word says in Psalm 5:12, "Surely, Lord, you bless the righteous; you surround them with your favor as with a shield." I declare that I am clothed in divine favor! I am shielded by favor! I walk in supernatural favor! Everywhere I go, favor goes before me! I am called, chosen, and set apart for such a time as this, and no good thing shall be withheld from me!

Father, I thank You for supernatural acceleration! What should take years, You will accomplish in days! What man says is impossible, You make possible! I align my life with Your divine timetable and declare that my destiny helpers will recognize me, seek me out, and be moved to bless and assist me, in Jesus' name!

I believe I receive this prayer, and I release my most holy faith to bring it to pass! Thank You, Father, for Your faithfulness! It is done, it is sealed, and it shall manifest, in Jesus' mighty name! Amen!

Victorious Living in God

Heavenly Father, I come to your Throne of Grace, through and by the blood Jesus Christ. I thank you that through faith, the blood of Jesus and the name of Jesus, that I can receive answered prayer. I have no reason to fear because you are with me. I will not be afraid because you are my God. You make me strong and you are protecting me with your arm and giving me great victories. I stand in victory in every area of my life. A thousand shall fall at my side and 10,000 at my right hand but it shall not harm or overwhelm me.

I navigate my life in victory. When I go through challenges in life, you are with me. Since you are with me, I come out of every challenge that I face stronger, better, wiser and richer. I am strong in you Lord and the power of Your might and the gates of hell shall not prevail against me or my family. I send the angels of heaven that have been assigned to my life and my family to surround us, guard, protect and keep us safe. I declare this is a day of supernatural victory, a week of supernatural victory, a month of supernatural victory, a season of supernatural victory, a year of supernatural victory and a decade of supernatural victory. I clothe myself in victory today.

In the name of Jesus Christ, I pray amen. I believe and I receive this and release most holy faith to bring it to pass.

Prayer to Pronounce Blessings Over the New Week

Heavenly Father, in the mighty name of Jesus, I come before You, lifting up this new week. Father, I thank You for Your unfailing love, Your faithfulness, and Your mercy that are new every morning. I stand on Your Word and declare that this week is blessed, overflowing with Your favor, provision, and goodness.

Lord, I decree and declare that every person connected to me is walking in divine alignment with Your perfect will. Their steps are ordered by You, and they are led by Your Holy Spirit in all they do. No weapon formed against them shall prosper, and every tongue that rises against them is condemned (Isaiah 54:17). They are surrounded by Your favor like a shield, and everywhere they go, they are walking into divine opportunities and Kingdom appointments (Psalm 5:12).

Father, I pronounce blessings of peace, strength, and clarity over every heart and mind. Your Word says that You will keep in perfect peace those whose minds are steadfast, because they trust in You (Isaiah 26:3). Let Your peace guard our hearts and minds this week, and let every decision we make be guided by Your wisdom (Philippians 4:6-7).

I declare that we are blessed in the city and blessed in the field, blessed when we come in and blessed when we go out (Deuteronomy 28:3-6). The work of our hands are prosperous, and every assignment I undertake is fruitful and effective. Let everything we put our hands to flourish under Your grace and anointing (Psalm 1:3).

Lord, I call forth breakthroughs in every stubborn situation and declare divine acceleration over our visions and dreams. Let the mountains be made low and the valleys raised up (Isaiah 40:4). You are the God of breakthroughs, and I declare that this week is filled with testimonies of Your faithfulness.

Father, let Your presence go before us, saturating every home, workplace, and environment. Let Your Holy Spirit empower us to walk in boldness and courage, proclaiming the good news of Your Kingdom. I thank You that signs, wonders, and miracles will follow those who believe, and that Your name will be glorified through our lives.

I seal this prayer in the name of Jesus Christ, declaring that Your Word will not return void but will accomplish everything it was sent to do (Isaiah 55:11). I believe I receive this prayer and release my faith to see it come to pass. Amen!

Faith Confessions for New Week

1. I declare that this week is blessed, and I walk in divine favor and purpose.
2. I am surrounded by God's protection, and no weapon formed against me will prosper. (Isaiah 54:17)
3. The peace of God guards my heart and mind, and I trust Him to guide me in every decision. (Philippians 4:6-7)
4. I am blessed coming in and going out, and everything I put my hands to will prosper. (Deuteronomy 28:3-6)
5. I walk by faith and not by sight, trusting that God is working all things together for my good. (2 Corinthians 5:7; Romans 8:28)
6. I am bold and courageous, acting in obedience to God's will, and His Spirit empowers me to succeed. (Joshua 1:9)
7. I declare that breakthroughs, blessings, and miracles are my portion this week in the name of Jesus.
8. I am a carrier of God's presence, and everywhere I go, His light and love shine through me. (Matthew 5:16)
9. The joy of the Lord is my strength and I face every challenge with confidence and peace. (Nehemiah 8:10)
10. I am like a tree planted by streams of water; I bear fruit in every season, and I prosper in all I do. (Psalm 1:3)
11. God has given me the wisdom and clarity I need to make the right decisions this week. (James 1:5)

12. I dwell in the secret place of the Most High and no harm will come near me or my household. (Psalm 91:1,10)
13. I am strong and courageous because the Lord is with me. I do not fear, for His presence goes before me. (Deuteronomy 31:6)
14. I call forth divine connections and destiny helpers to align with God's plan for my life. (Isaiah 60:3-4)
15. I declare that God is opening doors that no one can shut and closing doors that no one can open. (Revelation 3:8)
16. I will not grow weary in doing good, for my harvest is on the way, and I will reap in due season. (Galatians 6:9)
17. The Holy Spirit leads and guides me into all truth, providing clarity and direction for every situation. (John 16:13)
18. Every mountain in my life is being made low, and God is clearing the way for His plans to prevail. (Zechariah 4:7)
19. I declare that God's favor surrounds me like a shield, and blessings are overtaking me in every area of my life. (Psalm 5:12; Deuteronomy 28:2)
20. I walk in supernatural peace, power, and authority, knowing that greater is He who is in me than he who is in the world. (1 John 4:4)
21. The Lord is fighting my battles and I will stand still and see the salvation of my God. (Exodus 14:14)
22. I am a vessel of honor, sanctified and ready for the Master's use, prepared for every good work. (2 Timothy 2:21)
23. I decree that this week is filled with unexpected blessings, gifts and surprises. Joy is overflowing in my life.
24. The Word of God is alive in me, and I declare His promises with boldness, knowing they will not return void. (Isaiah 55:11)
25. I am more than a conqueror through Christ who loves me and nothing can separate me from His love. (Romans 8:37-39)
26. My household is blessed, my relationships are flourishing, and my family walks in unity and love. (Psalm 133:1)
27. I declare that this week is a week of open heavens, divine favor, and supernatural provision.

28. I am equipped and empowered to fulfill God's purpose for my life and no plan of the enemy can stop me. (Job 42:2)
29. I walk in the victory of Christ and I overcome every obstacle by the blood of the Lamb and the word of my testimony. (Revelation 12:11)
30. The Lord is my Shepherd and I lack nothing. His goodness and mercy follow me all the days of my life. (Psalm 23:1,6)

I believe I receive this and I release most holy faith to bring it to pass. In the mighty and matchless name of Jesus Christ I pray, amen.

Declaring Favor, Breakthrough, and Abundance

Father, in the mighty name of Jesus, I come boldly before Your throne of grace this morning, washed in the blood of the Lamb and filled with expectation for Your goodness and mercy to overflow in my life. I honor You as the source of every blessing, every breakthrough, and every miracle, and I thank You for this day that You have made. I declare it blessed and I rejoice in it!

Lord, I decree and declare that Your favor surrounds me like a shield (Psalm 5:12). Everywhere I go, I walk in divine favor. Doors that no man can shut are opening before me and opportunities for breakthrough are chasing me down. I thank You, Lord, that I am blessed in the city and blessed in the field, blessed coming in and blessed going out (Deuteronomy 28:3-6). Your blessings are overtaking me as I obey Your Word.

Father, I release faith for breakthroughs today! I declare that supernatural provision, restoration, and increase are manifesting in every area of my life. You are the God of more than enough, Jehovah Jireh, my Provider. I receive bonanza blessings, overflowing, pressed down, shaken together, and running over, just as Your Word promises in Luke 6:38. Lord, I decree that this is my season of abundant harvest!

I stand on the truth of Ephesians 3:20, that You are able to do exceedingly, abundantly above all I could ask or think. I declare that financial breakthroughs are mine, healing is mine, restoration is mine, and divine connections are coming forth. No weapon formed against me shall prosper and every plan of the enemy is canceled and reversed in Jesus' name (Isaiah 54:17).

Holy Spirit, I invite You to saturate this day with Your presence. Lead me, guide me, and show me the paths of favor and success that You have prepared for me. I declare that I walk in wisdom, strength, and boldness today, knowing that the hand of God is upon me. Father, I give You all the glory, all the honor, and all the praise. I believe I receive this prayer, and I release my most holy faith to bring it to pass, in the mighty name of Jesus. Amen!

Faith Confessions for Breakthroughs and Blessings

1. I declare that I am blessed and highly favored of the Lord. (Luke 1:28)
2. The favor of God surrounds me like a shield and opens doors that no man can shut. (Psalm 5:12)
3. I decree that breakthrough is manifesting in my life today, spiritually, financially, and physically. (2 Corinthians 9:8)
4. I am the head and not the tail, above only and not beneath. (Deuteronomy 28:13)
5. My God supplies all my needs according to His riches in glory in Christ Jesus. (Philippians 4:19)
6. I walk in divine increase, and the blessings of the Lord make me rich and add no sorrow with it. (Proverbs 10:22)
7. I declare that I live under an open heaven. Bonanza blessings are overtaking me and my household. (Malachi 3:10)
8. I decree that I am a lender, not a borrower, and every debt is canceled and paid in full in Jesus' name. (Deuteronomy 28:12)
9. I speak that unexpected checks, divine connections, and financial overflow are locating me today. (Luke 6:38)
10. I declare that I am walking in God's perfect will and His favor goes before me, making every crooked path straight. (Isaiah 45:2)
11. I am anointed for success, empowered for breakthrough, and positioned for blessings. (2 Corinthians 1:21)
12. I declare that this is my season of overflow, my time for restoration, and my moment for miracles. (Joel 2:25-26)
13. I decree that wealth and riches are in my house, and my righteousness endures forever. (Psalm 112:3)
14. The Lord is my Shepherd; I lack nothing. His provision is abundant in every area of my life. (Psalm 23:1)

15. I am fruitful in every good work, and my life reflects God's glory and abundance. (Colossians 1:10)
16. I declare that no good thing will the Lord withhold from me as I walk uprightly. (Psalm 84:11)
17. My steps are ordered by the Lord, and I walk into divine appointments and opportunities today. (Psalm 37:23)
18. I declare that all things are working together for my good because I love God and am called according to His purpose. (Romans 8:28)
19. I am chosen by God, and He has crowned me with glory and honor. Favor follows me everywhere I go. (Psalm 8:5)
20. I am an heir of God and a joint-heir with Christ. I inherit the promises of God in abundance. (Romans 8:17)
21. The blessings of the Lord overtake me and I live in the overflow of His goodness and mercy. (Deuteronomy 28:2)
22. I decree that everything my hands touch prospers and I walk in the prosperity of the Lord. (Psalm 1:3)
23. I declare that supernatural debt cancellation and financial freedom are manifesting in my life. (Proverbs 22:7)
24. My savings, retirement, and investment accounts are filled with plenty, and my bank accounts are overflowing with new money. (Proverbs 3:10)
25. I declare that the windows of heaven are open over my life, and blessings are pouring out abundantly. (Malachi 3:10)
26. I decree that healing and restoration are mine and I walk in divine health and wholeness. (Jeremiah 30:17)
27. I declare that I am more than a conqueror through Christ who loves me. (Romans 8:37)
28. I speak that wisdom, knowledge, and understanding flow freely in my life, and I make decisions aligned with God's will. (Proverbs 2:6)
29. I declare that the Lord fights my battles, and every enemy is defeated before me. (Exodus 14:14)
30. I decree that this is my season of supernatural breakthroughs, overflow, and divine acceleration. (Amos 9:13)

Blessings and God's Promises Over Our Bloodline & Seed

Heavenly Father, I humbly come before You, entering into Your presence with thanksgiving and praise. I lift up my bloodline and seed before You today, declaring that I am your covenant child who stands under the banner of Your promises. In the name of Jesus, I decree that my family walks in the fullness of Your blessing, favor, and divine purpose.

- **My seed is mighty in the land** (Psalm 112:2). I declare that every child, grandchild, and descendant is a shining light in this world, equipped and anointed to fulfill their God-given purpose. They will walk in power, authority, and influence for Your glory.
- **My bloodline is marked by righteousness and favor.** I proclaim that holiness and purity are our portion. Every generational curse is broken, and only generational blessings flow through our lineage. The favor of God surrounds us like a shield, and His glory is our rear guard.
- **I declare abundant provision** (Philippians 4:19). I decree that every need is met in abundance. Our family prospers in health, finances, relationships, and faith. We are lenders and not borrowers, above only and never beneath.
- **My family walks in divine health and strength.** I declare that every sickness, disease, and infirmity is rebuked in the name of Jesus. From the youngest to the oldest in our bloodline, I declare wholeness, vitality, and longevity.
- **My children are taught of the Lord** (Isaiah 54:13). I decree that my children walk in peace and wisdom. They are covered by Your Word and they grow in understanding, discernment, and the knowledge of God.
- **My family is blessed and highly favored** (Deuteronomy 28:3-6). I declare that Your blessings chase us down and overtake us in every area of lives.
- **My family leaves a legacy of faith** (Proverbs 13:22). I proclaim that we are building a godly legacy for future generations. Our

- lives, words, and deeds sow seeds of faith, hope, and love that will bear fruit for eternity.
- **We are established as a light to the nations.** I decree that our family rises in influence, shining brightly for Jesus. We are ambassadors of Christ, bringing His love, truth, and salvation to the world.
- **My lineage walks in unity and love.** I rebuke division, strife, and discord in Jesus' name. I release the love of Christ to flow freely, uniting our family in purpose and harmony.
- **My family fulfills God's divine purpose.** I declare that every member of our bloodline walks boldly in their calling, guided by the Holy Spirit. Every gift, talent, and resource are used to glorify You and advance Your Kingdom.

Father, I ask You to pour out Your Spirit upon our bloodline. Let every seed that comes from us be mighty in the land, carrying Your Word, walking in Your ways, and living in Your power. I declare divine favor over every child, grandchild, and descendant. They are the head and not the tail, above and not beneath.

I call forth blessings over my family, spiritually, physically, and financially. I speak life over every marriage, every relationship, and every generation. Lord, protect and preserve my family from every plan of the enemy. Surround us with Your angels, guard us with Your peace, and fill our hearts with Your joy.

I declare that every promise in Your Word is yes and amen for my family. Let the power of the blood of Jesus seal our lineage in righteousness, peace, and joy. Let my family be a living testimony of Your goodness and faithfulness.

I proclaim that my bloodline will never lack. The windows of heaven are open over us and we walk in the overflow of Your provision and grace. Thank You, Lord, for making us a family rooted and grounded in Your love.

I decree and declare that this prayer is established in Heaven and manifests on earth. I believe I receive it and release most holy faith to bring it to pass. In Jesus' mighty name I pray, Amen!

Prayer for Manifestation of Miracles, Signs, and Wonders

Heavenly Father, I come boldly before Your throne, lifting my heart in faith and expectation. Lord, You are the God of miracles, the One who spoke creation into existence, who parted the Red Sea, and who raised the dead to life. Today, I stand on Your promises, believing for miracles, signs, and wonders to manifest in my life, my home, and my community.

Your Word declares in Mark 16:17-18 that miraculous signs will follow those who believe. I declare today, I am a believer. I believe in Your power, authority, and ability to do the impossible. Let the sick be healed, the oppressed be set free, and the broken be restored by the power of Your name.

Holy Spirit, I invite You to move mightily in my midst. Stretch out Your hand, as declared in Acts 4:30, and let signs and wonders be done in the mighty name of Jesus. Break every chain, heal every sickness, and deliver every captive around me.

Lord, I reject every spirit of doubt, fear, and unbelief. I declare Matthew 19:26 over my life: *"With God, all things are possible."* I refuse to limit You with small thinking or weak faith. I choose to believe in Your limitless power and Your supernatural ability.

Let this be a season where I see miracles manifest daily. Heal the sick in my circle, restore broken relationships around me, provide supernatural resources, and break the chains of addiction, heaviness, and bondage.

I stand on the promise of John 14:12 that because I believe in you, I will do even greater works. Lord, empower me to be a vessel of Your miraculous power. Use my hands to heal, my mouth to speak life, and my heart to carry the fire of revival. Let dead places come alive again through the anointing on my life. Let barren places be revived to bring forth life.

Let Your presence fall so powerfully in my life that it becomes undeniable. Let those around me who doubt or don't believe, witness Your glory and come running to you. Let testimonies rise from my life, stories of impossible situations turned around, bodies healed, and lives transformed by Your power.

Lord, I declare revival fire is falling on me now, stirring my heart with passion, boldness, and unwavering faith. I speak supernatural provision, divine encounters, and open doors in the name of Jesus.

I align myself with Your will, believing that every promise in Your Word is *Yes and Amen*. I speak faith into the atmosphere and declare that I will see the manifestation of Your power in my life. I believe I receive this prayer, and I release my most holy faith to bring it to pass.

In the mighty and matchless name of Jesus, I pray, Amen and Amen!

Chapter 9 - Prayer for Revival & Fresh Outpouring

Revival & Fresh Outpouring

There is a cry rising in the earth for revival. A hunger is stirring in the hearts of God's people to see His glory manifest again, in our churches, homes, cities, and nations. True revival is more than just a series of church services or an emotional experience. Revival is the supernatural invasion of Heaven on earth, where hearts are set ablaze, sin is forsaken, lives are transformed, and the power of God is revealed in undeniable ways.

This chapter is a call to rekindle the fire of God on the inside of you. If you've ever felt dry, weary, or far from the presence of God, these prayers will reignite your pursuit and fan the flame again. It's time for a fresh outpouring. Time to ask God to breathe on us again.

Acts 2:17 (KJV) says, " And it shall come to pass in the last days, saith God, I will pour out of my Spirit upon all flesh: and your sons and your daughters shall prophesy, and your young men shall see visions, and your old men shall dream dreams." That promise is still active. We are in the last days, and the Spirit is still pouring. But we must posture ourselves hungry, yielded, surrendered, and in expectation.

Jesus is looking for those who will carry the fire. He's seeking a people who want more than surface-level Christianity. A people who desires to be baptized in the Holy Ghost and fire. A people who will contend until revival comes to their homes, their churches, their schools, their workplaces, and every place their feet tread.

These prayers are meant to draw you into deeper intimacy with God. Let your heart cry be, "Lord, do it in me first." Let every prayer in this section be a personal plea for transformation before it becomes a corporate cry. Revival begins in the secret place. Revival begins with each of us personally. It spreads from the altar of a burning heart.

Whether you've been walking with God for decades or you're seeking Him for the first time, may these words awaken your spirit, renew your fire, and release a fresh wind that causes you to live fully yielded, fully anointed, and fully alive in Him.

Father, let revival start in us. Let our lives be the evidence that You are still moving, still healing, still delivering, still baptizing, and still pouring out Your Spirit. We won't settle for a form of godliness without power. We are a generation that hungers for the real. Let revival come!

Baptized in the Holy Spirit and Fire

Heavenly Father, I come boldly before Your throne of grace, covered by the blood of Jesus and standing in the power of His name. I thank You for the precious gift of the Holy Spirit. Today, I posture my heart with expectancy, ready to receive a fresh baptism of the Holy Ghost and fire, just as You promised (Matthew 3:11).

Lord, I am hungry for your fire. Let it fall on me now. Let it burn away everything in my life that doesn't reflect You. Let it burn away fear, doubt, complacency, and heaviness. Set my heart ablaze for Your glory (Hebrews 12:29).

I lift my hands in surrender, asking You to ignite a fresh flame within me. Let the fire of Your Spirit purify me, empower me, and propel me into purpose. Stir up the fire within me until it burns bright with holy passion for you. (2 Timothy 1:6).

You said I would receive power when the Holy Ghost comes upon me, so today, I fully submit myself to you and ask that I receive the indwelling of the Holy Spirit. I receive power to be Your witness, to live holy, to pray boldly, to walk in authority, and to speak life with conviction (Acts 1:8).

Just as You did on the day of Pentecost, fill me to overflowing. Let Your presence rest upon me like tongues of fire. Let fresh utterance flow from my spirit as I speak what You give me (Acts 2:3–4).

I declare that I do not walk according to the flesh, but I live and move by the Spirit. Let the Spirit guide my decisions, my desires, and my direction (Galatians 5:16, Romans 8:14).

Holy Spirit, saturate every part of my being, my thoughts, emotions, will, and body. Let the fire of God touch every area of my life, my home, my family, my business, my calling, and my ministry (1 Thessalonians 5:23).

Let revival begin in me. Let the Holy Spirit overflow in power and boldness. Let everything around me be transformed by the fire You've placed within (Acts 4:31).

Father, I believe I receive a fresh baptism of the Holy Spirit and fire, and I release my most holy faith to bring it to pass (Mark 11:24, Jude 1:20).

In Jesus' mighty name, Amen and Amen!

Dead to Sin, Alive to God

Father, in the name of Jesus, I come boldly to Your throne declaring today that I am no longer who I used to be. Thank You for the finished work of the cross that didn't just cover my sin, but killed the power of it over my life. Because I died with Christ, I now live with Him, and I declare that sin no longer has dominion over me.

Lord, I declare that I am dead to sin, dead to shame, dead to cycles, and dead to compromise. The old me has been buried, and a new creation has risen. I no longer respond to the voice of the flesh, I respond to the voice of my Father. I no longer follow old patterns, I follow the leading of Your Spirit.

Let the same resurrection power that raised Jesus from the grave be stirred in me today. Let me walk in newness of life, boldness of spirit, and purity of heart. I don't serve sin anymore, I serve righteousness. I don't yield to the flesh, I yield to grace, to truth, and to the Spirit of the Living God.

Father, I throw myself wholeheartedly and full-time into Your will. I will not run errands for the old life. I will not play with what You've called me to crucify. Today, I take my position as one who is alive in You, set apart, made new, and empowered to walk holy.

Let revival begin in my heart again. Stir up a fresh hatred for sin and a burning love for truth. I don't live halfway. I live fully surrendered. I believe I receive this prayer, and I release my most holy faith to bring it to pass.

In the mighty name of Jesus, Amen and Amen!

Hunger and Thirst for God's Word, Prayer, Worship, and Praise

Heavenly Father, I come before You today with my heart wide open, declaring that You alone are the source of my satisfaction. Just as the deer pants for streams of water, so my soul longs for You. Let that longing be ignited deep within me, a holy hunger and an unquenchable thirst for Your Word, Your presence, and Your voice.

Lord, I hunger for Your Word. Let it be my daily bread, nourishing my spirit, soul, and body. Teach me to love Your Word, to meditate on it day and night, and to let it guide every step I take. I desire that it be the lamp to my feet and the light to my path.

Father, I thirst for moments in Your presence through prayer. Stir within me a passion for deep and intimate communion with You. Let prayer become my lifeline, not just an activity, but a sacred encounter where my heart connects with Yours. You are my hiding place and I long to dwell with You.

Holy Spirit, awaken in me a lifestyle of true worship. Let my worship go beyond the songs I sing and become a surrendered posture of my heart. Teach me to worship in spirit and in truth. Let my life reflect a heart bowed in reverence and awe before You.

Lord, I declare that praise will always be on my lips. In every season, whether in abundance or in lack, I will bless Your name. You invite me to come when I'm thirsty, and I know You alone can satisfy the deepest places in me. Let Your living water overflow and meet every longing of my heart.

Fill me, Lord, with all that You have for me. Pour into every dry place, every weary soul within me, every broken or lonely area. Overflow in me until I become a vessel of Your love, grace, and glory to everyone around me.

Today, I lay down distractions, idols, and anything that tries to compete with my desire for You. I choose You first. I seek You above all else. You are my portion, my pursuit, and my joy.

I believe I receive this prayer, and I release my most holy faith to bring it to pass. In the mighty and matchless name of Jesus Christ, I pray, Amen and Amen!

More Like Jesus

Heavenly Father, In the name of Jesus, I thank You for Your grace, the kind that doesn't just cover me but transforms me. I don't want to just say I know You, I want to reflect Your Character in my life. I want to walk like Jesus, talk like Jesus, and respond like Jesus in every situation.

Father, let Your grace do the deep work in me. Shape my heart, refine my character, and strip away anything that doesn't look like Christ. I yield to the process. Make me a vessel that carries Your nature, full of truth, love, boldness, and compassion.

Lord, even in my weakness, Your grace is working. I declare that I'm not striving to be perfect, I'm surrendering to be transformed. Day by day, You are changing me from the inside out. You are the potter and I am the clay. Father mold me into a vessel fit for your use. Let my posture be humble before you. Let my decisions reflect that I have been with You.

Holy Spirit, help me not to resist You. When You speak, I'll follow. When You convict, I'll respond. When You lead, I won't hesitate, I will follow. I trust that You are working in me both to will and to do according to Your good pleasure.

I declare by faith that I am becoming more like Jesus. Not by might, not by power, but by Your Spirit. I receive Your grace for today, grace to walk upright, grace to grow, and grace to become all that you have called me to.

I believe I receive this prayer, and I release my most holy faith to bring it to pass. In the mighty name of Jesus, I pray, Amen.

Prayer for Revival

Heavenly Father, I come boldly before Your throne of grace, crying out for revival. You said that if Your people humble themselves, pray, seek Your face, and turn from their wicked ways, You would hear from heaven, forgive their sins, and heal their land. So today, I humble myself before You, Lord, and I cry out for a mighty move of Your Spirit in my life and in the earth.

Father, I ask for revival to begin in my own heart. Set a fresh fire in me. Let every area that has grown cold or numb be reignited with passion for You. Remove every form of complacency, every distraction, and everything that has dulled my pursuit of You. Let nothing stand in the way of my hunger for Your presence.

Revive Your Church through me, Lord. Awaken every believer, every pastor, every leader and let it begin with me. Let Your Church rise in boldness, holiness, and unity. Let our gatherings be filled with Your glory. Let Your Word go forth with fire. Let souls come running to You in great numbers because the truth is being preached and lived out with power.

Father, I pray for revival in families beginning with my own. Heal what's been broken, restore what's been lost, and bring unity where there's been division. Turn the hearts of fathers to their children and children to their parents. Let Your love reign in every household.

Holy Spirit, move in my community. Let Your presence flood homes, schools, workplaces, and every public place. Break every stronghold of addiction, violence, oppression, and darkness. Release peace, love, healing, and righteousness everywhere my feet tread.

Lord, I cry out for revival across the nations. Let Your glory cover the earth as the waters cover the sea. Raise up voices, laborers, and messengers, including me, who will boldly proclaim the Gospel to every tribe, tongue, and people. Let miracles, signs, and wonders follow as Your Word is released.

You said in times of need, You would revive Your works. Do it again, Lord. Pour out Your Spirit just as You promised. Let dreams be awakened, visions be released, and prophetic voices rise with clarity and accuracy. Breathe on this generation. Let the fire of revival sweep across the land.

I repent for anything in me that has grieved You. I turn my heart fully back to You. Let times of refreshing flow from Your presence. Revive me again, O Lord.

I declare that revival is here. It is rising in me. Dry bones are coming alive. Weary souls are being renewed. Broken hearts are being restored. The harvest is ripe and I thank You for the wave of souls that will come into the Kingdom through this outpouring.

Holy Spirit, have Your way in me. Move freely. Speak loudly. Reign supremely in my heart, in my home, and in my nation. I believe I receive this prayer, and I release my most holy faith to bring it to pass.

In the mighty and matchless name of Jesus, I pray. Amen and Amen.

Prayer for Revival 2

Heavenly Father, in the mighty name of Jesus, we come boldly before Your throne, lifting up a cry for revival in our homes, our communities, our churches, and across this nation. Lord, You are the God of revival, and we declare that Your Spirit is moving mightily in this hour. We thank You that Your Word says You will pour out Your Spirit upon all flesh, that sons and daughters will prophesy, young men will see visions, and old men will dream dreams (Joel 2:28). Father, we stand on this promise, declaring that the time for revival is now!

Lord, we decree and declare that the fire of the Holy Ghost is being ignited in the hearts of Your people. We call forth a fresh outpouring of Your Spirit, a shaking that will awaken the Church and turn the hearts of the lost back to You. Let the dry bones come alive, Lord! Breathe new life into every weary and stagnant soul, reviving passion for Your presence and a hunger for Your Word (Ezekiel 37:4-6).

Father, we intercede for revival fire to sweep through our churches, transforming them into places of power, prayer, and miracles. Let Your glory rest upon every sanctuary, home, and gathering place where Your name is lifted high. We declare that strongholds are being broken, chains are falling, and lives are being transformed as Your Spirit moves (2 Corinthians 3:17). Lord, let Your people rise up in boldness and unity, proclaiming Your truth without compromise.

We speak revival into the nations! We call forth the awakening of entire cities and regions as Your power and presence invade. Father, we ask that You open the heavens and release a fresh outpouring of Your Spirit. Let salvation break forth like the dawn, and righteousness flow like a mighty river (Isaiah 58:8; Amos 5:24). We decree that multitudes are coming into the Kingdom, and the harvest is being gathered as Your Spirit draws them.

Holy Spirit, stir the hearts of leaders, intercessors, and every believer to step into their divine assignments. Raise up a generation of fire carriers who will not be silent, who will not back down, but who will proclaim Your Word with boldness and power. Let signs, wonders, and miracles follow the preaching of Your gospel, confirming Your Word and glorifying Your name (Mark 16:17-18).

Lord, we repent for anything that has hindered Your move in our midst. We humble ourselves before You, seeking Your face, turning from our wicked ways, and declaring that You will hear from heaven, forgive our sins, and heal our land (2 Chronicles 7:14). Let the purifying fire of revival cleanse Your Church, renewing our hearts and aligning us with Your perfect will.

We bind every work of the enemy that seeks to delay or disrupt revival. We take authority over apathy, division, and unbelief, and we declare that these things have no place in the Body of Christ. Instead, we release the Spirit of unity, faith, and expectancy for the mighty move of God (Matthew 18:18; Psalm 133:1-3).

Father, let revival begin with us! Set our hearts ablaze with love for You and compassion for the lost. Let our lives be living sacrifices, holy and pleasing to You (Romans 12:1). We declare that this is the season of revival, the time of Your visitation. Lord, have Your way! Do what only You can do. Shake the heavens and the earth with Your glory, and let Your name be exalted in all the earth (Haggai 2:6-7).

We believe we receive this prayer, and we release our most holy faith to bring it to pass. We seal it in the mighty, matchless name of Jesus Christ, and we declare that revival is here! Amen and Amen!

Preparing Hearts for a Fresh Outpouring

Heavenly Father, I come before You with a humble heart, fully aware of how much I need Your presence. Thank You for Your promise that You will pour out Your Spirit on all people. Today, I align my heart and position myself to receive a fresh outpouring of Your glory.

Father, I ask You to cleanse my heart just as David cried out for a clean heart and a steadfast spirit. Remove anything in me that hinders Your move, every distraction, every sin, every trace of pride or rebellion. Purify me, Lord, and renew a right spirit within me.

You promised to take away my stony, stubborn heart and give me a tender, responsive one. So today, I surrender completely to Your refining work. Make me receptive to Your voice, to Your leading, and to the flow of Your Spirit.

Holy Spirit, come and have Your way in me. Ignite a fresh hunger and a deep thirst for righteousness. I don't want surface-level encounters, I want the depths of You. Let every part of me long for what pleases You.

I declare in faith that every hindrance, every chain, and every stronghold that would block the flow of Your Spirit is broken off my mind, heart and desires in the name of Jesus. I rebuke the spirit of complacency. I stir up my heart to be alert and ready for revival fire.

Lord, I lift up every home, every family, every church, and every city connected to this journey of consecration. Prepare our hearts for a mighty move of Your Spirit. Let repentance fall like rain. Let worship rise like incense before Your throne. Let faith be stirred for supernatural encounters that shift atmospheres.

Father, I declare that I receive power when the Holy Spirit comes upon me. Let boldness rise in me. Let authority flow through me. Let unwavering faith take root in me. Use me as a vessel of Your glory. I carry revival fire wherever I go.

I declare that this outpouring will not be confined to church walls. It will overflow into my home, my workplace, and my community. It will bring healing to the brokenhearted, deliverance to the bound, and draw the lost to the feet of Jesus and ultimately to the Most High.

I refuse to settle for anything less than Your fullness, O' God. I will not be passive. I will not miss this moment. I am ready, expecting, and fully positioned for a supernatural encounter with You.

Father, let Your glory fall fresh upon us. Let Your Spirit move on our hearts. Let Your name be exalted in my life. I believe I receive this prayer, and I release my most holy faith to bring it to pass. In the mighty and matchless name of Jesus, I pray. Amen and Amen!

Graced to Win through the Leadership of the Holy Spirit

Father, in the mighty name of Jesus, I come before You with humility, gratitude, and great expectation, declaring that I am graced to win because of Your precious Spirit! Thank You for the Holy Spirit, my divine Counselor, Helper, and Guide. Holy Spirit, I acknowledge that true victory is found in surrendering to Your leadership and walking in step with Your perfect will.

Lord, I decree and declare that I will not be led by fear, emotions, or the pressures of this world. I am led by the Spirit of the Living God! Every decision I make is aligned with Your wisdom, every step I take is ordered by Your hand, and every battle I face has already been won through Jesus Christ! I do not lean on my own understanding. In all my ways, I acknowledge You, and You are making my path plain and straight before me.

By the power of the Holy Spirit, I walk in wisdom, strategy, and divine insight. No weapon formed against me shall prosper, because I am moving in divine alignment with Your will! Every obstacle is becoming a steppingstone and every challenge is an opportunity for supernatural victory. The Spirit of God goes before me, making the crooked places straight and opening doors that no man can shut!

I pull down every stronghold of confusion, hesitation, and doubt! I silence the voice of the enemy and tune my ears to the voice of the Holy Spirit. I declare that I have clarity, boldness, and supernatural confidence. The same power that raised Christ Jesus from the dead is at work in me, empowering me to overcome, persevere, and walk in dominion.

Father, I thank You that as I follow the leadership of the Holy Spirit, I will not be delayed, I will not be denied, and I will not be defeated! I am winning in my faith, in my family, in my assignments, and in my purpose because I walk by the Spirit and not by the flesh!

I seal this prayer by faith, declaring: "I believe I receive this prayer and release my most holy faith to bring it to pass!" In the mighty and matchless name of Jesus, AMEN!

Revival Fire in Our Lives, Churches, and Communities

Heavenly Father, I come before You with a humble and expectant heart, crying out for a fresh outpouring of revival fire in my life, church, and community. Lord, I have heard of Your mighty works, and I stand in awe of Your power. Today, I ask You to do it again in our generation, as You promised in Habakkuk 3:2.

Father, I repent for any apathy, complacency, or distractions that have kept me from fully pursuing You. According to 2 Chronicles 7:14, I humble myself, pray, and seek Your face. Heal our heart, heal our land, and let Your glory fall afresh upon us.

Lord, ignite our hearts with a holy passion for Your presence. Remove every barrier, every chain, and every hindrance that keeps us from walking in intimacy with You. Fill us with boldness to proclaim the gospel, courage to stand for truth, and compassion to love others unconditionally.

Holy Spirit, let times of refreshing come, as promised in Acts 3:19. Breathe fresh wind into weary souls. Pour out Your Spirit in homes, churches, workplaces, and communities. Father, let dry bones come to life, and let every dead place that should be awakened be revived by Your power.

Father, I cry out like the psalmist in Psalm 85:6, "Won't You revive us again, so Your people can rejoice in You?" Stir our hearts to worship You with passion, to pray without ceasing, and to seek Your face daily.

Father, in the name of Jesus, I cry out for more of You. Rend the heavens, Lord, and come down! Let Your glory fill this place. Let Your presence break through every barrier and saturate this atmosphere. I'm not satisfied with ordinary. I want a divine encounter. Let Your power fall, let Your fire burn, and let every heart be awakened to the weight of Your glory. Come like only You can, and move among us, Lord. We welcome You. We honor You. We need You, as in Isaiah 64:1. Let Your presence shake the foundations of our lives, our churches, and our cities. Break every stronghold, uproot every spirit of division, and let unity and love flow freely among Your people.

Father, I pray for pastors, leaders, and spiritual shepherds. Anoint them with fresh oil, give them divine wisdom, and empower them to lead with boldness and humility. Let pulpits across the world burn with the fire of Your Word and the fire of the Holy Ghost.

Lord, I intercede for entire communities and cities. May revival spread like wildfire, transforming churches, homes, schools, businesses, and government offices. Let every street, every home, and every heart become an altar for Your glory. I declare that this is the season of revival! I believe that families will be restored, prodigals will return home, marriages will be healed, and communities will witness Your glory in unprecedented ways.

Father, I refuse to settle for surface-level encounters. I am hungry for more of You. Fill me, saturate me, and overflow through me. I commit to being a carrier of revival fire, spreading Your love and power wherever we go.

Lord, let this revival bring lasting transformation, generational blessings, and eternal impact. I believe I receive this prayer, and I release our most holy faith to bring it to pass. In the mighty and matchless name of Jesus, I pray. Amen and Amen!

Chapter 10 – Prayers for Specific Areas and Situations

Prayers for Specific Areas and Situations

There are moments when prayer must be laser-focused, intentionally targeting specific areas that touch every part of our lives and the world around us. These prayers are designed to align our hearts with Heaven's agenda concerning our families, communities, governments, education systems, and more.

As believers walking in Kingdom authority, we cannot be passive or silent about the state of the world. God is calling intercessors to rise up with holy boldness, to speak what Heaven is saying, and to shift the atmosphere through prayer. When we intercede for the lost, the hurting, the oppressed, or those in positions of leadership, we stand in the gap as vessels of divine justice, peace, healing, and truth.

This chapter is about discerning the burden of the Lord and responding with prophetic precision. Whether you are praying over your school district, interceding for government leaders, crying out for the salvation of a loved one, or covering the seven mountains of influence, these prayers are assignments. They are Kingdom business.

Let's posture our hearts to hear the voice of the Lord clearly, and let's release the kind of prayers that shake nations, transform households, and usher in revival across every sector of society. You have been placed in this generation for such a time as this. Your prayers matter. Child of God, your voice carries weight and glory. Heaven is listening.

Get ready to pray with authority, compassion, and purpose, covering specific areas that impact generations, regions, and destinies.

Anoint Yourself

Anoint Your Head
I anoint my head in the name of the Father, Son Jesus Christ, and the Holy Spirit. I put on Christ and I have the mind of Christ. I hold the thoughts, feeling and purposes of his heart and mind. Holy Spirit think through my thoughts and illuminate my mind. Align my thoughts with your will.

Anoint Your Ears
I anoint my ears in the name of the Father, Son Jesus Christ, and the Holy Spirit. My ears are anointed to hear with prophetic accuracy on the heavenly frequency. I hear my Heavenly Father's voice, the voice of my Lord and Savior Jesus Christ, the voice of the Holy Spirit and angels of God that were sent to minister to me. I follow the leadership of the Holy Spirit in all that I do. As Jesus said, My sheep hear my voice and the voice of a stranger, they will not follow. I am his sheep; therefore, I hear his voice clearly.

Anoint Your Eyes
I anoint my eyes in the name of the Father, Son Jesus Christ, and the Holy Spirit. My eyes are anointed to see with the seers anointing. I see things accurately and I'm always able to see into the realm of the spirit. Therefore, I am able to discern the times and seasons. I am able discern between good and evil.

Anointed Your Mouth
I anoint my mouth in the name of the Father, Son Jesus Christ, and the Holy Spirit. My mouth is anointed to speak with prophetic accuracy. My words are like the pen of a ready writer. My words feed many and my thoughts are right. My words edify and build others up. I speak out of the abundance of my heart and my heart is full of faith and the word of God. My words bring life, my words produce blessings, prosperity, and abundance. My words bring healing. My words are seeds and produce a peaceable harvest that will remain.

Anoint Your Hands
I anoint my hands in the name of the Father, Son Jesus Christ, and the Holy Spirit. My hands are blessed and empowered to prosper. Everything I touch is successful, profitable, increasing, and abounding. My hands are anointed to heal the sick.

Anoint Your Feet
I anoint my feet in the name of the Father, Son Jesus Christ, and the Holy Spirit. My feet are covered under the promise of Joshua chapter 1. As God was with Moses and Joshua, so shall He be with me. My steps are ordered by the Lord. I am always in the right place, at the right time. Wherever I go, God's angels are with me and they work for me. God's mercy and goodness follows me all the days of my life.

Salvation of the Lost

Heavenly Father, I come boldly before Your throne today, interceding for the salvation of the lost. You said in Your Word that You desire no one to perish but for all to come to repentance. Lord, I cry out for souls today! Soften their hearts, Lord. Remove the stony, stubborn hearts and replace them with tender, responsive hearts that are open to Your truth. Let every wall of pride, doubt, and unbelief crumble, in the name of Jesus. Father, remove the spiritual blinders from their eyes so they can see the glorious light of the Gospel. Silence every distracting voice and let them hear Your voice calling them home.

I declare that the lost will have ears to hear Your voice and courage to respond to Your call. Holy Spirit, draw them with cords of love. Bring them to the feet of Jesus, where salvation, grace, and mercy flow. Lord, anoint us to boldly and effectively share the Gospel of Jesus Christ with those You place in our path. Let our words be seasoned with grace, filled with truth, and spoken in love. Give us divine opportunities, open doors, and prepare hearts to receive the message of salvation.

I declare that some will plant, others will water, but You, O God, will give the increase. I trust You to cause every seed of the Gospel to grow, flourish, and bear fruit for Your Kingdom. Father, I ask for divine encounters, dreams, visions, and timely conversations that will lead the lost to accept Jesus as their Lord and Savior. Let the love of Christ flood their hearts and break every chain of darkness. Send forth anointed laborers across their path to minister the gospel in a way that they will receive and I thank you in advance for the testimony of their names being written in the lamb's book of life.

Lord, I declare over every prodigal son and daughter, RETURN HOME in the name of Jesus! I call them back from the north, south, east and west, into the loving arms of the Father. I declare that they are free from any chains of lies and deception. I release my faith today that they are FREE NOW. They are on FIRE for JESUS! I speak revival over homes, families, communities, and nations. Let the fire of salvation spread like wildfire, and may multitudes come running to You.

I declare by faith, salvation is here NOW! This is our season to see hearts turned back to God. Lives are being transformed, and souls are being won for the Kingdom of God. Father, draw the multitude to you now. Draw them by Your Spirit. In the mighty and matchless name of Jesus, I pray. Amen and Amen! I believe I receive this prayer and release most holy faith to bring it to pass.

The 7 Mountains of Influence

Father, in the name of Jesus, I come humbly before Your throne of grace. I thank You that You have given us authority to advance the Kingdom and declare Your will in the earth. Today, I lift up the seven mountains of influence and I declare Your righteousness, Your wisdom, and Your presence over every sphere of society.

I decree Your Kingdom come and Your will be done in every mountain, just as it is in heaven. I plead the blood of Jesus over these mountains and release heavenly angels to guard, protect, and carry out Your assignments.

I lift up the mountain of Family. Lord, restore the foundation of the family. Heal marriages. Strengthen parents. Protect children. Let love, unity, and honor reign in households. I bind division, generational curses, abuse, and abandonment. I declare families will rise as strong, spirit-filled units that represent Your heart in the earth.

I cover the mountain of Religion. Raise up leaders who rightly divide the Word of Truth, who walk in power, holiness, and compassion. Purify Your Church. Expose deception and compromise. Let revival sweep through pulpits and pews. Reignite the fire of the Holy Ghost and let Your Word go forth with boldness and authority.

I speak over the mountain of Education. I declare that truth will prevail in classrooms and campuses. Raise up godly teachers, administrators, and students who will carry Your presence into every school. Expose ungodly agendas and protect the minds of our children. Let wisdom, creativity, and integrity flood our educational systems.

I intercede for the mountain of Government. Father, raise up righteous leaders who fear the Lord and walk in integrity. Remove those who oppose Your will and promote unrighteousness. I declare justice, truth, and righteousness will rule in our land. Let every law and policy align with Your Word. Turn the hearts of our leaders back to You.

I pray over the mountain of Media. Let truth and light break through the lies and darkness. We cancel the agenda of fear, confusion, and deception. Raise up voices that speak life, bring clarity, and reveal Your truth to the masses. Anoint Kingdom-minded media influencers, journalists, and creators for such a time as this.

I cover the mountain of Arts and Entertainment. Lord, purify this space. Raise up creative voices, musicians, writers, and artists who glorify You. Tear down idols and break the influence of perversion, violence, and rebellion. Let a sound from heaven rise in this generation that stirs hearts to repentance and worship.

I declare over the mountain of Business and Economy. Release Kingdom wealth strategies and bless the hands of Your people. Raise up entrepreneurs and executives who honor You with their resources and steward wealth for Kingdom advancement. Shift the economy to work in the favor of your people. Cancel debt and break cycles of poverty. Let favor, increase, and innovation be upon the righteous. Raise up leaders that are anointed to set captives free from poverty, lack and shortage.

Father, I thank You that You are releasing Josephs, Esthers, Daniels, and Deborahs in every mountain — leaders with wisdom, integrity, and divine influence. Let the Church rise up and take her place. Let revival shake every sector of the marketplace, government and ministry. Let the kingdoms of this world become the Kingdom of our God. In the mighty name of Jesus, I pray.

I believe I receive this prayer, and I release our most holy faith to bring it to pass.

The Educational System – Teachers, Administrators, and Students

Heavenly Father, I come boldly before Your throne of grace, lifting up every teacher, administrator, student, and educational institution into Your loving care. You are the source of all wisdom, knowledge, and understanding. Your Word declares in James 1:5 that if anyone lacks wisdom, they can ask You, and You will give it generously. Today, Lord, I ask for an outpouring of divine wisdom upon our educators and students.

Father, I plead the blood of Jesus over every school campus, classroom, and administrative office. Let the blood of Jesus be a shield against every threat, danger, or act of violence. Cancel every plot, plan, and scheme of the enemy designed to bring hurt, harm, fear, or confusion.

I declare Psalm 91:11 over every school, "For He will order His angels to protect you wherever you go." Lord, dispatch Your angels to guard every entryway, every hallway, and every corner of these campuses. Let Your divine protection cover every student, teacher, and staff member.

Father, I lift up teachers before You. Strengthen them physically, emotionally, and spiritually. Give them patience, creativity, and endurance to fulfill their assignments with excellence. Let their classrooms be filled with an atmosphere of peace, learning, and encouragement.

Lord, guard their hearts against discouragement, burnout, and stress. Fill them with fresh passion and purpose every day. Let them see the eternal impact of their labor, knowing that their work is not in vain.

I pray for administrators and school leaders. Father, grant them clarity, wisdom, and courage to make decisions that honor You and benefit the students and staff they serve. Let integrity and righteousness guide their leadership. May their lives be led by you. Father, lead them by your Spirit. Raise up Godly teachers and administrators and plant them in school systems around the world. Let your will be done in our school systems as it is in heaven.

Lord, I lift up students before You. Cover their minds with the blood of Jesus. Guard their hearts from fear, anxiety, and distractions. Grant them focus, discipline, and understanding as they pursue academic success. They will excel in the classroom and in their extracurricular activities.

Let every student know that they are valued, loved, and created for a divine purpose. Break every cycle of low self-worth, failure, and shame. Replace it with confidence, courage, and a hunger for knowledge and growth.

Father, I rebuke every spirit of confusion, peer pressure, bullying, and fear in our schools. I declare that no weapon formed against our students will prosper (Isaiah 54:17). I bind every evil and wicked plan and scheme trying to discourage our children. I declare that the angels are watching over your word to perform it in their lives. Hallelujah.

Lord, let Your presence saturate every campus. Let prayer rise in classrooms and hallways. Raise up students and staff who will boldly carry the light of Christ into their schools. I intercede for parents as they guide and support their children. Give them wisdom, patience, and strength to nurture their children's education and spiritual growth.

Father, I also pray for emotional healing for students and staff who have been affected by trauma, loss, or mental health struggles. You are the God who heals the brokenhearted and binds up their wounds (Psalm 147:3).

Lord, I pray for divine provision for every school. Meet their financial and resource needs. Equip every classroom with the tools necessary for effective teaching and learning.

Father, I ask that the Holy Spirit moves through schools, bringing transformation, revival, and awakening hearts and minds to the power of God. Let students and teachers experience Your love and truth in powerful ways. I declare Isaiah 54:13 over our students, "All your children shall be taught by the Lord, and great shall be the peace of your children."

Lord, I thank You for the testimonies that will come from our schools; testimonies of academic excellence, lives changed, and campuses transformed by Your power. I believe I receive this prayer, and I release our most holy faith to bring it to pass. In the mighty and matchless name of Jesus, I pray. Amen and Amen!

Prayer for Godly Leadership in Government and Authority

Heavenly Father, I come before Your throne of grace today, lifting up leaders in government, authority, and decision-making roles across our cities, states, nations, and the world. You are El Elyon, Most High and Jesus Christ is the King of kings and the Lord of lords, and all authority comes from You.

Father, Your Word in Proverbs 21:1 declares that the king's heart is in Your hands, and You guide it like a stream of water. Today, I ask You to guide the hearts of every leader, policymaker, and influencer according to Your will and purpose.

Lord, I lift up our national leaders, our state leaders, our local officials, and every individual who holds a position of authority. Fill them with divine wisdom, discernment, and integrity. Let them not be swayed by personal ambition, corruption, or greed.

Father, I declare 1 Timothy 2:1-2 over our leadership: "I pray for all those in authority so that we may live peaceful and quiet lives marked by godliness and dignity." Lord, let peace, justice, and righteousness flow through every governing body.

I bind every spirit of confusion, division, and manipulation operating in our leadership. I silence every voice of deception and command divine truth to prevail in boardrooms, council meetings, and legislative chambers.

Lord, I pray for godly counsel to surround leaders at every level. Raise up Josephs, Daniels and Esthers in every government, men and women who will stand boldly for truth and righteousness, even in the face of opposition and adversity.

Father, let every law, policy, and decision align with Your Word and Your perfect plan. Expose and dismantle unjust systems, hidden agendas, and oppressive laws that harm Your people. Replace them with policies that reflect Your heart for justice, fairness, and compassion.

I declare Psalm 33:12 over our nations: "Blessed is the nation whose God is the Lord." Lord, I ask You to position godly leaders in places of influence, leaders who will honor You and serve the people selflessly.

Father, I pray for protection over righteous leaders who are standing for truth. Shield them and their families from harm, threats, and retaliation. Strengthen their resolve and renew their courage daily. I intercede for leaders who have strayed from righteousness. Lord, convict their hearts, soften their spirits, and draw them back to You. Let the wooing power of the Holy Spirit draw them back into your presence. Show them the path of integrity and truth.

Father, I ask for divine intervention in political climates filled with chaos, conflict, and division. Let Your peace reign and let Your Kingdom rules be established. I declare Daniel 2:21 over every leadership transition, "You remove kings and raise up kings. You give wisdom to the wise and knowledge to the discerning." Lord, raise up righteous leaders and remove those who refuse to walk in integrity.

Father, let unity, collaboration, and peace prevail among leaders in every nation. Let egos be replaced with hearts to serve and let humility lead the way. Lord, let the Holy Spirit saturate every government building, every policy meeting, and every decision-making table. Move through lawmakers, advisors, judges, and officials with supernatural guidance and discernment.

I believe that every nation, every city, and every home will be touched by righteous leaders. I thank You in advance for laws that reflect justice, policies that honor Your Word, and leaders who bow before Your authority.

I believe I receive this prayer, and I release our most holy faith to bring it to pass. In the powerful and matchless name of Jesus, I pray. Amen and Amen!

Leadership in the Body of Christ

Heavenly Father, I come boldly before Your throne of Grace today, through and by the blood of Jesus, lifting up every leader in the Body of Christ; pastors, apostles, prophets, teachers, evangelists, and ministry workers. You have called them, anointed them, and set them apart for Your Kingdom work.

Father, Your Word declares in Jeremiah 3:15 that You will give us shepherds after Your own heart, who will guide us with knowledge and understanding. Lord, raise up leaders whose hearts beat in sync with Yours, leaders who seek Your face, love Your people, and walk in humility and integrity.

I plead the blood of Jesus over every pastor, ministry leader, and church worker. Protect them from burnout, discouragement, and every fiery dart of the enemy. Shield and protect their families, their health, and their minds from every attack of the wicked one and wicked people.

Lord, I pray for strength and endurance for every leader. In moments of weariness, refresh them with Your Spirit. In times of pressure, grant them peace that surpasses understanding. Help them stand firm on the promises of Your Word.

Father, release clarity and vision to every leader. Let them hear Your voice clearly, follow Your direction confidently, and lead their congregations with bold faith and divine wisdom. Remove every spirit of confusion, fear, and doubt.

Lord, I rebuke every spirit of division, strife, and offense that seeks to disrupt the unity of the Body of Christ. Strengthen leadership teams with love, mutual respect, and shared purpose.

Father, according to 1 Peter 5:2-3, may leaders care for the flock entrusted to them willingly and eagerly, with pure hearts and selfless motives. Let them not be driven by pride, greed, or personal ambition but by love and obedience to Your calling.

I pray for protection against the schemes of the enemy. Every plot, plan, and strategy of darkness aimed at pastors, ministry leaders and their families are canceled in the name of Jesus! I declare that no weapon formed against them will prosper.

Lord, let Your anointing rest heavily on every leader. Empower them to preach with boldness, counsel with compassion, and lead with integrity. Fill their mouths with Your Word, their hearts with Your love, and their spirits with divine courage.

Father, I ask for an outpouring of Your Spirit in every church, ministry, and gathering of your people. Let revival break out as leaders yield fully to Your direction and power. Strengthen their marriages, bless their children, and fortify their homes with Your peace. Let their personal lives be a reflection of Your grace and love.

Lord, remind every leader that their labor is not in vain, and that You are their great reward. Fill them with joy as they serve, knowing that You are the One who called, equipped, and sustains them.

I thank You, Father, for godly leadership rising in this hour. I thank You for the wisdom, strength, and anointing You are pouring out on every pastor, church leader, and ministry worker.

I believe I receive this prayer, and I release our most holy faith to bring it to pass. In the mighty and matchless name of Jesus, I pray. Amen and Amen!

Joy and Peace Over the Body of Christ

Father, in the name of Jesus, I lift up the Body of Christ before You today. I thank You that no matter what we face, the joy of the Lord is still our strength. I declare right now that joy is rising. Joy that breaks heaviness. Joy that restores strength. Joy that renews hope. Joy that lifts every burden and drives out weariness.

Your Word says in Nehemiah 8:10 that the joy of the Lord is our strength, so I speak that strength over every believer right now. Where there has been sorrow, let joy return. Where there has been fatigue and frustration, let joy overflow. I declare supernatural joy is filling hearts again. Joy that comes from knowing You are faithful. Joy that stands firm even when things don't make sense. Joy that remains because we trust in You.

Father, I declare the peace of God over the Body of Christ. Peace that passes all understanding. Peace in our homes. Peace in our minds. Peace in our emotions. Peace in every decision. Peace in the waiting. Peace in the unknown. I silence the voice of chaos, fear, and confusion, and I speak divine peace over Your people.

I declare that Your peace is guarding hearts and minds today. I come against anxiety, panic, discouragement, and emotional unrest. We will not be shaken. We will not be moved. We are anchored in You. You are our peace, and we receive it now.

Father, strengthen Your people today with joy and clothe them in peace. Let joy burst forth in the midst of trials. Let peace settle every storm. I declare refreshing. I declare restoration. I declare rest for the weary and strength for the journey ahead.

I believe I receive this prayer, and I release my most holy faith to bring it to pass. In Jesus' name I pray, Amen.

Prayer for the Lost, Hurting, and People in Need

Heavenly Father, in the mighty name of Jesus, I come boldly before Your throne of grace today, interceding for the lost, the broken, the hurting, and those in need. Lord, You are the Father to the fatherless, the Defender of the weak, the Restorer of broken hearts, and the Hope to the hopeless. Your Word declares in Psalm 34:18 that You are close to the brokenhearted and save those who are crushed in spirit. Right now, Lord, I lift up every soul that is lost in darkness, every heart that is weighed down by despair, and every life that is struggling under the burden of fear, lack, and confusion.

Father, I cry out for mercy! I stand in the gap and ask that You release a fresh outpouring of Your Spirit across this nation! Let the blinders be removed from the eyes of those who are deceived, and let the hardness of heart be shattered by the power of Your love. Lord, Your Word says in 2 Corinthians 4:4 that the god of this world has blinded the minds of unbelievers so they cannot see the light of the gospel. But I declare that the veil is being lifted! I call forth salvation, deliverance, and divine encounters with Jesus Christ! Holy Spirit, draw them to repentance! Let them hear Your voice calling their names and recognize that Jesus is the only way, the truth, and the life!

Father, I bind every spirit of fear, oppression, and confusion that has gripped this nation. Your Word says in 2 Timothy 1:7 that You have not given us a spirit of fear, but of power, love, and a sound mind. So, I take authority over every assignment of fear, chaos, and destruction, and I command it to be broken in Jesus' name! I release the peace of God that surpasses all understanding! I speak clarity where there has been confusion, strength where there has been weariness, and hope where there has been despair!

Lord, I pray for Your Church, Your remnant, the Body of Christ to RISE UP in this hour! Let Your people be awakened and positioned to be the hands and feet of Jesus. You said in Matthew 5:14 that we are the light of the world, a city set on a hill that cannot be hidden. So, I declare that the Church will not shrink back, but we will move forward with boldness, authority, and compassion! We will not be silent in the face of injustice, fear, or despair, but we will be voices of truth, healing, and redemption!

Lord, stir our hearts to be Your hands extended! Raise up laborers who will go into the harvest fields! Your Word says in Matthew 9:37-38 that the harvest is plentiful, but the laborers are few. So, I pray, Lord of the harvest, send out laborers! Send men and women who will feed the hungry, clothe the naked, embrace the broken, and proclaim the gospel with fire and conviction! Let Your Church be moved with compassion, just as Jesus was moved when He saw the multitudes scattered like sheep without a shepherd!

God, position us to be problem-solvers in this time of crisis! Give us divine strategies to bring Your solutions to a hurting world. Let the Church be a beacon of hope, a refuge for the weary, and a place where miracles, signs, and wonders flow. Your Word says in Isaiah 61:1-3 that the Spirit of the Lord is upon us to preach good news to the poor, to bind up the brokenhearted, to proclaim freedom for the captives, and to comfort those who mourn. So, Lord, empower us to walk in this anointing with power and love!

I declare that revival is here! That this is the hour for a great awakening! That souls will come flooding into the Kingdom! That those who have been cast aside will find a place at Your table! That the Church will be a voice of righteousness and healing in the land! That the Name of Jesus will be exalted, and every knee will bow and every tongue confess that Jesus Christ is Lord!

Father, I believe I receive this prayer, and I release my most holy faith to bring it to pass! I thank You that answers are on the way, strongholds are being broken, and transformation is happening even now! I give You all the glory, honor, and praise, in Jesus' mighty name! AMEN!

Faith that Moves Mountains

Heavenly Father, I come before You in the name of Jesus, standing on the authority of Your Word. I declare that my faith is unshakable, immovable, and mountain-moving. I refuse to be moved by what I see, hear, or feel. I am moved only by what You have spoken and what is in alignment with your will. I believe every promise You have declared over my life, and I release my faith to bring it to pass.

Lord, Your Word says that if I have faith as small as a mustard seed, I can speak to the mountains in my life, and they must move. Today, I speak to every obstacle, every hindrance, and every delay that has stood in my way. I command them to be cast into the sea. Every limitation, every stronghold, and every barrier is broken now in the name of Jesus.

I refuse to doubt. I reject fear. I silence every voice of unbelief that would try to weaken my faith. My trust is in You, Lord, and I stand on Your unchanging promises. My faith is the evidence of things not seen, and I declare that I will see manifestation, breakthrough, and divine acceleration in every area of my life.

I declare that nothing is impossible for me because I believe. Every door that was closed is now open. Every delay turns into divine timing. Every setback is becoming a setup for greater things. I call forth miracles, provision, healing, and supernatural favor. I align my words with Your Word, and I decree that my faith will produce results.

I stand in the authority You have given me, and I prophesy to the mountains in my life, be moved, be cast down, and be removed forever! My faith is alive, my prayers are powerful, and I walk in victory. I will not waver, I will not retreat, and I will not be shaken. My confidence is in the Lord, and I know that what I have asked in faith, I will receive. I believe I receive this prayer and release most holy faith to bring it to pass. In Jesus' name, Amen.

Prayer for Peace in Our Land

Heavenly Father, I come before You with a humbled heart, standing in the gap for our land, our communities, and our nation. You are the Prince of Peace, and You alone have the power to heal the deep wounds that divide us.

Lord, Your Word declares in **2 Chronicles 7:14** that if Your people humble themselves, pray, and turn from their wicked ways, You will hear from Heaven and heal our land. Today, I cry out for healing, restoration, and peace to flood every corner of our cities and nations.

Father, I plead **the blood of Jesus** over our land. Let Your blood cover our borders, our neighborhoods, and our homes. Every root of division, hatred, and violence must bow to the authority of Jesus' name.

I rebuke the spirit of fear, chaos, and confusion that seeks to stir unrest in our streets, our governments, and our institutions. Lord, silence every voice of hatred and every plan of destruction. Replace fear with faith, anger with love, and division with unity.

Lord, according to **John 14:27**, You have given us peace, not as the world gives, but a supernatural peace that surpasses understanding. Let this peace permeate every home, every school, every workplace, and every community gathering.

Father, I intercede for our leaders, local, state, and national. Grant them wisdom, humility, and compassion as they make decisions that impact lives. Remove any selfish ambition, pride, or corruption from their hearts, and replace it with a spirit of servanthood and responsibility.

Lord, I ask You to heal the racial, cultural, and economic divides in our nation. Let reconciliation flow like a river. Break the walls of prejudice, injustice, and inequality. Let forgiveness and compassion be the foundation upon which bridges of healing are built.

Father, I pray for protection against violence and unrest. Guard our schools, workplaces, places of worship, and public spaces from harm. Dispatch Your angels to encamp around us and let no weapon formed against us prosper (Isaiah 54:17).

I declare Psalm 122:6-7: "Pray for peace in Jerusalem. May all who love this city prosper." Lord, let peace reign not only in Jerusalem but in every city and every nation around the world.

Father, I ask for revival to break out across our land. Turn hearts back to You and let repentance sweep through our communities. Let the fear of the Lord return to our nation and let righteousness and justice be established as the foundation of our society.

I pray for the peacemakers, Lord, the leaders, pastors, and ordinary citizens working tirelessly to bring peace and reconciliation. Bless their efforts, amplify their voices, and surround them with Your favor and protection.

Lord, let Your Word in Isaiah 32:18 come to pass: "My people will live in safety, quietly at home. They will be at rest." Grant us safety in our homes, peace in our streets, and rest in our hearts.

I declare that love will triumph over hate, unity over division, and peace over chaos. Let Your kingdom come and Your will be done in our land as it is in Heaven.

Father, I thank You because I know that You hear our prayers, and Your Word will not return void. I stand in faith, believing that transformation is taking place even now.

I believe I receive this prayer, and I release our most holy faith to bring it to pass. In the mighty and matchless name of Jesus Christ, I pray. Amen and Amen!

Prayer for Restoration

Father, in the name of Jesus, I thank You for being the God of restoration. You are faithful to restore everything that was stolen, everything that was delayed, and everything that the enemy tried to shut down. I put my faith into action today and I declare that I will recover all. I will not sit in regret. I will not stay stuck in what was. I rise up in faith and move forward expecting restoration.

I call back the time. I call back the strength. I call back the opportunities and the resources that belong to me. I speak to every area that looked like it dried up and I command life to flow again. You promised that if I pursue, I will overtake, and without fail recover all. So, I pursue. I move. I act in obedience and I speak what You said.

I declare that this is my season of supernatural restoration. Everything attached to my assignment, everything connected to my purpose, and everything I need to finish strong is being restored now. I speak to loss and I say no more. I speak to closed doors and I command them to open. I speak to broken places and I declare healing and restoration now in the name of Jesus.

Holy Spirit, lead me. Give me divine strategy and clear instructions. I thank You that restoration is not coming, it is already here. I step into it by faith. I walk in it with confidence. I believe I receive this prayer and I release my most holy faith to bring it to pass. In the name of Jesus, Amen.

CHAPTER 11 – Declarations and Confessions

Declarations and Confessions Introduction

There is supernatural power in your mouth. As believers, we don't just pray, we **declare**. We **decree**. We **confess** God's Word and his promises with boldness, knowing that our words shape the atmosphere, command results, and call forth Heaven's will into the earth. Life and death are in the power of the tongue, and in this final chapter, we are putting our mouths to work for the Kingdom of God.

These declarations shift mindsets, break cycles, and release prophetic power over your life, family, and future. As you speak the Word of God aloud, your faith will rise, fear will flee, and the atmosphere around you will respond to the sound of truth and authority.

This chapter is your arsenal. It's your reminder that you were never meant to live on defense. God has given you the ability to call things that be not as though they were. You have authority to bind and loose, to uproot and plant, to speak light into dark places and watch dead things come alive.

So, open your mouth. Let every declaration rise from a place of conviction, not convenience. Speak as one who believes what God said. Use these confessions daily. Declare them over your mornings, your family, your ministry, your business, and your destiny. Don't just say them, *own* them.

You are blessed. You are anointed. You are chosen. You are walking in victory. You are filled with wisdom, surrounded by favor, and covered by the blood. Every promise is "yes and amen" in Christ Jesus. Now declare it until you see it!

Declaration and Faith Confession of Blessings Over the Day

Heavenly Father, in the mighty name of Jesus, I declare that this is the day that the Lord has made, I will rejoice and be glad in it! I decree that blessings, favor, and divine opportunities are assigned to me today. Goodness and mercy are following me all the days of my life (Psalm 23:6).

I declare that I am blessed in my coming in and blessed in my going out (Deuteronomy 28:6). Everything I put my hands to prospers and succeeds because of the favor of God on my life. I walk in divine health, supernatural wisdom, and uncommon favor. Doors of opportunity are opening for me, and I walk through them with boldness and confidence.

No weapon formed against me shall prosper, and every tongue that rises against me in judgment is condemned (Isaiah 54:17). The joy of the Lord is my strength (Nehemiah 8:10), and His peace guards my heart and mind (Philippians 4:7).

I declare that I am the head and not the tail, above only and never beneath (Deuteronomy 28:13). Today, I walk in purpose, on assignment, fully equipped, and anointed to conquer every challenge. Blessings chase me down and overtake me because I am favored by God.

I believe I receive this declaration, and I release my most holy faith to bring it to pass. In Jesus' mighty name, Amen!

Declaration of Victory Over Your Life

Heavenly Father, I come before You in the mighty name of Jesus, declaring that victory is mine! I stand on Your unshakable Word, knowing that You have already gone before me and made the crooked places straight. I decree and declare that no weapon formed against me shall prosper and every tongue that rises against me in judgment is condemned. I am more than a conqueror through Christ Jesus.

I take my place in the spirit, standing firm on the promises You have spoken over my life. Every battle I face has already been won because You fight for me. I don't fight for victory. I stand in victory because of what Jesus Christ already won. I will not be moved by what I see, hear, or feel. I stand on the truth that I walk in divine victory. I cast down every lie of the enemy, every scheme, every plot, and every form of opposition that tries to hinder my progress. I overcome by the blood of the Lamb and the word of my testimony!

I declare that I am victorious in my mind — I have the mind of Christ, and my thoughts align with Your truth. I reject fear, doubt, and confusion, for You have given me power, love, and a sound mind. My emotions are steady, my faith is unwavering, and my spirit is strong.

I declare that I am victorious in my body — every sickness, disease, and infirmity must bow to the name of Jesus. I walk in divine health, strength, and wholeness. I am whole from the crown of my head to the soles of my feed. My body is the temple of the Holy Spirit, and no sickness can dwell here. The life of God is flowing throughout my whole body bring healing to every part of my being.

I declare that I am victorious in my finances — You are Jehovah Jireh, my provider, and You supply all my needs according to Your riches in glory. I lack nothing because I am blessed and highly favored. All of my needs are met in God's divine plan. When I rise and when I rest, provision is made available to me. Wealth, resources, and open doors are my portion, all the days of my life.

I declare that I am victorious in my relationships — peace, love, and unity surround me like a shield. Every toxic connection is severed and divine relationships that align with my destiny are being established. I walk in love, wisdom, and discernment. My life is filled with people who love me, support me and care for me.

I declare that I am victorious in my calling — I will fulfill every assignment God has placed on my life. Nothing and no one can stop what You have ordained for me. My steps are ordered by the Lord. My purpose is established and I move forward with boldness, clarity, and authority.

Satan, I serve you notice, you are defeated, and you have no power or influence over my life. I resist you, and you must flee! Every chain is broken, every stronghold is torn down, and every demonic plan is overturned. The gates of hell will not prevail against me, my family, my ministry, my business or my destiny.

Lord, I thank You for the victory that is already mine! I will not shrink back, I will not waver, and I will not retreat. I step into this day with confidence, knowing that greater is He who is in me than he who is in the world. I walk in triumph, I walk in power, and I walk in complete victory!

I believe I receive a victorious in Christ Jesus and release most holy faith to bring it to pass. In Jesus' name, Amen.

Declaring God's Rule Over the Day

Father, in the name of Jesus, I come boldly before Your throne of grace this morning, taking my rightful place as Your ambassador and joint heir with Jesus Christ. I declare that this is the day You have made, I will rejoice, I will be glad, and I will walk in total victory. I stand in the full armor of God, clothed in righteousness, and armed with the sword of the Spirit, which is the Word of God.

I take authority over this day and command the morning to align with the divine will of God. Every demonic agenda that was plotted in the night, every scheme of the wicked, and every word curse spoken against me is overturned, dismantled, and destroyed by the fire of the Holy Ghost. Let the heavens declare the righteousness of God over this day, for Your Word says in Psalm 19:1, "The heavens declare the glory of God; the skies proclaim the work of His hands."

No weapon formed against us shall prosper, and every tongue that rises against us in judgment is condemned (Isaiah 54:17). I release the blood of Jesus over my home, family, businesses, ministries, finances, health, and destinies. The blood of Jesus speaks on our behalf, silencing the voice of the accuser and nullifying every demonic decree (Hebrews 12:24). Every satanic embargo placed on my progress is lifted now in the name of Jesus, for according to Matthew 18:18, "Whatever we bind on earth is bound in heaven, and whatever we loose on earth is loosed in heaven."

I take dominion over the airways, the highways, the railways, and the waterways. I decree that every portal of darkness attempting to infiltrate our regions is shut down by the power of God. I declare Psalm 24:7-8 over this land: "Lift up your heads, O ye gates! And be lifted up, O ancient doors, that the King of Glory may come in. Who is this King of Glory? The Lord, strong and mighty, the Lord, mighty in battle." I decree that every demonic interference operating through technology, social media, and mass communication is exposed and dismantled. Let every hidden work of darkness be brought to light (Luke 8:17).

I push back the forces of darkness attempting to operate in our homes. Every spirit of strife, division, confusion, and oppression must go now in the name of Jesus. Your Word declares in Joshua 24:15, "As for me and my house, we will serve the Lord." I release the peace of God, the joy of the Lord, and an atmosphere saturated with the presence of the Holy Spirit. I declare that families are walking in unity, marriages are strengthened, and children are covered under the blood of Jesus Christ.

I take authority over the spiritual climate in businesses, workplaces, and industries. Every spirit of corruption, dishonesty, oppression, and manipulation is cast down, for Proverbs 11:1 declares, "Dishonest scales are an abomination to the Lord, but a just weight is His delight." I release the favor of God over those who walk in integrity, and I decree that promotions, contracts, and financial breakthroughs are being released. The wealth of the wicked is laid up for the righteous (Proverbs 13:22), and divine provision flows freely to the people of God.

I release the power of God into hospitals and healthcare systems. I rebuke the spirit of infirmity, disease, and premature death. I command healing to manifest in hospital rooms, intensive care units, emergency rooms, and nursing facilities, for it is written in Isaiah 53:5, "By His stripes, we were healed." I speak life over every sick body and declare that the same Spirit that raised Jesus from the dead dwells in us and gives life to our mortal bodies (Romans 8:11).

I declare that revival is sweeping through the streets, schools, courthouses, and government institutions. The spirit of deception is broken, and the light of God's truth is shining in dark places. I call forth a spirit of repentance to fall upon this land, for Your Word declares in 2 Chronicles 7:14, "If My people who are called by My name humble themselves, and pray and seek My face and turn from their wicked ways, then I will hear from heaven and will forgive their sin and heal their land." Let hardened hearts be softened. Let blind eyes be opened. Let captives be set free.

The earth is the Lord's and the fullness thereof (Psalm 24:1). I decree that every territory and every domain where the enemy has set up his throne is being reclaimed for the Kingdom of God. The Lord strong and mighty, the Lord mighty in battle, has gone before us. I release warring angels to contend with every demonic power, to overthrow every stronghold, and to enforce the will of God in the earth (Psalm 91:11).

I cancel every assignment of the enemy over this day. I bind accidents, tragedies, sudden attacks, and demonic delays. I decree divine protection over those traveling by land, air, and sea, for Psalm 121:8 declares, "The Lord will watch over your coming and going both now and forevermore." I release the hand of God over legal battles, court cases, and governmental decisions. I decree that righteousness will prevail, and every evil agenda is overturned.

Father, let Your glory invade this day. Let Your fire fall upon our altars. Let signs, wonders, and miracles be released. Let divine encounters take place. Let the hearts of men be drawn to You in repentance and total surrender. As You declared in Habakkuk 2:14, "For the earth will be filled with the knowledge of the glory of the Lord as the waters cover the sea."

I decree and declare that this day is set apart for the purposes of God. It is blessed, it is prosperous, and it is victorious. I command the morning to yield the fullness of what has been ordained in Heaven, and I call it into manifestation now. It is so, and it shall not be otherwise. In Jesus' mighty name, amen. I believe I receive this prayer and release most holy faith to bring it to pass.

The Power of Speaking Good Things

Heavenly Father, I come before You in the name of Jesus, thanking You for the gift of speech and the power You have placed in my words. Your Word declares that life and death are in the power of the tongue (Proverbs 18:21), and today, I choose life. Lord, help me to guard my words and align my speech with Your truth and promises.

Forgive me for any careless or negative words I have spoken and cleanse my heart so that my words overflow with faith, hope, and love. Holy Spirit, fill my mouth with words that build up, encourage, and speak life into every situation (Ephesians 4:29). Let my words be seasoned with grace and reflect Your goodness and mercy (Colossians 4:6).

Father, I decree that my tongue will not speak defeat, lack, or fear but will declare Your promises and victory over my life and the lives of others. Empower me to speak healing, hope, and restoration in every conversation. May my words honor You and bring peace and unity to those around me (Proverbs 16:24).

Thank You for the authority You have given me to declare Your will on earth. I call forth blessings, favor, and divine alignment in every area of my life, believing that what I speak in faith will come to pass (Romans 4:17). I believe I receive this prayer and release my most holy faith to bring it to pass. In Jesus' name, amen.

Faith Confessions: The Power of My Words
1. I declare that my words are powerful, and I choose to speak life, truth, and blessings (**Proverbs 18:21**).
2. My mouth is filled with wisdom and grace, and my words bring healing and encouragement to others (**Proverbs 16:24**).
3. I refuse to speak negativity, doubt, or fear; instead, I speak faith, hope, and victory in every situation (**Mark 11:23**).
4. I decree that my words are aligned with God's Word and bring His promises to life in every circumstance (**Romans 4:17**).

5. My tongue is a tool of righteousness and peace, used to glorify God and declare His goodness (**Proverbs 10:11**).
6. I speak peace into my relationships, favor into my career, and abundance into my finances (**Philippians 4:8**).
7. I declare that no corrupt or idle words will proceed from my mouth, only words that build up and bless (**Ephesians 4:29**).
8. My words are a reflection of my faith, and I call things that are not as though they were (**Romans 4:17**).
9. I declare blessings over my family, my future, and all that I put my hands to do (**Deuteronomy 28:8**).
10. My speech honors God, and with my words, I decree His will and His promises over my life (**Isaiah 55:11**).
11. I declare that my words are guided by the Holy Spirit and produce good fruit in every area of my life (**Matthew 12:36-37**).
12. I will not let fear or anxiety shape my speech; I will declare that God has not given me a spirit of fear, but of power, love, and a sound mind (**2 Timothy 1:7**).
13. I decree that my words release healing and restoration wherever they are spoken (**Proverbs 15:4**).
14. I speak joy and strength into my life because the joy of the Lord is my strength (**Nehemiah 8:10**).
15. I declare that my words are established in heaven, and they bring God's Kingdom to earth (**Matthew 6:10**).
16. I speak boldness and confidence into my heart because I am fearfully and wonderfully made (**Psalm 139:14**).
17. I speak truth and reject deception, for the truth sets me free (**John 8:32**).
18. I declare that my words are a light in the darkness, bringing clarity and direction to others (**Psalm 119:105**).
19. I speak God's promises over my children and future generations, declaring that they will walk in His ways (**Isaiah 54:13**).
20. I proclaim that my words are a shield of faith because I speak the word of God, extinguishing every fiery dart of the enemy (**Ephesians 6:16**).

Faith Confessions for Resisting Fear, Anxiety, and Worry

1. I declare that God has not given me a spirit of fear but of power, love, and a sound mind. (2 Timothy 1:7)
2. I refuse to be anxious about anything, but I bring my requests to God with thanksgiving, and His peace guards my heart and mind in Christ Jesus. (Philippians 4:6-7)
3. The Lord is my light and my salvation, whom shall I fear? The Lord is the stronghold of my life, of whom shall I be afraid? (Psalm 27:1)
4. I cast all my cares upon the Lord because He cares for me. (1 Peter 5:7)
5. I am strong and courageous; I will not be afraid or discouraged, for the Lord my God is with me wherever I go. (Joshua 1:9)
6. I declare that no weapon formed against me shall prosper, and every tongue that rises against me in judgment is condemned. (Isaiah 54:17)
7. Even though I walk through the valley of the shadow of death, I will fear no evil, for You are with me, Lord. Your rod and Your staff comfort me. (Psalm 23:4)
8. The peace of God that surpasses all understanding fills my heart and mind, and fear has no place in my life. (Philippians 4:7)
9. I decree that fear and worry must bow to the name of Jesus, and I walk boldly in the confidence of His promises. (Philippians 2:10)
10. I am more than a conqueror through Christ who loves me, and no circumstance can separate me from His love. (Romans 8:37-39)
11. I take up the shield of faith and extinguish every fiery dart of fear and doubt from the enemy. (Ephesians 6:16)
12. The Lord fights for me, and I hold my peace. I will not be shaken by fear, for the battle belongs to the Lord. (Exodus 14:14)

13. I dwell in the secret place of the Most High and abide under the shadow of the Almighty. No evil will befall me, and no plague will come near my dwelling. (Psalm 91:1,10)
14. Perfect love casts out all fear, and I am filled with God's perfect love. (1 John 4:18)
15. I declare that God's promises are "yes" and "amen," and I trust Him to deliver me from every fear and anxiety. (2 Corinthians 1:20)
16. The joy of the Lord is my strength, and I will not be moved by fear or discouragement. (Nehemiah 8:10)
17. I lift my eyes to the hills; my help comes from the Lord, the Maker of heaven and earth. (Psalm 121:1-2)
18. The Spirit of the Lord is upon me, and He fills me with boldness, strength, and confidence. (Isaiah 61:1)
19. I set my mind on things above, not on earthly things, and the peace of Christ rules in my heart. (Colossians 3:2,15)
20. I declare that fear and anxiety have no place in my life, for I am hidden in Christ, and His perfect peace surrounds me like a shield. (Isaiah 26:3)

50 Declarations and Decrees for Your Prayer Call

1. I decree that everyone under the sound of my voice walks in the peace of God that surpasses all understanding. (*Philippians 4:7*)
2. I declare that the Holy Spirit is saturating this call, filling every home and heart with His presence, anointing, and power. (*Acts 2:4*)
3. I decree that no weapon formed against them will prosper, and every tongue that rises in judgment is condemned. (*Isaiah 54:17*)
4. I declare that each person on this call is walking in divine alignment with the will and plan of God for their lives. (*Jeremiah 29:11*)
5. I decree that the peace of Christ rules in every heart and mind, silencing fear, anxiety, and confusion. (*Colossians 3:15*)
6. I declare that everyone here is seated in heavenly places with Christ Jesus, walking in authority over all powers of darkness. (*Ephesians 2:6*)
7. I decree that the joy of the Lord is strengthening every individual, empowering them to overcome every challenge. (*Nehemiah 8:10*)
8. I declare that the favor of God is resting upon this group, opening doors of opportunity and blessing. (*Psalm 5:12*)
9. I decree that the blood of Jesus covers every person here, their families, and everything and everyone connected to them. (*Revelation 12:11*)
10. I declare that every person here is more than a conqueror through Christ who loves them. (*Romans 8:37*)
11. I decree that every stronghold of fear, doubt, or discouragement is broken in the name of Jesus. (*2 Corinthians 10:4-5*)
12. I declare that this is a day of divine breakthroughs, miracles, and testimonies for every person on this call. (*Isaiah 43:19*)
13. I decree that everyone here is walking by faith and not by sight, trusting fully in God's promises. (*2 Corinthians 5:7*)

PROPHECY THE PROMISES OF GOD

14. I declare that everyone here is anointed, equipped, and empowered to fulfill their God-given purpose. (*Philippians 4:13*)
15. I decree that the peace of God guards every heart and mind, protecting against worry and fear. (*Philippians 4:6-7*)
16. I declare that healing flows into every life, bringing restoration to spirit, soul, and body. (*Isaiah 53:5*)
17. I decree that this group is united in love, walking in the unity of the Spirit and the bond of peace. (*Ephesians 4:3*)
18. I declare that the presence of God surrounds each person like a shield, bringing divine protection. (*Psalm 91:4*)
19. I decree that every tongue that speaks against them is silenced, and they walk in vindication. (*Isaiah 54:17*)
20. I declare that every step they take is ordered by the Lord, leading them into victory and success. (*Psalm 37:23*)
21. I decree that the light of God shines in every life, driving out all darkness. (*John 8:12*)
22. I declare that hope is rising, faith is stirring, and courage is strengthening in every heart. (*Romans 15:13*)
23. I decree that angels are encamped around this group, protecting and guiding them into God's will. (*Psalm 34:7*)
24. I declare that the power of the Holy Spirit is filling every believer here, equipping them for every good work. (*Acts 1:8*)
25. I decree that God's glory is being revealed in and through every person here. (*Habakkuk 2:14*)
26. I decree that every person here walks in the fullness of their God-given authority and purpose. (*Luke 10:19*)
27. I declare that divine strategies and wisdom are being released to solve problems and make decisions with clarity. (*James 1:5*)
28. I decree that each person is surrounded by the favor of God like a shield, drawing blessings and breakthroughs. (*Psalm 5:12*)
29. I declare that hearts are being renewed and minds transformed by the power of the Word of God. (*Romans 12:2*)

30. I decree that faith is rising in every individual, breaking every chain of doubt and unbelief. (*Mark 11:22-24*)
31. I declare that the goodness and mercy of God will follow everyone here all the days of their lives. (*Psalm 23:6*)
32. I decree that strongholds of fear, worry, and anxiety are demolished by the power of the Holy Spirit. (*2 Timothy 1:7*)
33. I declare that open heavens are over this group, and blessings are being poured out abundantly. (*Malachi 3:10*)
34. I decree that every person here is clothed with the full armor of God, standing strong against all schemes of the enemy. (*Ephesians 6:11*)
35. I declare that rivers of living water are flowing from within each person, bringing life and refreshing. (*John 7:38*)
36. I decree that financial breakthroughs and provision are being released over every household. (*Philippians 4:19*)
37. I declare that every hidden obstacle is removed, and every crooked path is made straight. (*Isaiah 45:2*)
38. I decree that boldness and courage are being released to declare the truth and walk in victory. (*Proverbs 28:1*)
39. I declare that the Lord is fighting battles on behalf of every person here, and victory is assured. (*Exodus 14:14*)
40. I decree that every dream and vision God has placed in their hearts is coming to fruition. (*Habakkuk 2:3*)
41. I declare that healing flows freely in every life, bringing wholeness to spirit, soul, and body. (*Jeremiah 30:17*)
42. I decree that every word spoken against them is rendered powerless, and they walk in vindication. (*Isaiah 54:17*)
43. I declare that God's light is shining through each person, dispelling darkness and attracting others to Him. (*Matthew 5:14-16*)
44. I decree that doors of opportunity and favor are opening, and no one can shut them. (*Revelation 3:8*)
45. I declare that each person is rooted and grounded in the love of Christ, unshaken by circumstances. (*Ephesians 3:17*)
46. I decree that peace rules every heart and home, silencing confusion and strife. (*Colossians 3:15*)

47. I declare that the power of the Holy Spirit is empowering each person to fulfill their divine assignments. (*Acts 1:8*)
48. I decree that the fire of God is consuming every hindrance and igniting fresh passion for God. (*Hebrews 12:29*)
49. I declare that the promises of God are yes and amen, and they are being fulfilled in every life. (*2 Corinthians 1:20*)
50. I decree that this is a season of breakthrough, overflow, and divine acceleration for everyone on this call and everyone connected to them. (*Amos 9:13*)

50 Faith Confessions for Live Out Your Faith Nation with Scriptures

1. I declare that the Live Out Your Faith Nation is blessed, protected, and thriving under the mighty hand of God. (Psalm 84:11)
2. We are led by the Holy Spirit into all truth, and our footsteps are ordered by the Lord. (John 16:13; Psalm 37:23)
3. No weapon formed against us shall prosper, and every tongue that rises against us is silenced in Jesus' name. (Isaiah 54:17)
4. We walk in the abundance of God's blessings, and no curse can reverse what God has ordained for us. (Numbers 23:23)
5. We are contagiously blessed, abounding in the goodness, favor, peace, and provision of God. (Deuteronomy 28:1-6)
6. God is adding to our numbers daily, and we are growing exponentially with faithful, Holy Ghost-filled, committed members. (Acts 2:47)
7. The four winds of heaven are releasing divine connections, destiny helpers, and Kingdom partners to assist in the work of the ministry. (Isaiah 60:3-4)
8. We have all the finances, resources, and abilities needed to accomplish God's plans for us, and we always have more than enough to bless others. (Philippians 4:19)
9. Every event, prayer call, and gathering is overflowing with people hungry for the truth and obedient to God's voice. (Matthew 5:6)
10. Signs, wonders, and miracles follow us because we walk in faith and obedience to God's Word. (Mark 16:17-18)
11. We are unified in vision, faith, and purpose, and we are known by the love we have for one another. (John 13:35)
12. Revelation knowledge flows freely among us, unhindered by any satanic or demonic force. (Ephesians 1:17-18)

13. We speak the truth of the gospel in love, and the anointing of God rests on our words, transforming lives for His glory. (Ephesians 4:15)
14. We are like trees planted by streams of water, bearing fruit in every season and prospering in all we do. (Psalm 1:3)
15. The Word of Christ dwells richly in us, guiding us with wisdom and filling our hearts with songs of praise. (Colossians 3:16)
16. We are protected by an impenetrable wall of Holy Ghost fire and angelic protection. No evil can come near us. (Psalm 91:10-11)
17. We are more than conquerors through Christ Jesus, and we walk in His authority and power. (Romans 8:37)
18. God's favor surrounds us like a shield, and we are walking in divine opportunities and supernatural breakthroughs. (Psalm 5:12)
19. We declare that everything we do prospers and succeeds because we are aligned with God's will. (Joshua 1:8)
20. The Live Out Your Faith Nation is a beacon of light and hope, drawing people from all nations into the Kingdom of God. (Isaiah 60:1-3)
21. We walk by faith and not by sight, trusting in the unchanging promises of God. (2 Corinthians 5:7)
22. The peace of God rules in our hearts, and His joy strengthens us daily. (Philippians 4:7; Nehemiah 8:10)
23. We are equipped and empowered by the Holy Spirit to fulfill every Kingdom assignment. (Acts 1:8)
24. Every obstacle before us is removed, and we walk in divine acceleration. (Zechariah 4:7)
25. God's glory is upon us, and His light shines through us to the world. (Matthew 5:16)
26. We declare that we are debt-free and operating in supernatural financial overflow. (Deuteronomy 28:12)
27. We are anointed to preach the good news, heal the brokenhearted, and set captives free. (Isaiah 61:1)
28. Our gatherings are filled with the presence of the Holy Spirit, and lives are transformed. (2 Corinthians 3:17)

29. We are rooted and grounded in love, and Christ dwells richly in our hearts. (Ephesians 3:17)
30. The Lord is our Shepherd; we lack nothing. (Psalm 23:1)
31. The joy of the Lord is our strength, and we are filled with His unshakable peace. (Nehemiah 8:10; John 14:27)
32. We declare that the Word of God is alive and active in our ministry, cutting through every hindrance. (Hebrews 4:12)
33. We stand firm in faith, knowing that the Lord is fighting for us. (Exodus 14:14)
34. The Holy Spirit teaches us all things and reminds us of the promises of God. (John 14:26)
35. We are steadfast, immovable, always abounding in the work of the Lord. (1 Corinthians 15:58)
36. We are chosen, royal, holy, and set apart to proclaim the praises of God. (1 Peter 2:9)
37. We declare that strongholds are broken, and freedom reigns in our midst. (2 Corinthians 10:4)
38. We are victorious in every battle, for the Lord goes before us. (Deuteronomy 20:4)
39. We honor the Lord with our wealth, and He fills our barns with plenty. (Proverbs 3:9-10)
40. God's Word is a lamp to our feet and a light to our path. (Psalm 119:105)
41. We decree that families within Live Out Your Faith Nation are blessed, restored, and unified. (Psalm 133:1)
42. We declare that God is raising up intercessors to stand in the gap and pray for the nations. (Ezekiel 22:30)
43. Our ministry events draw multitudes who are hungry for the Word of God. (Isaiah 55:1)
44. We are faithful stewards of God's blessings, and He multiplies the resources we have. (Luke 16:10)
45. We stand boldly in the face of opposition, knowing that God is our defender. (Psalm 46:1)
46. We declare that the nations are our inheritance and the ends of the earth our possession. (Psalm 2:8)
47. We have the mind of Christ and our thoughts are aligned with His purposes. (1 Corinthians 2:16)

48. We are filled with Holy Ghost power and walk in boldness, faith, and authority. (Acts 4:31)
49. We declare that revival is breaking forth in the Live Out Your Faith Nation, transforming lives for God's glory. (Habakkuk 3:2)
50. Signs and wonders follow us all the days of our lives and we dwell in the house of Lord forever and ever.

We believe we receive every promise of God for Live Out Your Faith Nation, and we release our faith to bring it to pass. (Mark 11:24)

In the name of Jesus Christ of Nazareth, we pray and say amen.

Faith Confessions for Live Out Your Faith Nation

Heavenly Father, we come before you right now with our voices lifted in praise and adoration to you. We thank you for your grace and mercy which you have so lasciviously given to us. We lift up the Live Out Your Faith Nation family and community of believers to you. We thank you that your mighty hand is upon us and that you are leading and guiding us into all truth. Father, we ask that you order our footsteps and guide our way. We ask for your hand to rest mightily upon every leader, intercessor, administrator, member, and ministry partner.

We ask for your protection and safety to surround our lives as a shield. We decree and declare that no weapon formed against us shall proper and every tongue that rises up to speak against us, will be proven wrong. We pull down, rebuke and reverse every negative word curse that has been spoken against us and through the power of Jesus Christ, we declare that we are so blessed that no curse can reverse it. We are contagiously blessed and walking in the abundance that Jesus Christ came to give us. We are abounding in the goodness of God, the favor of God, the Peace of God and the Provisions of God.

Father, we thank you for your love that you have for us and your love is abounding richly in our lives. In the name of Jesus Christ, we believe we receive this and have no doubt in our hearts.

Growth:
In the name of Jesus Christ, We declare that we are growing by leaps and bounds. We decree and declare that God is adding to our growth daily. Father, we thank you for drawing the multitude. The people that you have ordained to partner with us are being drawn to us in the name of Jesus Christ. We speak to the north, south, east and the west and we declare that people are released by the hand of God and ushered by the angels of God.

We thank you for faithful, committed, and loyal people that are full of the Holy Ghost, people of integrity, people of honor and people that are on fire for Jesus to come now in the name of Jesus. Like a divine magnet, we call them from the north, south, east and west. We declare that the 4 winds of heaven are blowing them in our direction. They are coming NOW in the name of Jesus.

People that are from all around the world. People that are hungry for the truth and will be obedient to your voice oh God. People that will thrive in prayer and yield to the leadership of the Holy Spirit. We have a minimum of 1000 people that are joining our prayer calls each day, we have a minimum of 100,000 people that are connected to this ministry around the world. Our online and in person events always reach or exceed capacity in the name of Jesus. We are experiencing supernatural accelerated growth by the hand of the most high God. God is adding people to our ministry daily in the name of Jesus Christ.

Finances:
In the name of the Lord Jesus Christ, we decree and declare that Live Out Your Faith Nation has all the finances, resources and abilities to accomplish the plan that God has for our lives. We decree and declare that destiny helpers will come forth swiftly to assist us in our Kingdom work. We decree and declare that we always have more than enough money to meet our needs and plenty left over to be a blessing to others. We decree and declare that we have favor with people of influence, affluence, and power that will grant us favor whenever we need it. We have no lack or insufficiency in our lives or in this ministry.

Our ministry endeavors are always financed in the name of Jesus Christ. We have the finances and resources to meet or exceed our budget requirements. We pay our bills on time or in advance every month. All of our events are paid in full, and our members and guests can attend without financial limitations in Jesus' name. We declare an overflow of favor be upon us NOW in Jesus' name. We declare that financial resources are pouring in. We have an abundance of financial resources and plenty left over to be a blessing to others. We have everything we need to carry out the Great Commission and reach people globally. We declare that the Live Out Your Faith Nation has a net-breaking anointing upon our finances in the name of Jesus Christ. Amen. We believe we receive this and release most holy faith to bring it to pass.

Power of the Holy Spirit:
We decree and declare that we are filled with the Holy Ghost fire and teach the word of God in a way that others will be able to hear and understand. We declare that signs, wonders, and miracles are manifesting when we come together. Holy Spirit, you are always welcome every time we gather. We are being transformed by the renewing of our minds. We declare that we are doing the greater works which Jesus Christ said that we would do because he is with the Father in Heaven.

We are yielded and submitted to the voice of God and voices that are strange and contrary to His will; we will not follow. We live a life that is led by the Holy Spirit of God. We have the mind of Christ and hold the thoughts, feelings, and purpose of God's heart.

We thank you for your unity within the Live Out Your Faith Nation. We are united in vision, we are united in faith, we are united in the Holy Ghost, and we are united in our Kingdom purpose. We are known by the love that we have for each other.

We speak the truth of the gospel in love, and the anointing of God is on our lips. When we teach the word of God, people are transformed and renewed. We declare that revelation knowledge is given to us and it flows freely, unhindered by any satanic or demonic force. When we teach the word of God, it falls on the good ground of the hearts of those who hear it and grows up to produce a peaceable harvest. We are like trees planted by the rivers of water and we produce fruit in our season. Our leaves shall not wither or fade away, and whatever we do shall prosper and succeed.

Let the word of Christ dwell in us richly in all wisdom, teaching and admonishing one another in psalms and hymns and spiritual songs, singing with grace in our hearts to the Lord. And whatever we do in word or deed, we do all in the name of the Lord Jesus, giving thanks to God the Father through Him.

In the name of Jesus Christ, we stand protected by an impenetrable wall of Holy Ghost fire and angelic protection. We are more than conquerors in Christ Jesus. In the name of Jesus Christ and on the authority he has given us, we pray and say amen! Be it unto us according to all that we have prayed. This or something better comes forth in God's perfect timing, according to God's rich good for us. We believe, we receive this and release most faith to bring it pass.

Declaring Blessings Over a New Year

(Say the Year) is a BIG YEAR for me. I will receive unexpected blessings, good news and miracles all year long. I will be happy again. I will heal. I will grow. I will flourish into the person I am destined to be. I will abide in peace all year long. This or something better will come forth in God's perfect timing.

(Say the Year) is my due season year. Lord, I thank you that **(Say the Year)** is my due season. Suddenly out of the ordinary things will work in my favor. I will get new breaks and divine connections. Things out of the ordinary will happen for me. God will give me ideas, creativity, and supernatural grace. This is my year to see my increase. I will experience unexpected blessings and creative miracles.

This is my year to meet the right people. This is my year for divine connections. I am at the right place at the right time in the right frame of mind. This is my year for supernatural favor. This is my due season year to get breakthroughs in my life. This is my year to see restoration. This is my year to experience God's best.

I am a magnet for goodness and good breaks. God is going to show up and turn it around. I am moving into leadership positions. My health will be better than ever. My relationship will be better than ever. My hope will be better than ever. God's blessings are chasing me down and overtaking me. I am releasing my faith and in great expectation today for the manifestation of my promised season.

In the name of Jesus!

Prayer Declaring Who I Am in Christ

Heavenly Father, I come before You with a heart full of thanksgiving, boldly declaring the truth of Your Word over my life. Thank You for calling me out of darkness into Your marvelous light and for choosing me to be a royal priesthood, a holy nation, and Your special possession. I rejoice in the identity You have given me in Christ Jesus, and I align myself with Your promises.

Lord, I declare that I am a new creation, redeemed by the blood of Jesus, and seated in heavenly places with Him. I am Your workmanship, created to do good works and bear much fruit. I stand in the authority You have given me, knowing that I am victorious, more than a conqueror, and filled with Your Spirit.

Father, I renounce every lie of the enemy and proclaim that I am strong, courageous, and unshakable in Jesus Christ. I am rooted in Your love, justified by faith, and empowered to walk in the fullness of my calling. Thank You for equipping me with all I need to live for Your glory and reflect Your character to the world.

Today, I embrace my identity in Jesus Christ and declare that I am unstoppable, unshakeable, immovable and always abounding because Christ Jesus lives in me. I give You all the honor, praise, and glory. In Jesus' mighty name, I pray. Amen.

Faith Confessions Declaring Who I Am in Christ

1. I am a new creation in Christ; the old has passed away, and the new has come. (2 Corinthians 5:17)
2. I am part of a royal priesthood, a holy nation, and God's special possession. (1 Peter 2:9)
3. I am fearfully and wonderfully made, created in the image of God. (Psalm 139:14)
4. I am loved with an everlasting love and drawn to God by His unfailing kindness. (Jeremiah 31:3)
5. I am chosen by God and called by name. (Isaiah 43:1)

6. I am forgiven and redeemed by the blood of Jesus. (Ephesians 1:7)
7. I am the righteousness of God in Christ Jesus. (2 Corinthians 5:21)
8. I am seated in heavenly places with Christ. (Ephesians 2:6)
9. I am God's masterpiece, created for good works. (Ephesians 2:10)
10. I am strong and courageous because God is with me. (Joshua 1:9)
11. I am free from condemnation because I belong to Jesus Christ. (Romans 8:1)
12. I am the temple of the Holy Spirit, filled with God's presence and power. (1 Corinthians 6:19)
13. I am victorious through Jesus Christ who strengthens me. (Philippians 4:13)
14. I am healed by the stripes of Jesus. (Isaiah 53:5)
15. I am filled with the joy of the Lord, which is my strength. (Nehemiah 8:10)
16. I am called to bear much fruit that glorifies God. (John 15:16)
17. I am an heir of God and a co-heir with Christ. (Romans 8:17)
18. I am the light of the world, shining brightly for God's glory. (Matthew 5:14)
19. I am rooted and grounded in God's love. (Ephesians 3:17)
20. I am more than a conqueror through Christ who loves me. (Romans 8:37)
21. I am blessed and highly favored. (Luke 1:28)
22. I am complete in Christ Jesus, lacking nothing. (Colossians 2:10)
23. I am equipped with everything I need to do God's will. (Hebrews 13:2)
24. I am protected under the shadow of God's wings. (Psalm 91:1)
25. I am redeemed from every curse and walk in God's blessing. (Galatians 3:13)
26. I am filled with peace that surpasses all understanding. (Philippians 4:7)

Declaring the Lord is Good (Psalm 118)

Father, I come boldly to Your throne of grace with a heart full of gratitude. You are good, and Your mercy endures forever. I declare it with everything in me; You are faithful, You are mighty, and You are good! No matter what I see or feel, I know that You are working all things together for my good because I belong to You.

I declare Psalm 118, this is the day that You have made, and I will rejoice and be glad in it! I thank You for Your unfailing love that surrounds me like a shield. You rescued me when I was in distress, and You brought me into a spacious place. You are my strength and my song, and You have become my victory!

I declare that I will not die but live and proclaim what the Lord has done. You are my defender, my refuge, and my strong tower. I will not be shaken because the Lord is on my side. Even when people turn on me, even when things don't go as planned, I stand on this truth: the Lord is good and His love never fails.

Open up the gates of righteousness, Lord, and I will enter in with praise. I lift my hands and bless Your name. You have done marvelous things in my life, and I will testify of Your goodness. You are my God, and I will exalt You. You are my God, and I will praise You!

So, I declare right now, the Lord is good! His mercy endures forever! His truth stands through all generations! I believe I receive this prayer and release most holy faith to bring it to pass. In Jesus' name, I pray, amen.

The Lord's Prayer Faith Confession

Father, we come before You with hearts lifted, saying, "Our Father who art in heaven, hallowed be Your name." We honor You, Lord, and exalt Your holy name above all. You are our Creator, our Sustainer, and the One who loves us with an everlasting love.

Let Your Kingdom come and let Your will be done in our lives as it is in heaven. Lord, we align ourselves with Your purpose. We submit to Your perfect plan, asking that You would guide our steps and bring Your glory into every part of our lives. Father, let Your presence overflow in us, transforming every corner of our hearts and minds.

Give us this day our daily bread, for You are our Provider, the One who meets every need according to Your riches in glory. I ask for Your provision in every area; our spiritual, physical, and emotional needs. Let us never lack but have more than enough to bless others, showing Your goodness to those around us.

Forgive us our trespasses, as we forgive those who trespass against us. Lord, help us to release every hurt and offense. Teach us to walk in the freedom of forgiveness, to show the mercy You have shown us, and to extend grace just as You have lavished it upon us.

Lead us not into temptation but deliver us from evil. Holy Spirit, strengthen us in every moment of testing. Guard our hearts and minds and keep us rooted in Your truth. I declare that no weapon formed against us shall prosper, and we stand secure in Your protection.

For Yours is the Kingdom, the power, and the glory, forever. Father, I lift You high. All honor and praise belong to You, now and for all eternity. May Your name be glorified in our lives and may we walk as living testimonies of Your faithfulness.

We believe we receive this prayer and release our most holy faith to bring it to pass. In Jesus' mighty name, amen.

Prophetic Prayer to Declare Blessings Over the Day

Heavenly Father, I step into this day with confidence, knowing that You have gone before me and made every crooked place straight and rough place smooth. I prophesy blessings over my life today. I declare that this is a day of divine favor, supernatural breakthroughs, and overwhelming victories! Every moment of this day is saturated with Your presence, and I will walk in the fullness of Your promises.

I decree and declare that today is fruitful and productive. Everything my hands touch prospers, and everything I set my mind to is accomplished with excellence. Doors of opportunity are swinging open for me, and I walk into rooms filled with divine connections and destiny helpers. I am at the right place, at the right time, with the right people, in the right mind.

I prophesy over my health; my body is strong, my mind is sharp, and my spirit is refreshed. Every system in my body functions in divine order, and I am walking in supernatural strength and vitality. No sickness, no disease, and no affliction can attach itself to me because I am covered by the blood of Jesus.

I declare that abundance follows me. Resources, finances, and provisions locate me effortlessly. I lack nothing, for my God supplies all my needs according to His riches in glory. I am a lender and not a borrower. Wealth and increase flow into my hands, and I steward it wisely for Kingdom purposes.

I speak favor over my relationships; peace, love, and unity surround me. I attract people who align with God's perfect plan for my life, and I disconnect from every distraction and hindrance. Divine alignment is my portion.

I take authority over this day. I bind every plot, scheme, and attack of the wicked spirits and wicked people. No weapon formed against me shall prosper, and every tongue that rises against me in judgment is condemned. Every demonic assignment sent to delay, distract, or discourage me is canceled now in the name of Jesus.

I declare that joy of the Lord is my portion. The peace of God is my foundation. Victory is my reality. I will not be shaken, I will not be moved, and I will not be defeated! The hand of God is upon me, and His goodness and mercy follow me all the days of my life.

I prophesy that my future is bright, my destiny is secured, and my path is filled with divine acceleration. The favor of the Lord surrounds me like a shield, and I walk boldly into every good thing that God has ordained for me.

I believe I receive this prayer and release most holy faith to bring it to pass. In Jesus Christ name I pray, amen.

Due Season Declaration

This is my due season year. Lord, I thank you that year is my due season. Suddenly out of the ordinary things will work in my favor. I will get new breaks and divine connections. Things out of the ordinary will happen for me.

God will give me ideas, creativity, and supernatural grace. This is my year to see my increase. I will experience unexpected blessings and creative miracles. This is my year to meet the right people. This is my year for divine connections. I am at the right place at the right time in the right frame of mind.

This is my year for supernatural favor. This is my due season year to get breakthroughs in my life. This is my year to see restoration. This is my year to experience God's best. I am a magnet for goodness and good breaks. God is going to show up and turn it around. I am going to move into leadership positions. My health will be better than ever. My relationships will be better than ever. My hope will be better than ever. God's blessings are chasing me down and overtaking me.

I am releasing my faith and in great expectation today for the manifestation of my promised season. I release most holy faith to bring this to pass.

Release the Prophetic Anointing and the Gift of Prophecy

Father, in the mighty name of Jesus, I enter into Your presence with thanksgiving and reverence. I thank You for the blood of Jesus that gives me access to your throne of grace and I stand under an open Heaven, expecting to receive fresh oil upon my life.

Holy Spirit, I welcome You into this moment, into this prayer time, and into every space I step into today. Saturate my life with Your presence. Lord, I ask for a supernatural stirring within me. Let a fresh wind from Heaven blow on my gifts, calling, and everything in me that's been lying dormant. Wake it up, Father God. Breathe on me and let me rise in power, boldness, and purpose.

Lord, Your Word declares in Joel 2:28, you will pour out your Spirit upon all people, our sons and daughters will prophesy, so I declare, let it be so in our lives! I ask that you release the prophetic oil upon us now. Let there be an awakening of dreams, visions, and divine utterance. I decree and declare that the spirit of prophecy is rising within us, not for performance, but for kingdom purpose. Not for fame, but for the glory of God!

I declare that our ears are open to hear what the Spirit is saying. Our mouths are anointed to speak only what You speak, Lord. Our hearts are aligned with Heaven and we surrender our voices as prophetic vessels, set apart to build, to edify, to warn, to equip, and to declare Your will in the earth.

Father, ignite the fire of prophecy within us. Let there be an impartation of boldness and clarity. May we prophesy with boldness, accuracy, humility, and love. May we discern the times and speak Your truth without fear. I cancel confusion, fleshly ambition, and false prophecy. We receive a fresh outpouring of your anointing right now, in the name of Jesus Christ.

I call forth prophetic dreams, words of knowledge, words of wisdom, divine interpretation, and supernatural insight. Raise up intercessors, watchmen, prophetic scribes, teachers, and leaders who will not be silenced. Let a fresh anointing fall upon us now, from the crown of our heads to the soles of our feet.

I prophesy over our lives:
We are God's mouthpieces.
We hear clearly.
We speak boldly.
We discern wisely.
And we prophesy only what aligns with the written and revealed Word of God.

Lord, let Your prophetic glory fill our homes, our gatherings, our churches, and our families. Let Your power rest on us to release breakthrough and shift atmospheres. May signs, wonders, and confirmations follow every prophetic word You give us to release.

I seal this prayer with faith and great expectation. We receive it and we walk in it.

I believe I receive this prayer and release most holy faith to bring it to pass. In Jesus' name I pray, amen.

Declaring the Spirit of Power and Might

Father, in the mighty name of Jesus, I thank You for the fullness of Your Spirit resting upon me. You have not given me a spirit of fear, so I cancel every lie, every torment, and every hesitation that would try to grip my soul. I rise up today and I decree and declare that I am strengthened with all might according to the Spirit of Power, the Spirit of Might and Your glorious power.

Lord, You are my strength and my shield, and because Your Spirit dwells in me, I will not back down. I walk in divine ability, divine authority, and supernatural confidence. I am clothed with boldness, equipped to cast out devils, destroy yokes, and shift atmospheres. The Spirit of Might causes me to stand firm, declare the word of God and finish every assignment You've placed in my hands.

Holy Spirit, rest on me like never before. Let Your power ignite a holy fire in every area of my life; my thoughts, my words, my walk, and my witness. I thank You for fresh oil and divine stamina. Even when I feel weak, I tap into your might. Even when the enemy comes in like a flood, I lift up the standard of Your Word and remind hell that no weapon formed against me shall prosper.

I will not faint. I will not fold. I will not fear. I am filled with the Spirit of the Lord, the Spirit of Wisdom, the Spirit of Understanding, the Spirit of Counsel, and yes, the Spirit of Might. I walk in dominion and authority and I speak with fire in my mouth.

Let miracles, breakthroughs, and supernatural acceleration be my portion. Let signs and wonders follow my obedience. I speak to every weary place and command the breath of God to blow fresh wind. Strengthen my hands to build. Strengthen my knees to pray. Strengthen my spirit to stand.

This is not the season to fall apart, this is my season to rise in power and might! I believe I receive this prayer and release most holy faith to bring it to pass. In Jesus' name I pray, amen.

Prayer for Endurance, Tenacity, and Unwavering Faith

Heavenly Father, in the mighty and matchless name of Jesus, I come boldly before Your throne of grace, thanking You for being the Author and Finisher of my faith. Lord, You are my refuge, my strength, and the source of my endurance. Today, I declare that I will not quit, I will not back down, and I will not be moved because greater is He that is in me than he that is in the world (1 John 4:4).

Father, Your Word declares in Hebrews 10:36 (NLT), *"Patient endurance is what you need now, so that you will continue to do God's will. Then you will receive all that He has promised."* I decree that I am clothed with patient endurance. I refuse to faint in the face of adversity. I am steadfast, unmovable, always abounding in the work of the Lord because I know my labor is not in vain (1 Corinthians 15:58).

Holy Spirit, stir up a fresh fire within me! Light a blaze that cannot be extinguished. When the enemy tries to wear me down, I rise up with the tenacity of a warrior, declaring, *"I can do all things through Christ who strengthens me"* (Philippians 4:13). My strength does not come from my circumstances; it comes from the One who conquered death, hell, and the grave.

I break every assignment of discouragement, defeat, and demonic delay. I cancel the lies of the enemy that whisper, *"It's too hard,"* because nothing is too hard for my God (Jeremiah 32:17). I speak life to every dry place. I declare strength where there's been weakness, boldness where there's been fear, and faith where doubt has tried to creep in.

Lord, Your Word says in Galatians 6:9 (ESV), *"And let us not grow weary of doing good, for in due season we will reap if we do not give up."* I prophesy over my life: THIS is my due season! I'm reaping because I refused to quit. I'm walking into promises because I didn't faint. I'm standing in victory because I held on when it was easier to let go.

I declare that my spirit is fortified, my mind is renewed, and my heart is fixed, trusting in the Lord. I am a finisher. I endure. I overcome. I win.

I believe I receive this prayer, and I release my most holy faith to bring it to pass. In Jesus' mighty, powerful, matchless name I seal this prayer, amen!

Faith Confessions for Endurance, Tenacity, and Unwavering Faith

1. I am strong in the Lord and in the power of His might and the gates of hell shall not prevail against me; I will not faint, for my strength is renewed daily (Ephesians 6:10; Isaiah 40:31).
2. I endure with patience and persistence, knowing that God's promises are yes and amen in my life (2 Corinthians 1:20; Hebrews 10:36).
3. I am steadfast, unmovable, always abounding in the work of the Lord because my labor is not in vain (1 Corinthians 15:58).
4. I can do all things through Christ Jesus who strengthens me; nothing can stop me from fulfilling my purpose (Philippians 4:13).
5. Greater is He that is in me than he that is in the world; I am victorious in every battle (1 John 4:4).
6. I press toward the mark for the prize of the high calling of God in Christ Jesus; I will not be distracted or discouraged (Philippians 3:14).
7. I walk by faith and not by sight; I am not moved by what I see, but by what God has spoken (2 Corinthians 5:7).
8. The joy of the Lord is my strength; I am filled with supernatural joy, even in the face of challenges (Nehemiah 8:10).
9. I am more than a conqueror through Christ who loves me; defeat is not my portion (Romans 8:37).
10. I will reap my harvest in due season because I refuse to give up; my breakthrough is inevitable (Galatians 6:9).

11. My heart is fixed, trusting in the Lord; I am rooted and grounded in His love and faithfulness (Psalm 112:7).
12. No weapon formed against me shall prosper, and every tongue that rises against me in judgment is condemned (Isaiah 54:17).
13. I am filled with the Spirit of power, love, and a sound mind; fear has no place in me (2 Timothy 1:7).
14. I stand firm in the faith, courageous and strong, knowing God fights my battles (1 Corinthians 16:13).
15. I am a finisher; I complete every assignment God has given me with excellence and perseverance (2 Timothy 4:7).

I believe I receive this prayer, and I release my most holy faith to bring it to pass. In Jesus' mighty, powerful, matchless name, amen!

A Prayer to Unleash Divine Progress and Provision

Father, in the mighty name of Jesus, I come boldly before the throne of grace to release heaven's authority over my life. I take my rightful place in the Spirit and declare that every demonic blockade, every wall of resistance, every wicked spirit of delay, and every chain of lack is broken right now by the fire of God! I bind every hindrance, every assignment of the enemy sent to stall my progress, sabotage my provision, and block my answered prayers. I take authority over it, and I shut it down in Jesus' name!

Every force standing in the way of my progress be dismantled now! Every mountain of intimidation, confusion, debt, doubt, or distraction, I command you to be cast into the sea by the Word of the Lord! I command open doors, divine connections, angelic reinforcements, and supernatural strategies to manifest in my life today. I decree and declare that my steps are ordered by the Lord, my resources are released on earth as they are loosed in heaven, and my destiny helpers are arriving on time. Hallelujah.

Lord, let there be a divine overturning. Let what's been held up be released. Let what's been locked down be loosed. Let every spiritual embargo be broken by the power of the blood! I declare that I walk in unstoppable momentum. I make supernatural progress. I decree my breakthrough is now. I decree my provision is now. I decree my favor is now!

I prophesy, no more dry places, no more closed doors, no more cycles of delay. I break the back of stagnation, and I call forth divine movement and momentum. I declare supernatural results. I declare that the heavens are open over me, and I operate in kingdom authority, led by the Holy Spirit, backed by the Word, and covered in the blood of Jesus!

Jesus paid the full price for my victory, so I rise with boldness and walk into the fullness of everything God has for me. Progress is mine.

Provision is mine. Promotion is mine and no devil can stop what God has ordained for me!

I believe I receive this prayer and release most holy faith to bring it to pass. In Jesus' name, Amen!

Declaration: Who We Are in Christ

I am a child of the Most High God, chosen, called, and set apart for such a time as this. I am redeemed by the blood of Jesus, forgiven, washed clean, and made righteous in Him. I am no longer a slave to fear, sin, or shame. I am free. I am victorious. I am loved. I am the head and not the tail, above only and never beneath. I walk in Kingdom authority, backed by Heaven.

I am filled with the Holy Spirit. I carry His power, His wisdom, and His presence everywhere I go. I have the mind of Christ. My thoughts are aligned with His will. I hear His voice and follow His lead. I am the light of the world and the salt of the earth. I shine for Jesus. I influence atmospheres. I am a joint heir with Christ, and every spiritual blessing in heavenly places belongs to me.

I am healed. I am whole. I am strong in the Lord and in the power of His might. I am equipped. I am anointed. I am appointed. I am unstoppable in my assignment. I am a vessel of honor, fit for the Master's use. Signs, wonders, and miracles follow me. I am not defined by my past. I am defined by God's promises and His purpose for my life.

I walk in love, I live by faith, and I overcome by the blood of the Lamb and the word of my testimony. I am who God says I am, I have what God says I have, and I will do what God says I will do. In Christ, I lack nothing. In Christ, I am complete. In Christ, I always win!

Declaration of Divine Acceleration and Restoration

I decree and declare that this is my appointed time of divine acceleration. God is moving in my life, and it won't be long now. Things are happening so fast my head will swim one blessing on the heels of another, breakthrough after breakthrough!

Everywhere I look, I see the hand of God restoring, rebuilding, and releasing overflow into every area of my life. I declare that what was broken is being rebuilt, what was lost is being returned, and what was delayed is being supernaturally accelerated!

I call forth blessings pouring like wine off the mountains. I speak to every dry place and declare fruitfulness, increase, and divine recovery. The ruined places in my life are being restored, my hands are blessed to plant, build, harvest, and rejoice.

I shall not be uprooted from my place of purpose. I am planted in the promises of God, and I am firmly rooted in victory. This is my harvest season. This is my purposed season. I walk in it boldly.

I believe I receive it, and I release most holy faith to bring it to pass. In Jesus' name, Amen!

Scripture Acknowledgments

Unless otherwise noted, Scripture quotations are from the **King James Version (KJV)** of the Bible. Public domain.

Other Scripture quotations are taken from:

- **The Holy Bible, New International Version® (NIV)**
  Copyright © 1973, 1978, 1984, 2011 by Biblica, Inc.™ Used by permission. All rights reserved worldwide.
- **New Living Translation (NLT)**
  Copyright © 1996, 2004, 2015 by Tyndale House Foundation.
  Used by permission of Tyndale House Publishers, Carol Stream, Illinois 60188. All rights reserved.
- **English Standard Version (ESV)**
  Copyright © 2001 by Crossway, a publishing ministry of Good News Publishers. Used by permission. All rights reserved.
- **New King James Version (NKJV)**
  Copyright © 1982 by Thomas Nelson. Used by permission. All rights reserved.
- **The Passion Translation® (TPT)**
  Copyright © 2017, 2018, 2020 by Passion & Fire Ministries, Inc. Used by permission. All rights reserved. ThePassionTranslation.com.
- **New American Standard Bible (NASB)**
  Copyright © 1960, 1962, 1963, 1968, 1971, 1972, 1973, 1975, 1977, 1995 by The Lockman Foundation. Used by permission. www.Lockman.org.
- **The Message (MSG)**
  Copyright © 1993, 1994, 1995, 1996, 2000, 2001, 2002 by Eugene H. Peterson. Used by permission of NavPress. All rights reserved. Represented by Tyndale House Publishers.

About The Author

Angelia Brown is a speaker, author, trainer, and certified life coach with a passion to see God's people walk in purpose, financial freedom, and Kingdom authority. As the founder of Live Out Your Faith Nation and AMB Coaching, Angelia equips men and women to boldly step into their divine assignment and build a life rooted in faith, wisdom, and supernatural breakthrough.

Her journey is marked by both corporate success and personal transformation. After walking away from a six-figure salary to pursue entrepreneurship, Angelia experienced both the heights of achievement and the depths of loss. But through it all, she discovered that true victory comes from obeying God, trusting His timing, and standing firm on His promises. That revelation became her mantle — to teach others how to rise, rebuild, and live in alignment with God's Word.

Angelia is known for her powerful prayer life, faith declarations, and practical wisdom that merges biblical truth with real-world application. She leads a vibrant daily prayer call that has touched lives across the nation, hosts the Ignite Your Life Conference, and continues to mentor leaders, visionaries, and believers who are ready to shift from survival to supernatural living.

She is a devoted wife, mother, and grandmother. Whether through books, coaching, or ministry, Angelia's heartbeat remains the same, to empower people to live boldly, walk in purpose, and create lasting Kingdom impact.

Stay Connected with Angelia: www.angeliabrown.com
Social Media Platforms @coachangelia

www.ingramcontent.com/pod-product-compliance
Lightning Source LLC
Chambersburg PA
CBHW070620160426
43194CB00009B/1324